THE DIVIDED MIND
OF MODERN THEOLOGY

BOOKS BY JAMES D. SMART

PUBLISHED BY THE WESTMINSTER PRESS

*The Divided Mind of Modern Theology:
Karl Barth and Rudolf Bultmann, 1908–1933*

*History and Theology in Second Isaiah:
A Commentary on Isaiah 35, 40–66*

*The Old Testament in Dialogue
with Modern Man*

The Creed in Christian Teaching

The Interpretation of Scripture

*Servants of the Word: The Prophets of Israel
(Westminster Guides to the Bible)*

The Rebirth of Ministry

The Teaching Ministry of the Church

The Recovery of Humanity

What a Man Can Believe

A Promise to Keep

Jesus, Stories for Children

IN COLLABORATION WITH DAVID NOEL FREEDMAN

God Has Spoken

THE DIVIDED MIND
OF
MODERN THEOLOGY

Karl Barth and Rudolf Bultmann
1908–1933

BY
JAMES D. SMART

THE WESTMINSTER PRESS
PHILADELPHIA

Library of Congress Catalog Card No. 67–10614

Published by The Westminster Press®
Philadelphia, Pennsylvania

PRINTED IN THE UNITED STATES OF AMERICA

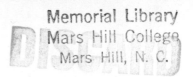
CONTENTS

PREFACE

A BOOK that examines in detail the writings of Karl Barth and
Rudolf Bultmann during the twenty-five-year period between
their graduation from university and the onset of the Hitler era — with
some essays by Friedrich Gogarten thrown in — may require some justification. Why, at this late date, look with such closeness at the early development of these theologians? If the purpose is comparison of their theologies, would it not be more to the point to examine the more familiar and
extensive writings of the postwar years in which one can see their thought
in its most fully developed form?

The answer is that in our present theological situation in the English-
speaking world the Barth and Bultmann of this early period speak to us
with an unusual pertinence. There are remarkable parallels between the
European mood of the twenties and the English and American mood of
the sixties: God seemed to have gone into hiding; religious and theological
language out of the past had become wooden and unconvincing; men felt
themselves suspended between a world that had died and a new world that
was waiting to be born; a church indifferent to the plight of the masses
was recognized as unworthy of the name Christian; the identification of
Christianity with Western civilization, and of divinity with the higher elements in man, had become highly suspect; in various forms the hunger
for a new world *now* was felt, and some understood it as hunger for a
living God. In that kind of world Barth and Bultmann became theologians whose one endeavor was to find the word that would unlock the
future, the word that would bring wholeness of faith and creative power
by being the very truth of the living God. No one who reads their writings
with an open mind can question the integrity with which each of them
faced the theological task. For them it was a life or death matter, not just
for the church but for humanity. Therefore, there was a ruthlessness in

the way in which they forced their way forward on the road that opened
before them. Compromise was a word unknown to them. And now it is
history that in the twenties they accomplished a breakthrough in both
Biblical interpretation and theology which radically changed the course of
European theology. The influence of that breakthrough has reached beyond Protestantism into the Roman Church and bears at least some responsibility for the reformation which it has been experiencing in recent
years.

The influence has, of course, made itself felt widely also in Britain and
America, but in muted forms and more often as an influence of Barth,
Bultmann, Brunner, or Gogarten on particular theologians rather than as
a parallel theological revolution in the American or British situation,
fought through in American or British terms. Indicative of this is the extent to which our Biblical scholarship remains at a purely historical level
with an untheological, if not sometimes a definitely antitheological character, or, in the field of religious education, so much of the literature is
theologically innocuous and even irresponsible. It is not surprising that
today there is a widespread reversion to something strangely like the theological attitudes of the liberal era. The question must be asked: Is this
because we never rightly or with integrity fought our way out of the liberal era? We tried to absorb the theological fruits of the European revolution in theology without having to take responsibility for it in our own
situation.

One cannot skip grades in the ongoing school of theology in which the
Holy Spirit seeks to guide the church of Christ into all truth. The Roman
Church is learning today that it cannot skip the lessons of the Reformation if it is to be ready for life in the twentieth century. Perhaps we need
to emulate their humility and acknowledge that even as the Roman Catholics are trying to answer the questions Luther asked, we have to go back
a step and face profoundly the issues that Barth and Bultmann raised in
the twenties and thirties of this century. Those were the years of ferment
and decision. The writings of Barth and Bultmann take us into the very
heart of the struggle.

But why the title " The Divided Mind of Modern Theology "? Surely
no one will deny that modern theology has a seriously divided mind, not
divided in the healthy sense which produces fruitful dialogue but into
two streams which go their way largely in isolation from each other. The
one stream stems from Barth and the other from Bultmann. For some reason, what should be two poles of Christian thought has become two irreconcilable theological movements, each of which is seriously weakened by
its isolation from the other. Perhaps this is one reason why no command-

ing figure comparable in stature to a Tillich or a Barth or a Brunner or a Bultmann is to be found anywhere today. What made them commanding was the boldness and integrity with which they cut their way through the theological morass of the present into the future, always aware of the road that lay behind them and unwilling to turn back even for a moment, or rather, only turning their eyes backward in order to move more surely forward. If, then, we would be freed from this divided mind, we must go back into this early twentieth-century era of decisive change and see how the cleft originated — and perhaps in the understanding of its origin find how it may be surmounted, though that is something that no one can promise. To look only at the writings of the postwar period would be more likely to reinforce the sharpness of the division.

Because so many of the essential documents are not likely to be translated, I have tried to give an accurate digest of their contents that students may have before them not just my evaluation of the ongoing discussion but a report of the discussion itself. I realize that such digests can misinterpret and also that the condensation of the argument may make difficult reading, but it seemed to be the only way in which I could offer the reader who is without access to the original documents an opportunity to listen in on this epoch-making dialogue between theologians and to form his own judgments on the issues.

My thanks are due to Union Theological Seminary for the sabbatical which provided time for writing, and to the Presbyterian congregations of Beaverton and Gamebridge in Ontario whose hospitality and considerateness greatly expedited the work.

J. D. S.

Beaverton, Ontario

CHAPTER I

BARTH AND BULTMANN IN THE ENGLISH-SPEAKING WORLD

THERE WAS A TIME when Karl Barth and Rudolf Bultmann were widely regarded as colleagues in a common quest for a new approach to Scripture and proponents of a radically new movement in theology. In fact there were a few years when they regarded each other as allies with almost the whole theological world ranged against them. But those years were in the early 1920's, more than forty years ago. Today in the European scene the theological world that has been reshaped largely by the work of these two men is split into two sharply separated camps, the one stemming from Barth and the other from Bultmann. Hermann Diem in his *Dogmatics* [1] describes this division as so far-reaching that the two groups of theologians have ceased even to hear each other, each going its own way in disregard of the other, with serious results for the theological dialogue of our time.

There have been attempts to bridge the gap. Diem himself devotes his volume to an analysis of the work of the two men in its historical context, hoping to make possible a more fruitful relation. Heinrich Ott, Barth's successor in Basel, who professes a critical loyalty not only to his teachers, Barth and Bultmann, but also to the philosopher Heidegger, and whose first writings [2] have been concerned to establish his relation with each of them in a thoroughgoing fashion, undoubtedly has aimed to bring the divergent streams into some kind of unity. But neither succeeds. Diem's strictures on Bultmann are so much more severe than those on Barth that he is labeled a partisan, while the increasing influence of Heidegger on Ott seems to be carrying him into the neighborhood of the existentialist theologians who out-Bultmann Bultmann. Helmut Gollwitzer makes no attempt at mediation in his *The Existence of God as Confessed by Faith* [3] but, rather, a slashing attack on the tendency of the Bultmann school to let the transcendence of God become indistinguishable from the transcendence of an element in man's own existence, but he has at least succeeded in provoking a discussion: the transcript of a public debate between him and the disciple of Bultmann, Herbert Braun, has been published.[4] There is a definite reluctance, however, to debate the theological issues that can be traced in Bultmann and also in some of his disciples. It is notable that while Bultmann has pushed on with his own scholarly program since 1925 with little attention to his differences with Barth, Barth has constantly in his *Dogmatik* and in other publications been taking account of Bultmann's thought, often without naming him specifically. Then, in his pamphlet " Rudolf Bultmann, an Attempt to Understand Him "[5] he focused directly on the problem. In its concluding pages he somewhat plaintively commented that, while he has been struggling for years to understand Bultmann, Bultmann has maintained something of the attitude of a sphinx and has shown little concern to understand him in return.

1. An Essay in Understanding

What, then, is my intention in considering these two theologians together? The fact that our study is to be focused on the early period in their development, from 1908–1933, before either of them was much known in the English-speaking world and largely before there had been any open break between them, might suggest an intention to show how close they were to each other in the beginning in their basic positions and how much their subsequent separation has been the product of unfortunate misunderstandings. Arnold B. Come in his *An Introduction to Barth's* Dogmatics *for Preachers*[6] expresses a viewpoint of this kind, asserting that they were originally in close agreement and will eventually be recognized as standing together in spite of all differences. The evidence is contrary to this. As it unfolds, it will show that even when they were closest to each other, they were each of them aware of profound theological differences which separated them, that the period of closeness was remarkably brief, and that the issues dividing them even then were of such a nature that if they remained unresolved, they would carry them eventually in widely divergent directions. The cause of theological understanding will not be served if we smudge over the points of difference.

Again, it might be thought that the intention in considering the two men together is to attempt once more to bridge the gap between them, to recognize their points both of agreement and of divergence, and then perhaps to establish a theological position in line with their points of agreement but reconciling somehow their separate contributions where they diverge. That would be much too ambitious a project even if it were practicable. My aim is much more modest: simply an essay in understanding. Both in Great Britain and in America theologians young and old are forming judgments on the issues which are raised by the writings of these two men. But there is nothing available in our theological literature that enables the student who has no command of German to go back into the early period when the ferment of theological revolution was swirling round the two and to follow step by step the process by which they reached the positions that have been associated with their names for the last twenty-five years. The present frequently takes on new meaning when seen in the light of the past and can be thrown quite out of focus by the removal of that background. The name of Bultmann suggests to most students of theology today only the projects of demythologizing and existentialist interpretation of Scripture that began to command attention in 1941, though they had their roots much earlier. The name of Barth suggests to them the systematic theologian whose twelve ponderous volumes of dogmatics stand on the shelf in German, English, and other languages, like a veritable Mount Everest which only the boldest would attempt to conquer. Bultmann is "the demythologizer" and Barth "the awesome dogmatician." It is forgotten that long before they gained this repute, they were joint participants in a far-reaching revolution in Biblical scholarship and in theology, which shook the theological world like an earthquake and turned its endeavors into decidedly new channels. It is forgotten that Barth, once he had broken loose from the nineteenth century, began his career as a New Testament expositor, that Biblical exegesis displaced systematic theology as his first love, that in his first years as a professor he divided his courses between New Testament exposition and systematic theology, and that he has published more commentaries on New Testament books than Bultmann has. It is forgotten that what set Bultmann apart from his New Testament colleagues of the 1920's and made him a revolutionary force was not so much his work in form criticism as his interest in the larger problems of theology, his concern about the failure of preaching to communicate the gospel, and his insistence that the nature of the Biblical text forced him to be both a theologian and a historian.

2. Significance for the English-speaking World

The essay in understanding, however, has to do not just with the development of these theologians in Europe between 1908 and 1933 but also with their significance in the Biblical and theological situation of the English-speaking world. There are voices which have been telling us that Barth, if not Bultmann too, has had his day. H. Richard Niebuhr in his later years was heard saying that while in the thirties and forties we needed Barth's contribution to draw us away from the liberal ditch on the left side of the theological highway, now in the sixties we need once more the contribution of Schleiermacher to keep us from falling into the orthodox ditch on the right side of the highway. Schubert Ogden [7] calls for us to go beyond Bultmann's demythologizing to a dekerygmatizing of the gospel, which he himself recognizes as in a large measure a return to the early twentieth-century naturalism of Henry Nelson Wieman. Indeed, what is disturbing is that the call which is heard in many quarters to " go beyond Barth and Bultmann " turns out frequently to be a call to go back to the 1920's as though the past forty years theologically and Biblically had been a journey down a road that ends in an impasse. Certainly we must go beyond both Barth and Bultmann, but not without going *through* them, not by skirting round them, not by retreating from them into a repristination of some earlier theology. They both did their work for their day with an amazing thoroughness, and we cannot find our way into the future without first settling our theological accounts with them.

It may seem at least a little odd to allege that American theology has not as yet taken adequate account of Barth and Bultmann. When these pages were written Barth was eighty and Bultmann eighty-two. They have been lecturing and writing for over fifty years. How can two such men be expected to make a fresh and lively contribution to our American theological discussion? Surely they have been squeezed dry by this time. But that is a false impression. It can be shown, and it will be the task of this chapter to do so, that on the whole we are only now beginning to explore the issues which these two men were opening up so boldly more than forty years ago. Individual theologians have become well acquainted with them but somehow our American theological discussion has never quite discovered and faced their questions as its own questions in more than a fragmentary fashion. There is reason to suspect that the next twenty years may be the period of their greatest influence in our midst. Different as they are and irreconcilable in their theologies, they have each of them a ministry to fulfill toward us, not just among professional students of theology in the seminaries but also and more urgently in the life of our churches, in laying open to us the drastic problems that afflict our preaching and teaching and setting us at least a few steps on our way toward a solution of those problems.

We frequently marvel at the speed of communication in our modern world, the racial riot in New York being seen and discussed in Singapore within a very few hours, which ill prepares us to recognize the painful slowness of theological communication from one part of the world to another, and in particular between the Continental and the English-speaking churches. Even the associations generated by the World Council of Churches have done only a little to overcome the obstacles. First among them is the time lag caused by the language barrier, since few books are translated within fifteen or twenty years of their origin. Bultmann's *The History of the Synoptic Tradition*[8] appeared in English forty-five years after its publication in German. Sir Edwyn Hoskyns' translation of Barth's rewritten commentary on Romans (1922) was published in England in 1933[9] when Barth had already moved on to a new stage in the development of his thought. The "Romans" of 1919, which he so quickly put behind him and yet is so important in tracing his growth, and the "Christian Dogmatics" of 1927, which shows how far he had moved in five years from the "Romans" of 1922, have neither of them as yet been translated. But an even greater impediment to communication than the slowness of translation has been the difference in theological context, the difference in presuppositions, in what is taken for granted in theological discussion, which in turn reflects the difference in the stages that theological conversation has reached in various areas. In the mid-nineteenth century, German theological developments were regarded with such distrust in England that it was dangerous to the career of an English churchman to translate a German work, and some antipathy seems to linger on in a weakened form even a century later. The American churches, many of which were still paralyzed theologically in the grip of a naïve, literalistic fundamentalism as recently as 1930, have had to cram into a few years a growth in Biblical and theological scholarship that on the Continent was spread in a more leisurely fashion over two and a half centuries. It is little wonder then that books written in the Continental context have had to wait until the questions to which they were addressed became the live questions of the new environment. Perhaps one day there will be a single world context for theological thought, but that day has not yet arrived and we have continually to take into account not only the problems of translation of the words into another language but also the problem of interpreting the thought into another context.

Both of our theologians have made their way slowly in our English-speaking world. By 1933, Bultmann was known only as one of three initiators of form criticism in the study of the Gospels whose radical skepticism about the possibility of reconstructing a life of Jesus was highly offensive in most English and American quarters, and Barth was known only as the author of a strange commentary on Romans which was engendering either furious anger, helpless frustration, or incoherent ecstasy. The anger was produced by his seemingly impertinent contradiction of many of the " assured results " of liberal scholarship, the frustration by his complicated and paradoxical way of saying things, and the ecstasy by his passionate exposition of Pauline theology as a viable alternative for modern man. The general impression of both men among the most respectable scholars in Britain and America was that although one had to credit them with certain valuable " emphases," their views were of such an extreme nature that they could have little appeal or influence in our religious situation. From 1933 to 1945 Barth became much more favorably known, not because of his theological achievements but because of his powerful leadership in the German Confessional Church and his encouragement of the free world to resist Hitler. With the abolition of Nazism in 1945, his star quickly waned, particularly when he refused to turn against Communism the incisive polemic with which he had fought Nazism for twelve years. But even during the years of his popularity there is little evidence that most American and English theologians had read beyond his " Romans " of 1922. An anthology of their judgments concerning him would make interesting, and perhaps embarrassing, reading today. A sample criticism, one which was frequently repeated and which is ludicrous for anyone who has read extensively even in the writings of the 1920's, was that he created such a gulf between God and man that there could be no relation between them. It was unfortunate that neither the " Dogmatics " of 1927 nor the half volume in which he began to rewrite it in 1932 were translated before the war, since either of them would have prevented the misconceptions that were created by the commentary on Romans from gaining such wide circulation and would have provided a balanced introduction to his theology. Only the comparatively recent appearance of the many-volumed *Dogmatics* in English has made possible an adequate understanding of Barth in the British and American scene.

Another factor that has delayed the influence of Barth in America has been the preference of many of our teachers of theology for Brunner. Until recently in many seminaries students were introduced to Brunner rather than to Barth as representative of the renewal in Reformed theology. Brunner had been here, first as a student, then later as a visiting lecturer, and had established a personal relation with many theologians. Through him they became acquainted with what he called " the theology of crisis," so that they took him to be a valid interpreter of Barth's theology who made it more comprehensible to American minds than Barth himself could. They paid no heed to the fact that in the mid-twenties Barth was already

critical of Brunner's approach to theology.[10] In 1924, Barth published a severely critical review [11] of Brunner's book on Schleiermacher, *Der Mystik
und das Wort,* and in the early thirties he attacked both Brunner's concept of a connecting point in man for revelation (in which he scented a
pretext for the reintroduction of natural theology) and his inclination to
turn theology into apologetic assaults against the isms that seemed to
threaten Christianity. These, however, were only preliminary to Barth's
" No! Answer to Emil Brunner," [12] published in 1934 when the struggle
with Nazism on behalf of the church was just beginning and he saw in
Brunner's concessions to natural theology a dangerous compromising of
the faith. In America this last publication was widely interpreted as an
inexcusable attack by Barth on a colleague for not agreeing with him on
all points, so that, instead of serving as a warning not to assume that
Brunner spoke for Barth, it merely strengthened the preference for Brunner. But eventually it will have to be recognized that Brunner is preferred
basically because he disturbs us less and fits more comfortably into our
theological world, encouraging us as he does in our confidence in Western civilization and leaving us at least a vestige of natural theology as a
theological support for that confidence. But recently, students, at least in
some seminaries, have begun to read Barth for themselves and, particularly in the *Dogmatics,* they are aware of a voice that has been strangely
silent until now in their theological world.

Also, since 1960, students have begun to have available to them, in translation, writings of Eduard Thurneysen which are of great value in understanding Barth. Rarely have men been so close to each other in their thinking as these two. Their first book [13] was a joint publication of sermons in
which they did not distinguish their separate products, since all the sermons were the outcome of their intimate collaboration. They thought
their way together through the problems that confronted them as the Neo-
Protestantism of the nineteenth century became untenable for them and
they had to break open new theological channels. Thurneysen, however,
has remained all his life in the pastorate (though he lectured in homiletics
and pastoral theology during his years in Basel), and because of his more
open style of writing and his constant focus upon the theological problems
that underlie the work of a pastor, he is for many readers much easier to
understand than Barth. He is no parrot of Barth but from the beginning
has done a distinctive theological work of his own. His *Theology of Pastoral Care* [14] stands by itself as a critical examination of the pastoral rela-
tionship in the light of the principle that man is justified by grace alone
through faith alone. Yet until 1960 Thurneysen's writings were almost unknown in the English-speaking world! The present author must confess

that in 1933, after the sermons in the volume *Come, Holy Spirit* had captured his interest and raised his hopes, he was completely frustrated in his attempt to read Barth's "Romans" of 1922, but fortunately came upon Thurneysen's essays [15] and found in them a more convenient way of access to a new world of theological thought.

Much less need be said to show that Bultmann too is not at the end but just at the beginning of his period of greatest influence in American theology. The debate on demythologizing began in Germany in 1941 and for twenty years now Hans Werner Bartsch has been publishing his volumes of essays, six in all, entitled *Kerygma und Mythos*.[16] With somewhat less than the usual time lag, the first volume in English appeared in 1953.[17] The sixties, however, have seen a perfect spate of literature on the subject in Britain and America. Bishop Robinson with his *Honest to God* has interested literally hundreds of thousands in the subject, and the remarkable circulation of his book demonstrates that the questions which Bultmann has long been posing belong not to a past era but very decidedly to the present and are unfinished business in the American scene. Whatever we may think of Bultmann's (and Robinson's) answers, there is no escape for us from his questions.

From yet another angle we can establish a present relevance for both Bultmann and Barth. The subject of hermeneutics is claiming for itself a place of central importance in theological discussion. James M. Robinson [18] has attempted to commandeer the term "hermeneutic" for a new development that he is confident is the theological "wave of the future," but his purposes require an unfortunate and illegitimate narrowing of meaning. Nothing should be allowed to obscure the fact that "hermeneutics" is simply a technical name for the complex problem of understanding and interpreting texts. In the Christian realm it applies primarily to the text of Scripture but is involved in every aspect of the work of theology. It would be as sensible to try to reserve the term "exegesis" for some one school of theology as to accede to Robinson's proposal. But Robinson in America and Ernst Fuchs and Gerhard Ebeling in Europe have at least focused attention on the problems of interpretation. By bringing the philosopher Heidegger into the picture, they may seem at times to have made the interpretation more difficult to understand than the texts they are interpreting. But at least they are working at the right problem, and any adequate approach to it must recognize that the pioneer work in laying it open was done by Barth and Bultmann forty years ago. What could be more valuable than to see how the problem appeared before Heidegger came in to complicate and obscure the picture? It may well be that what is needed to bring clarification in the hermeneutical discussion is to go back and trace the steps by which it first began to open up. What contribution had Bultmann made before ever he launched his demythologizing project? What had Barth in common with him and where did the two part company? The present discussion of hermeneutics is too narrow; it needs broadening, and the men to give it that broadening are the two who initiated the discussion.

3. The Focus on the Problem of Preaching

If the influence of Barth and Bultmann is only in its first stages in our theological seminaries, it is not surprising that it has barely touched the life of our churches as yet. The theological lag between the seminaries and the laity in the churches is even greater than the lag between Continental developments and our seminaries. For instance, historical and critical scholarship in the study of Scripture, which was well established in the theological faculties in Germany and Switzerland early in the nineteenth century, was fighting its way to acceptance in Britain and America in the last quarter of that century but was still new and revolutionary to most of the laity of our churches in the mid-twentieth century. In fact a seminary professor has been expelled from his position only recently because of his critical views! One of our most serious problems is the slowness with which what is taught in the seminaries becomes what is taught in the churches and church schools. Church schools in particular have frequently been allowed to remain bastions of outworn theologies. This in turn reacts upon the seminaries in two ways: first, students find not just a gap but more often a painful contradiction between what they have learned in their home churches and what they are taught in seminary, so that much of their precious three years' training is spent in trying to close the gap and overcome the contradictions; and second, when they return to the local church as ministers or directors of education they are under pressure to revert to a standpoint that is congenial to the mind of the congregation and too often they accede to that pressure or make what seems to be a reasonable compromise, rather than undertake the difficult task of the reeducation of the laity. The theologian, therefore, needs to visualize more clearly the radical character of the tension in which the seminary graduate is likely to find himself when he steps out of the theological world of the seminary into the very different theological world of the local congregation, which may be fifty, or one hundred, or even two hundred and fifty years [19] removed from the one he has lived in in seminary.

Both Barth and Bultmann have important contributions to make in overcoming this divorce between seminary and church. One point at which they stand together is in the emphasis that they place upon preaching; in fact, for them the whole work of theology is focused upon the task of preaching. One has only to think of the place that the kerygma occupies in the thought of Bultmann. " Kerygma " is simply a name for the preaching of the early church, its proclamation of Christ crucified and risen, but for Bultmann the word designates rather the event of divine revelation which occurs uniquely in that preaching and alone has in it the power to liberate man from his past and open to him a new future. The kerygmatic event remains *God's* action and is therefore hidden in the preaching that in its conceptuality is merely a temporary expression for it. The kerygma is the word of God himself in which he comes to men and redeems them out of death into life, or, to use existential language, out of inauthentic into authentic existence. The task of theology is to translate the kerygma ever afresh into the language and concepts that are meaningful to each new age. The preachers of the early church, whose voices are heard in every part of the New Testament, were necessarily limited to the language and thought forms of their age, which have ceased to be those of the modern age. Therefore, merely to repeat what they said is to erect insuperable barriers to the hearing of the kerygma, the modern mind being offended and repelled not by the word of God himself which it needs to hear but by the alien phraseology and concepts. The whole project of demythologizing is thus not to be dismissed as an accommodation of the gospel to the mind of modern man but must be seen as a sincere attempt to find the words through which the gospel that created the church of Jesus Christ in the beginning may create it afresh today.

In a different way the whole theological enterprise of Barth focuses upon the preaching of the gospel. The present preaching of the church in all its ambiguity is the starting point of theology, and the bringing of that preaching into accord with the original gospel is its goal. It must not be thought that he separates preaching from teaching, worship, works of charity, and all else that makes up the life of the church. Preaching is simply the form in which the church's existence comes most clearly to expression. The church's true being is Jesus Christ. Only insofar as he lives and speaks and acts in and through its life and words and actions is it truly the church. It has its true existence only in his ever-renewed coming to it. In each moment of its life it is confronted by the dilemma of its unfaithfulness. Theology is the activity in which the church grapples with the desperate and inescapable problem of the mingling of truth and falsehood in its existence. It focuses upon preaching because preaching brings the church's unfaithfulness out into the open and because the renewal of the church always begins with the recovery of its gospel. The task of theology is to bring the church of today under the judgment of the word of God in the witness of the prophets and apostles that through repentance and rebirth it may once more stand in continuity with the church of God that was revealed in them. We are challenged, therefore, in two different ways to rethink the very structure of our theological work and its relation to the life of the church.

Then there is the problem of language. Here the *Honest to God* debate, plus the discussion of demythologizing, plus British linguistic analysis, have set the currents flowing. We may find Bishop Robinson superficial and confused, and we may differ radically with Bultmann's definition of the mythological and with many of the conclusions at which he arrives, but surely no one who is honest with himself can deny that the Scriptures face all of us with a problem of language which is acute. The words and practices that meet us in Scripture are appropriate to the world of their day but their transfer *simpliciter* to our world does not necessarily preserve their meaning. Jesus' action in girding himself with a towel and washing his disciples' feet was highly meaningful in a world where this was the service of a slave to guests in the household, but such a ceremony, transferred intact to one of our churches, would not have the same quality of Christian witness. The words of Jesus and of the disciples by which they exorcised demons were the very words that had to be spoken in a world in which men conceptualized the evil forces that obstructed their lives as personal demonic spirits, but the same words spoken today would only make men laugh and would leave them still imprisoned by the evil forces in their modern guise. The tragedy of literalism is that it tries to preserve the original meaning and redemptive power by holding fast to the original words and practices. But already within the New Testament itself the words and practices had begun to change as faithful witness had to be borne in a new environment. Different words had to be found if the church was to continue to preach the same gospel.[20] Once admit the basic principle, and it has far-reaching consequences for our preaching and teaching, and in fact for all that we do in the church. It has been the merit of Bultmann that he has thrust this problem upon us with such forcefulness that we can no longer evade it, and, what is equally important, that he has warned us against a mere discarding of the ancient language and practices in which we would lose our hold also upon their content and meaning and so impoverish the gospel for our day.

What do American and British churches and churchmen do with this problem? In general they fall into two categories: the literalists, who close their eyes to the existence of the problem and repeat the Biblical language untranslated as though the meaning were obvious to any attentive person, thereby leaving the listeners in serious confusion; and those who, having abandoned literalism, think it sufficient merely to discard all the ancient terminology, and with it the theology that is implicit in it, and in the manner of Harnack to offer people a simple modern code of religion and morals. Both alike produce a church to which the Scriptures have become a closed book. But Bultmann seems already to have caught the ear of many in our churches, awakening them to the problem in a new way, and they may yet discover that Barth too has something important to say to them about how the revelation which is hidden and imprisoned in the language of Scripture is to be liberated that it may be heard in its full meaning in the language of our time.

4. The Uniqueness of the Christian Revelation

A third point at which Barth in particular, but Bultmann as well, has still a contribution to make to the American and British churches is in the area of Christology. Both men insist upon the absolute uniqueness of God's revelation in the gospel and reject natural theology as irreconcilable with the maintaining of that uniqueness — though Bultmann seems to make concessions to natural theology in his concept of the philosophic preunderstanding. The twelve volumes of Barth's *Dogmatics* could validly be described as one vast essay in Christology, an elaboration of the thesis that only in and through Jesus Christ does man rightly know either God or himself or his fellowman or his world. His negation of natural theology and natural revelation is offensive to many British and American theologians. But few seem to grasp that the negation is the necessary corollary of Barth's radical and thoroughgoing Christology. The question is whether it is any more radical than the New Testament itself: than Matthew's assertion that no one knows the Father except the Son and he to whom the Son chooses to reveal him, or John's that no man comes to the Father except by Jesus Christ, or Paul's that Christ crucified and risen is the only foundation upon which we can build, the only way of access to the power and wisdom of God. In all three the negation is inseparable from the affirmation. The uniqueness of God's revelation in Jesus Christ is such in its nature that nothing can be added to it without taking from it. To make "revelation" a general term to cover a variety of religious phenomena is to destroy its usefulness for the Christian who confesses that in Jesus Christ, God is known to him as Father, Son, and Holy Spirit. The Trinity, far from being an outworn theological formulation, is the necessary expression of the uniqueness of the Christian's faith in God.[21] While this is the source of Barth's intransigeance against natural theology, his opposition has been reinforced by his experience of the way in which a partial revelation of God in nature, reason, conscience, or orders of creation can provide the religious validation of an order of life that men desire to sustain and to protect from the judgment of the gospel. " Christ and conscience " was the formula that permitted his Göttingen colleague, Emanuel Hirsch, to become the passionate devotee of Hitler's nationalism. Friedrich Gogarten in the early twenties seemed to stand close to Barth in his Christology, but by making room for the orders of creation he was able to compromise for a time with Nazism in spite of his Christology. The question of natural theology is not an abstruse theoretical consideration but can be a matter of life or death for the church.

So deeply rooted is natural theology in both the British and American churches that any challenge of its validity is likely to be dismissed as an absurdity. Western man has had a persistent affection for a natural revelation that seems to him to undergird the values of his civilization even as the peculiarly Christian revelation undergirds the values of his religion. It does not occur to him that this may be an unconscious strategy of defense by which he protects an order of life that is based on his own insights and preferences against the radical claims which God makes upon the whole of man's life in Jesus Christ. Surely it must be said that although Barth's attack on natural theology has made itself felt among the theologians, it has generated no lively discussion and has barely touched the life of the churches.

A personal experience may illumine the situation. A young minister who had been reading Barth reacted sharply against his complete negation of natural revelation. It seemed to him much too sweeping. " We must leave at least an entering wedge for the truth which in all ages men have apprehended apart from Jesus Christ " was his considered judgment. He was prepared to admit that in the history of the church natural theology had again and again reduced the gospel to a religion of common sense and that always in it there was a threat against which one had to be on guard. But it seemed to him equally dangerous to deny to natural theology its entering wedge. What he failed to grasp was that in the situation which confronts us in our churches it is not natural theology that requires an entering wedge but the New Testament gospel in its radical distinctiveness.

If we define natural theology not in technical terms but simply as what a man assumes that he knows concerning God and man and life by the light of his own conscience and reason, surely we must recognize in this the basis of the rocklike resistance of good religious men to the unique promises and claims of the gospel. Jesus Christ offers them a costly fellowship with God, a share in the life that he himself has in God, a life in which God's own love and mercy and redemptive compassion will be reflected. Why are professing Christians uninterested in that offer except that they have already established for themselves a much less demanding and more comfortable fellowship with God by means of their own? Jesus Christ offers them eternal life, life in which there is no death, his own free and victorious life, but to receive that life is to be bound to him so that one dies to the old life of self and rises with him into a new life in the family of God. But the offer leaves men cold because they have already a confidence in their own immortality which is based not on any decision in relation to Jesus Christ but rather upon their own record of goodness and/or religiousness. Where do earnest Christians who defend racial segregation get their assurance except in consciences that have been culturally conditioned for generations, and have they not been told over and over that the voice of conscience is the voice of God? We might also ask why so many American churchmen find it so easy to identify the American way of life with Christianity, an identification that confuses our political and economic thinking, exposes us to the scorn of other nations and compromises the gospel itself. Has it any other source than that the values of our society are taken to be a direct revelation of the divine order for all human life? Natural theology may have been challenged and put on the defensive in recent years among the theologians but in our churches it is still persistently, and one might almost say arrogantly, dominant. Here again, there is a debate that is only in its beginnings if our theological discussions in the future are to deal with issues in which the very life of the church and of humanity is at stake.

CHAPTER II

BEFORE THE EARTHQUAKE

IF WE ARE TO MEASURE the dimensions of the revolution which, beginning in 1919, shook the theological world like an earthquake, we need to get some conception of what that world was like before the earthquake. It was roughly divided into liberal and conservative camps, with quite considerable variation in each camp, and the theological faculties in Germany reflected this division. Tübingen, Marburg, and Berlin were the leaders in liberal scholarship, and the fact that both Barth and Bultmann had their education in these three shows the theological orientation with which they began. Barth also attended the University of Bern where his father was a professor of theology. The father's theology was in the conservative tradition but was quite open to the advances of critical scholarship. It needs always to be remembered that the liberal-conservative antithesis in nineteenth-century Europe was very different in character from the American liberal-fundamentalist impasse. By the middle of the nineteenth century many conservative scholars had accepted the necessity of a historical approach to Scripture, participating in the work of historical criticism merely in a more conservative fashion and combining their critical work with an orthodox theology. Men such as Beck, Tholuck, and von Hofmann in mid-century, who tried to solve the problem of how there could be an absolute revelation in a sea of historical relativity by their concept of a sacred history in the midst of secular history, prepared the way for scholars such as Adolf Schlatter and Martin Kähler at the end of the century. Conservatism was not tied as it has been in America to the paralyzing identification of the text of Scripture with revelation which was to generate a hostility to all historical-critical scholarship. But there was no inclination of either Barth or Bultmann toward the conservative schools. It is interesting that Barth, even though his father belonged largely in the conservative tradition, discovered Beck and

Tholuck first during the war years [1] when he was working on his first draft of the commentary on Romans and was then considerably influenced by them for a time, so much so that he expected Schlatter would find his commentary congenial. But as a student he seems to have been unaware of their existence. He had ears only for the liberal theologians.

The difference between a Lutheran and a Reformed origin was of some consequence. Bultmann as the son of a German Lutheran pastor bears the marks of Lutheran tradition at a number of points — an intense concentration upon justification by faith alone, the finding of a more restricted canon within the canon of Scripture, and a rather sharp separation of the two kingdoms. Barth, in spite of the fact that for years he was in constant rebellion against the existing order in his Swiss Reformed Church, has found no reason to transfer his allegiance from the Reformed tradition, seen in its longer perspective. Its basic emphases continue in his theology, the sovereignty of God having a special prominence, the whole of Scripture being interpreted as essential to the church's witness, and no area of life being allowed to fall outside the authority and direction of the church's message. But it is doubtful if either of the two was particularly conscious of the shaping influence of his Lutheran or Calvinistic tradition during the university years. The liberal theologians most respected by them were men who had to qualify their loyalty to the Reformers in a very high degree.

The difference between German and Swiss has also played its part. Bultmann has spent his whole life in Germany and is completely at home in his German context. During the conflict of 1914–1918 he could speak of the war revealing " a greatness in mankind such as we never dreamed of " and could assert that " what the war has once again given us is the crowning glory of the tragic." [2] The sermons in the volume " This World and the Beyond " were most of them preached between 1933 and 1945, the years of Hitler's dominance, and one remarkable thing about them is that, though Bultmann stood with the Confessional Church in its resistance to the nazification of the German churches, there is little indication in the sermons that preacher and people were in the midst of such a conflict. Barth, however, never ceased to be a Swiss who had to make himself at home in his German situation during his professorships in Göttingen, Münster, and Bonn, and never wholly succeeded. In 1914 he was deeply offended by the readiness of prominent German theologians to put a Christian validation on the Kaiser's war. Upon settling in Göttingen in 1921 he entered sympathetically into his new situation but could not help viewing many German customs and practices with a critical Swiss eye. He kept himself in close communication with his Swiss friends. He was particularly sensitive to the presence of a passionate nationalism in some of his new colleagues and saw the peril of it very early. Perhaps his greatest service to the German Church, his sounding of the alarm in 1933, owed much to his ability as an alien to stand above the situation, above it but not apart from it. But perhaps also the decline of his influence in Germany owes something to resentment of the Swiss whose pen was for so long a weapon poised against Nazi Germany.

1. Education in a Liberal Context

Differences of church tradition and of nationality, however, counted for little in the university years when both men were directly under the influence of the leading liberal scholars of the time. From 1900 to 1914 was a period of triumphant confidence for liberal theology in Germany. The work of a century was coming to its culmination. The nineteenth century seemed in retrospect an era of the most remarkable progress in every department of theology. Biblical studies had more and more established themselves as historical sciences, evaluating the texts critically in the light of their origin and producing a radically new conception of the history both of Israel and of the beginnings of the Christian church. Early in the nineteenth century the Biblical scholar had considered himself a theologian as well as a historian but as the century advanced he divested himself of the former concern in order to be more objectively scientific in his investigations. His task was to lay bare the facts, in the Old Testament and other Jewish literature concerning the phenomena of Israelite and Jewish religion, and in the New Testament and early Christian literature concerning the complex of religious forces that brought the Christian church into being. The deciphering of cuneiform and hieroglyphic writings had opened up the other ancient Near Eastern cultures with their religions so that the Old Testament no longer stood in isolation but was seen against the background and in the context of a wide variety of religious ideas and practices. So also the religions of the Greco-Roman world became the context of New Testament developments. If in this process it became increasingly difficult to recognize what was unique and distinctive in Biblical religion and the whole took on the aspect of a succession of stages in religious syncretism, there was at least the consolation that Christian scholarship was being ruthlessly honest about its Bible, and the church was being emancipated from obsolete religious ideas that a naïve approach to the Bible had long perpetuated. It became a problem, however, how the Bible could continue to exercise anything of its traditional authority in determining the church's faith, but this was seen not as a loss but as a liberation of the church to serve a truth that was more comprehensive than Biblical truth.

Parallel with these Biblical developments was the reconstruction of theology begun by Schleiermacher and continued throughout the century. He came out of a world in which the theological alternatives were a rational orthodoxy that identified faith with adherence to traditional doctrines, a rationalism that was mainly concerned to accommodate Christianity to the enlightenment of modern man, and a pietism that nurtured a warm personal faith centered upon Jesus but was hopelessly naïve in its attitude to Scripture and doctrine. All three lost the church the respect of cultured men and set up a false antithesis between the intellect and faith. Schleiermacher gave theology a new starting point and basis. He appealed to men to begin their thinking not with the Scriptures or doctrinal traditions that had become so debatable and the occasion of so much alienation for modern man, but with man's experience in confrontation with the world's totality. Christian experience he interpreted as an intensified form of the universal experience of man in which self-realization is possible only within the larger realization of one's unity with the power that moves the universe. Doctrines received their significance as expressions of experience. On this basis there could be no conflict between Christian knowledge and all other knowledge. The different sciences were different ways of experiencing the world, each with its own validity, and the dignity of theology was that it dealt with man's profoundest, most intimate, and most decisive experience of the world. Since this made the focal point of theology religious experience rather than a revelation in the Scriptures, it compensated for the disappearing authority of Scripture, but, more important, it seemed to bring theology down to earth as a practicable science with the describable phenomena of human religious experience as its subject matter.

On this basis a new unity was found for the theological enterprise as the century advanced. It came to conceive of its task as the investigation and understanding of religion. The religion or religions of man rather than a specific revelation of God held the center of interest. The Old Testament scholar was finished with his responsibility when he had traced the religion of Israel through its various periods until it finally issued in the religion of Judaism. The New Testament scholar then proceeded to define the religion of Jesus, of Paul, and of the early church in its Jewish and Hellenistic stages. The church historian continued with a description of what had happened to the Christian religion through the centuries. At every step the contemporary religions were brought into the picture, but eventually the scope of investigation had to be widened to take in all the

world's religions. Topping the whole structure was a philosophy of religion with the task of bringing order out of the chaotic mass of phenomena
and relating it to the immediate problem of the Christian's understanding
and practice of his own religion. A certain optimism dominated the whole
proceeding. No one had any anticipation that an honest science of religion might reduce Christianity to a status equal or inferior to any other
religion. Just as a progress of religious development was traced in the
Scriptures, reaching its climax in Jesus, so a similar progress was found
in the history of the church with a rapid culmination in the nineteenth
century. The religions of man were arranged in the form of a pyramid
with Christianity at its apex. And the glory of it all was that the Christian now had a theology which gave him assurance that his confidence in
his religion had a scientific basis. Religious optimism of this kind was
combined with cultural pride, for it seemed obvious that Western civilization under the impetus of Christianity had produced an order of life in
comparison with which all other cultures were decidedly inferior, if not
barbarous.

One inevitable effect of making religion and religious experience central was that man rather than God became the focal point of concern and
God became just one of the elements in man's religion. Optimism concerning man had been one of the vital forces of the Enlightenment and now
it was intensified as evolutionary thinking seemed to open infinite possibilities for man's natural development. For religious men, God was the
explanation of man's greatness and the crucial question was where in
man's religious and cultural consciousness the reality of God was to be
located. It was difficult to make any hard-and-fast distinction between God
and the profoundest moral and spiritual depths in the human consciousness. In various degrees, therefore, God was conceived as immanent in
man. Every man had in him an element of the divine. With this, man's
optimism concerning himself had its theological basis and no longer was
he likely to take quite in earnest the Biblical and Reformation doctrine
concerning man's universal involvement in sin.

This threefold optimism of man, concerning his religion, his culture,
and himself, extended also to his church. Had not the nineteenth-century
church spread the benefits of a Christian religion and a Christian civilization (their inseparableness assumed) across the whole world by its heroic
missions? There were still vast areas to be Christianized, but the work
was well under way. Closer to home there was the social task of applying
the principles of the gospel to the problems of a changing society. But the
church was the fountainhead out of which all these benefits sprang. In
Western lands where the church had been long established, it was recog-

nized by the civil powers as indispensable to the health of society, and it
returned the compliment by speaking of the world that environed it as
"our Christian world" or "Christendom." A world which had been so
long under the influence of Christianity and which granted so many fa-
vors to the church could not be considered a non-Christian world even
when it withheld itself from active participation in the life and worship
of the church. Evangelism, therefore, was something to be practiced still
in the non-Christian areas of the world but was rather out of place in a
"Christian" country. Here where high moral and spiritual values were
evidence of the advance of God's Kingdom, the task was to push on until
the none too distant goal could be reached. The Kingdom being identified
with such values in human life, Christianity and civilization seemed almost interchangeable terms.

As theology took on more and more the character of a science and philosophy of religion, it steadily became more remote from the life of the
church. While its general effect was to give Christians confidence in the
superiority of their religion, it was hard pressed to maintain its relevance
for pastor and people in their day-to-day life. Having established its validity as a science in the university, it began to be less and less interesting to
the church. The scientific commentary on Scripture, which dealt with
such thoroughness with the linguistic, literary, and historical problems of
the text, stopped short of the point where the church's interest became
most intense, that is, where the text speaks its message into the present situation of man's life. That was regarded as a homiletical task which lay
outside the scope of Biblical science. The preacher was expected to take
that step alone, to step all the way from the eighth or sixth century B.C.,
or the first century A.D. to the vastly different twentieth century! So also
the study of religious phenomena through the ages could be a fascinating
intellectual pursuit that enabled a Christian to be much more intelligent
in his religious outlook, but it was not exactly essential to the Christian
life. Theology became an elective interest for the churchman, more at
home in a university situation than in the church.

The increasing complications of theology as a science of religion may
by reaction have produced the demand for a simplification of the gospel.
One of the aims of historical science was to reach back beyond the theological debates and formulations of the centuries and show what Christianity was in its original state in the historical person of Jesus. Men of all
theological colorations were agreed on the decisive importance of the
figure of Jesus and on the possibility and necessity of finding in him the
foundation in history for their religion. They merely differed in what
they found. They might have been warned by the findings of Reimarus

and Strauss that the problem of establishing a firm historical picture of Jesus was not at all simple. But it was not until Schweitzer [3] demonstrated at the end of the century that each theologian was finding in the records the Jesus who provided a foundation and authority for his own theology that the extent of the difficulty began to be recognized. Even then the idea persisted that the modern Christian could find liberation from the burdensome structure of traditional doctrine and guidance in discerning the nature of true religion in the labyrinth of religious ideas and practices by recovering for himself the simple religion of Jesus.

2. Teachers of Barth and Bultmann

Against this background we must now place several of the theologians under whom both Barth and Bultmann studied. None was more eminent than *Adolf von Harnack*. Unrivaled as a church historian, he had been professor in Berlin since 1888. Before that time he had already produced two volumes of his *Outlines of the History of Dogma* and more than a hundred articles. He had a genius for organizing large scholarly projects and enlisting the cooperation of others in their execution. For twenty-nine years he edited the *Theologische Literaturzeitung,* which kept the entire theological field under constant survey, and at the same time he regularly published volumes of his own. But his widest influence came from a series of lectures on " The Essence of Christianity " which he delivered in the winter of 1899 and 1900 to six hundred students of all faculties in Berlin and which was a masterly statement of the liberal point of view for laymen in the church.

For Harnack the definition of the Christian religion was a purely historical question. The historian had simply to show what religion was in the teaching and person of Jesus. Christianity " had a founder who himself was what he taught — to steep ourselves in him is still the chief matter." [4] To reach the simple essence of Jesus' religion, however, the historian had to strip away the temporary expressions of it that concealed what was of permanent value. The Jewish forms in which it first clothed itself, and then the Hellenistic ones that followed, did not belong to the essence, but Harnack was confident that " anyone who possesses a fresh eye for what is alive and a true feeling for what is really great " will have no difficulty in distinguishing the essence from the temporary elements. " The Christian religion is something simple and sublime: it means one thing and one thing only: eternal life in the midst of time, by the strength and under the eyes of God." The Kingdom of God preached by Jesus was the immediate rule of the Father in the hearts of his children. He pointed men not to himself but to the Father, and in assuring them of their status as God's children, he "was the first to bring the value of every human soul to light." As children of one Father their life had to have love as its ruling principle. The gospel, thus, had to do only with the two relationships, between God and man, and between man and man. The parable of the prodigal, according to Harnack, had no place in it for Jesus but only for the Father and his two sons. Jesus is the "personal realization" of the gospel, the one in whom men see what it means to be a "son of God," but he cannot be made the central figure of his own gospel. It was Paul who began the obscuring of Jesus' simple religion, concocting "the speculative idea that not only was God in Christ, but that Christ himself was possessed of a peculiar nature of a heavenly kind." The Greek philosophic mind, introduced into the church, went one stage farther and devised such doctrines as the Trinity, the incarnation of the logos, and the pre-existence of Christ. With one stroke Harnack stripped away the whole structure of traditional doctrine and reduced the religion of a Christian to a handful of simple truths of which Jesus was the first expositor in word and life.

As early as 1883, Harnack was defining faith as "trust in God's fatherly goodness" and was dismissing Trinitarian and Christological doctrines as "speculations." Jesus was simply the mirror of God's Fatherly heart. To know Christ was not to know two natures in him, one human and one divine, but to have learned that he is the only way to the Father. The only life worth having comes from Jesus Christ, but it comes not by trusting doctrines about his nature but by obedience to his commands. It is not surprising that Harnack, although he commanded an international circle of devoted followers, roused widespread distrust and antagonism in the church. Not only the orthodox but also the only moderately conservative churchmen saw in his teaching a reduction of Christianity to a form of humanistic unitarianism. When a controversy broke out concerning the trial of a young minister for failing to use the Apostles' Creed in the baptismal service, Harnack spoke out on behalf of the offender and called for a simpler creed, but when he was urged to set forth some such new confession of faith, he demurred, pleading that he was no reformer. Parallel with the reduction which he effected in doctrine was an equally radical reduction in the canon of Scripture. The Lord's Prayer and the Sermon on the Mount were the central fortress of his religion. The miracles, the eschatology, the mythical representations, and the doctrinal formulations in the New Testament were all dispensable. The Old Testament, which he agreed had served as a safeguard for Christianity in the early centuries of its life, was now a burden to it and could be set aside. To some in the church who had been imprisoned in a narrow and lifeless doctrinal orthodoxy and Biblicism such teaching was a liberation, but to others it seemed to be an abandonment of the apostolic and Reformation faith. At one point Harnack resisted the trend of liberal thought: he insisted upon the uniqueness and superiority of the Christian religion. For him it was not one religion among many but *the* religion, and on this basis he opposed the introduction of the history of religions into the theological curriculum.

Wilhelm Herrmann of Marburg seems to have made a much deeper impression upon both Barth and Bultmann than did Harnack. Barth, having read Herrmann's *Ethics* in 1905 and heard his lectures in 1908, considered him *the* theological teacher of his student days. He says that from his first contact with him in 1905 " I consider that I began to work at theology with an independent attentiveness." [5] When the fourth edition of the *Ethics* came to him as a gift from Herrmann five minutes before he went into the pulpit in his first charge, he regarded it as a " dedication for all the future." Bultmann, however, shows the influence of Herrmann in his early writings even more plainly than Barth.

Herrmann, five years senior to Harnack, had settled in Marburg in 1879 and remained there for the rest of his life. For him as for Harnack doctrinal orthodoxy was the chief enemy of a genuine Christian faith and the polemic against it is constant in his writings. The church authorities, in forcing from candidates an affirmation of a traditional creed, seemed to him to be doing violence to men's very souls. Simple integrity demanded that a man call nothing true until it was true for him in his own existence. Faith as an ineffable reality in each individual could not with honesty take over its form of expression ready-made from anyone else, not even from prophets and apostles. But Herrmann did not count himself a liberal. Liberals, to him, were theologians who rejected the authority of any special revelation of God either in Scripture or in tradition and proposed " a religiosity based in the being of the human spirit." [6] They were rationalists and mystics who held that we must find something in our own existence that makes us sure of God. They were philosophers of religion like Troeltsch who thought they could make theology a science like any other science and arrive at the truth of religion in an objective fashion. They were New Testament scholars who by their historical inquiry left the person of Jesus wholly problematical so that all we have on which to build is his gospel or his religion. In opposition to such liberalism Herrmann insisted upon the transcendence of God and the reality of a revelation in Jesus in which man is confronted with God and not

just with some divine element in his own being. He rejected the possibility
of a science of religion, since religion discloses itself as a reality only to
the one who experiences it and in each of its disclosures has a uniqueness
that is not objectively comprehensible by other persons. To reduce theology to a science of religion would be to focus it upon the observable external expressions of religion but to miss the inner reality which alone
makes it comprehensible. But, more important, he demanded for Jesus a
centrality for faith as the One through whom alone God is fully known
to man and man comes to the fulfillment of himself, and, starting from
this center, he found meaning in doctrines such as the Trinity and the
incarnation, which liberals like Harnack had been ready to cast aside.

Elements from Schleiermacher, Kant, and Ritschl were built into Herrmann's theology, but his starting point was Kant's basing of belief in God
upon man's conscience. God is revealed in goodness. Character grows from
ethical decisions, and in such decisions one is conscious of being grasped
by the eternal. Bowing to the ethical and finding in the eternal law its
own law, the soul is made free and stands on the threshold of Christian
faith. The child meets God in the goodness of his parents. But only in the
perfect goodness of the man Jesus is God perfectly revealed, so that our
faith remains always dependent upon the Jesus who meets us both in the
Scriptures and in those whose lives have been shaped by what they found
in him. Herrmann agreed with Martin Kähler that though critical scholarship made impossible the writing of a life of Jesus and left many elements in the New Testament picture uncertain, there remained still an
incomparable figure the power of whose ethical majesty was inescapable.
Every man has the ability to find in the New Testament traditions about
Jesus "the picture of a man who holds us over the abyss by the power of
his personal life." [7] Even the most critical New Testament scholar has a
picture of Jesus in his mind which he agrees represents the highest he has
ever known in this world. Christian faith, then, is man's response to the
grace of God which he experiences in the ethical goodness of the inner life
of Jesus. All goodness that meets us in other men has in it a self-contradiction which negates its power, but the perfection of Jesus' goodness, the
conformity of his life with his ideal, the purity of his love, the strength
of his will, the firmness of his convictions, make him the ultimate revelation of God that compels our repentance and brings to us a redemption
in which we learn a new kind of thinking, feeling, and willing, and see
the world in a new light. While Herrmann held that this revelation
could be mediated through a succession of persons for whom it had become living reality, he emphasized in his later years the importance of
the Scriptures if men were to be brought into immediate relation with the

inner life of Jesus. But, having defined the divine revelation in Jesus as the redemptive power of the ethical quality in his human character, it was hard for him to maintain the uniqueness of Jesus as the Christ or to escape the immanentalism of his opponents, since a similar though lesser ethical quality in other men would have to be interpreted as a similar though lesser presence of God in them.

For Herrmann, however, faith does not *begin* with the confrontation with Jesus but with a proper confrontation of man with himself. He has to become a self if he is to have anything to give society, but when he faces the truth, he has to acknowledge the absence of his true self. The concealment of this central dilemma is the real godlessness of man. Religion begins not with great emotions but in the integrity with which we face the present reality of our life and own to ourselves our longing for the one reality that would bring us wholly to our fulfillment. Herrmann seems to assume this starting point as already present in every man who will be honest with himself. Each man can know his dilemma and should be impelled by it to seek the resolution of his inner contradiction in Jesus. He cannot think his way through to it but has to experience it in a complete surrender to the true good that brings the self its freedom. It is strange that Herrmann should attribute to man the possibility of thus grasping the reality of his own situation and of making this knowledge the starting point from which he moves to the knowledge of God when his chief criticism of Schleiermacher was that he posited the feeling of absolute dependence as naturally present in every man instead of recognizing that it exists only in response to revelation and comes to a man in his conscious surrender to God. Applying the same evangelical criterion to his own assumption, he would have had to own that man has true and saving knowledge of his self-contradiction only in and with his knowledge of God.

Herrmann owed much to Schleiermacher, above all, his understanding of faith as a determination of the spiritual life of the Christian that finds expression in doctrines or ideas rather than as an adherence to doctrines of themselves, but also his confidence that with this definition of faith the split between Christianity and culture is overcome and faith illuminates the whole of God's dealings with man in his historical existence. Schleiermacher combined modern scientific knowledge with Christian faith and so inaugurated a new era, but it seemed to Herrmann that he did not sufficiently grasp either the dynamic character of faith, that it is not a static entity out of the past but is constantly in movement and manifesting itself in new forms, or its dependence on the life that meets us in Scripture and is ever beyond us. In an age when everything in Christianity was being defined in terms of man's religion, Herrmann held fast to the conviction that man's coming to his true life depends upon the unique and decisive revelation of God in Jesus Christ. It is not difficult then to see why Barth in 1925 could say that he was not conscious of any " conversion away from him " but only that he had had to say differently what he learned from him. And when we hear Herrmann say, " God reveals himself to us only in the inner transformation which we experience. . . . The religious man is certain that God has spoken to him, but what he can say of the event always takes the form of a statement concerning his transformed life . . . since religion is the transition from what only seems to be life to what is truly life," [8] we seem to be hearing the voice of Bultmann.

A third theologian who looms large in the immediate background is *Ernst Troeltsch,* against whose radical historicism and determination to make theology wholly a historical science Herrmann was in vigorous rebellion.[9] For Troeltsch, the medieval period in Christianity came to an end not with the Reformation but with the eighteenth-century Enlightenment. The turning point in the life of modern man was the period just before and after 1700 when he threw off the shackles of the old supernaturalism and authoritarianism and began to think for himself in a new way. Historical method, applied to the Scriptures and to Christian tradition, had simply dissolved the old authorities and made impossible the old theological structures of both Protestantism and Roman Catholicism. A work of reconstruction had to be done by theology using the best of modern scientific methods, and the theologian had to be free of ecclesiastical restraints that would interfere with his progress or deflect his scientific judgment. To this end Troeltsch himself transferred from the theological to the philosophical faculty when he went from Heidelberg to Berlin. The first duty of the historian was to lay bare the facts of religious history no matter how disturbing they might be, and Troeltsch was quite aware how disturbing his facts were to the mind of the church. So uncertain had the picture of Jesus become that it was no longer possible for theologians to build upon it, and when they retreated to the apostolic interpretation of Jesus as a foundation for their faith, the historian had in turn to question its legitimacy, since it seemed to be derived from diverse sources. Nowhere in history could one any longer put down his foot on solid ground that would provide a foundation for Christian faith. Religious history, including Biblical history, belonged in the context of general history and all was subject to the same forces and the same laws of development. There were no absolutes anywhere in history, only relative phenomena. To absolutize the inner life of Jesus as a historical phenomenon as Herrmann did was to make him unhistorical and therefore something other than human. Equally inadmissible was it to absolutize Christianity in any of its historical forms. The most the historian could say was that within the relativities of Western culture Jesus Christ represented the highest religious development that men had yet known. It was in this ruthless assertion of the relativity of all that is historical that Troeltsch exerted his primary influence on both Barth and Bultmann.

His positive theological judgments were of less significance. He had cleared the ground for reconstruction and had indicated that a theology which took account of the full breadth of religious phenomena in and beyond Christianity must take the form of a science of religion, but he was never very clear what this meant for the reformulation of the Christian faith itself. There was a mystical cast to his religion that had its basis in a direct feeling of God's presence, but when he came to define religion, his starting point was a psychological analysis of the religious consciousness that took the form of a critique of the successive stages of religion in history. With Hegel he regarded history as an unfolding of Infinite Spirit so that history itself was revelation and God the power behind the world's evolutionary advance. A theology based on such revelation naturally had to be a philosophy of history. Christian revelation was merely the culmination of this general revelation, Jesus Christ having a primacy as the man who had pierced through to the highest truth of spirit. Christianity was not necessarily the ultimate in religion since in the future it might be transcended, but for all practical purposes it could be regarded as final and unconditional for man in the present as he has nothing beyond it. Thus, in spite of his radical conclusions, Troeltsch ended on an optimistic note, reassuring Christians that a scientific evaluation of all the religions of the world through all history showed the superiority of Christianity (at least for the present) over every other religious affiliation. He also reinforced men's confidence in the inseparability of Christianity from Western culture. Only when one takes account of the direction in which theology was going in the work of men of the eminence of Troeltsch and Harnack does one appreciate the dimensions of the revolution that was to come.

3. SOME EXAMPLES OF NEW TESTAMENT SCHOLARSHIP

We need now to look at some samples of New Testament scholarship at the beginning of the century, and it will serve our purpose best to examine what two distinguished and representative scholars made of Paul who was to be of such crucial significance for both Barth and Bultmann. In an essay on "The Meaning of Paul for the Modern Christian,"[10] published in the same year that Barth brought out his first commentary on Romans, Johannes Weiss, who taught in Marburg until 1908, was mainly concerned to show how wide a gap loomed between Paul and the twentieth-century Christian. There were six points at which it seemed to him that the modern Christian must put Paul behind him: (1) Paul's doctrine of redemption had as its context a mythological world view that he had taken over from Gnosticism, the world being conceived as standing under the power of Satan so that Christ had to descend from heaven into this evil world in order to liberate men and then reascend to heaven. Mythology of this kind belongs to an ancient world to which we cannot return. (2) Conversion to Christianity meant a sharp break in the life of Paul, but no such break is necessary for us. Most of us live in the constant consciousness of the divine grace so that no conversion of any kind is necessary. (3) The idea that the Holy Spirit as a divine reality should invade man's person and actually take up residence in him belongs in the category of primitive animism in which men and things are inhabited by alien spirits. Man, however, is an autonomous being for whom the presence of God can mean no more than a heightening of his own spiritual powers. (4) Paul is in some degree pantheistic in his belief in a revelation of God in nature, but this actually is an advantage for him in the modern scene where so many intellectuals are pantheistic in their conception of God. (5) Paul's doctrine of justification by faith alone had a real point in the first century in antithesis to Pharisaic legalism, but such legalism is a thing of the past. It no longer exists in our situation, so that Paul's doctrine of justification is bound to be strange to us, the occasion for it having departed. (6) Paul's worship of Jesus Christ is as idolatrous as the Roman Catholic worship of Mary. Jesus ought not to be an object of worship for us but only an ethical awakener and guide. Again we meet an essentially unitarian and humanistic theology, complacent about the spiritual condition of Western man who has had the benefit of Christianity for centuries and in its complacency so alien to Paul's theology that he becomes largely incomprehensible.

Wilhelm Wrede, writing in 1907,[11] interpreted Paul as "the second founder of Christianity." For him, the break between Jesus and Paul was even more radical than for Weiss. Paul knew nothing of Jesus and wanted to know nothing. Before ever he became a Christian, he believed in a celestial being, the divine Messiah, and his conversion experience merely convinced him that the Jesus of the Christians was this celestial being. He thereupon transferred all the attributes of his Messiah to Jesus and in doing this transformed the simple ethical religion of Jesus into a religion of supernatural redemption. Insofar as the religion of Paul has any elements in common with the religion of Jesus, these are to be explained by the influence of Judaism on both of them. The only event in Jesus' life that was significant for Paul was his death and even it had importance only "as an occurrence in a world above that of sense." Paul's Christology he held to be a Gnostic mythology. The Son of God, a superhuman divine figure, active in the original creation of the world and preexistent with God, is conceived as taking the form of a man for a time, resigning his divine status in order to do it. In his human form he is not really human but is an impalpable phantom with no human thought, feeling, or will of his own. He descends into the realm of man's captivity in order to redeem him. By his death he is set free to return to his divine existence, and men in solidarity with him receive their freedom through identification with him in his death, though their freedom does not become actual until they die. Paul's conception of salvation as an objective achievement, already accomplished by God in the person and work of Jesus Christ, was declared by Wrede to be entirely alien to modern thought. Salvation could not be identified with a past historical event, since it was reality only when it was an inner experience of man.

Both scholars were confident that they were arriving at their conclusions concerning Paul by a purely scientific historical methodology. They were laying bare the facts, uninfluenced by theological presuppositions. But today it requires little discernment to recognize that their objectivity was something less than perfect and that from where they were standing theologically it was impossible to see very far or even very accurately into the mind of Paul. Historical evaluations and theological judgments are not as easily separable as they assumed.

Barth and Bultmann would have heard a somewhat different account of Paul from Adolf Jülicher, long a colleague of Weiss at Marburg. Jülicher was against any radical separation between Jesus and Paul. He had no objection to Wrede's historical methodology, which claimed the same kind of objectivity as was possible in natural science.[12] He also agreed that the Pauline concepts of redemption, reconciliation, and justification had no place in the gospel of Jesus. Paul undoubtedly thought he was proclaiming the gospel Jesus would want proclaimed, but he was mistaken. Jesus called men to faith but not to faith in himself. He did not tell the rich young ruler that he needed only to believe in him; he commanded him to sell all he had. But, having recognized this difference between the gospels of Jesus and Paul, Jülicher saw a legitimacy in the Pauline development. He was certain that Paul's Christ-myth did not shock the apostles or the Jerusalem church. They understood his emphasis on the risen Lord and had no objection to extending Jesus' divine story with accounts of his preexistence and of his miraculous birth. They differed with Paul concerning the authority of the law, but, where he developed doctrines of atonement, redemption, and life in Christ, they stood with him. Jülicher then proceeded to emphasize the points of unity between Paul and Jesus. While Paul could not and did not find a basis for his doctrine of the freedom of the Gentiles from the law in the teachings or example of Jesus, he at least was true to the spirit of Jesus, truer than the apostles who opposed him. Also, he must have known much concerning Jesus' ministry through his close association with Barnabas and Mark and the two weeks he spent with Peter. He was no second founder of Christianity but built upon foundations that were already laid in the early church at Jerusalem. In spite of all differences, Jesus and Paul were one in faith, hope, and love. Hope for the Kingdom dominated the minds of both and for both it was present as well as future. Paul may have used the term " kingdom " rarely, but his expectation was focused upon a day when evil would be destroyed and man's life would be brought to its fulfillment. The same unconditional faith in God possessed Paul that came to its perfect expression in Jesus and was claimed by him from every man. And the same infinite love toward God and man was the ultimate secret of life for Paul as for Jesus.

Here, then, was a very different estimate of Paul, but there was coupled with it the same antagonism to New Testament Christological developments that we have observed in the other scholars. The power of Jesus' great personality is central for Jülicher as it was for Herrmann, and the power resides in Jesus' ethical ideals which are able even to make a victory out of his death. Jesus' purpose was not to found a church but to bring a new piety, a new ideal, to birth among men. Jesus planted a garden; Paul built a wall around it.

It may be of value to look also at the views of Paul Wernle under whom Barth was introduced to New Testament scholarship in Bern and against whose standpoint he rebelled during the early years of his Swiss pastorate. Like Harnack, Weiss, and Wrede, Wernle [13] was concerned to strip off the temporary and transitory elements in the early formulations of the gospel in order to liberate its eternal substance. The early Christians were naïve in their geography, expecting the world to be evangelized in one generation, and naïve in their supernaturalism, letting a superstitious belief in the miraculous run riot. Their doctrines of inspiration and atonement were products of a childlike psychology. Their conceptions of demons and of a Holy Spirit were a legacy from paganism. The author of John's Gospel was polytheistic, placing a divine logos alongside the supreme God. The whole development of Christological doctrine in the early church was a perversion and a concealment of original Christianity. Jesus was a religious genius, "endowed with a self-consciousness more than prophetic" and "more than human." What this "more" signified is not clear, since the rise of Christianity under his influence was explained by Wernle as a purely human phenomenon. "He stands altogether a man on the side of men, with the feeling of the division that separates all things created from God." His humility before God, his ability to give new values to things and to scatter new thoughts which were energized by his person, his possession of healing power, especially in regard to mental diseases, his emancipation from outworn Jewish theological ideas, all served to draw men to him in an unusual way. "Revelation, redemption, forgiveness, help — he has all those and offers them to such as shall surrender themselves to the impression of his personality" (41). Jesus conceived of himself as a mediator, "God's final messenger after whom none higher can come." While discarding the New Testament Christology, Wernle attempted thus to salvage the ultimacy and absolute superiority of Christianity. But the most he could attribute to Jesus was a "superhuman self-consciousness . . . which knows nothing higher than itself save God" (45). The Kingdom originally proclaimed by Jesus was Jewish in concept, primarily future and for Israel alone, but Jesus showed his greatness in liberating himself from such narrowness. In a happy period of his ministry when "Jesus felt himself to be in harmony with all the good influences at work amongst his people," when "patriotism and religion were one and hope ran into vision," he taught that the Kingdom whose substance was everlasting life and unbroken communion with God was already present (66). This, however, was followed by a period of disenchantment in which the Kingdom receded into the future and gladness gave way to gloomy judgment, the people as a whole being regarded by him as hopelessly lost. In order to declare that God was on his side and that he was in the right, Jesus adopted the Jewish teaching of a return of the Messiah, "a fantastic and erroneous conception" and a mistaken compromise by Jesus with contemporary superstition.

Jesus' teaching, according to Wernle, was directed entirely to the individual and his inner life. Jesus had no social ethic. He accepted poverty and injustice as inevitable in human life. Not social reform but self-reform was his aim. Jesus' ethical achievement was in separating the universal, human element from the rest of the Jewish law, the moral from the ceremonial law, but his ethic was simply what every man's conscience sanctions. His teaching was so simple that even a child could understand him. He asserted nothing but what was obvious to the human conscience. Thus, the individual who was roused by Jesus' call "was made dependent simply upon himself and his own conscience." Jesus' aim was "to unite God and man as he himself was united with God." By his death he freed his disciples from their old inadequate interpretation of death and fear of death as divine punishment. The resurrection visions were too questionable to be the basis of faith but merely " enabled his disciples to recover from their perplexity " (116). Their faith was based on " the earlier impression which death had not been able to efface." Jesus was, as Lagarde had written, " too great that he should die." Jesus had had faith in the power of his word and the influence of his personality to ensure the continuance of his work. His office of mediation he expected to be taken over by the apostles, not as originators of a new tradition but in subordination to him as agents of his gospel. " The church originated in a hero-worship — theologians call it faith " (127). But obedience to God's will as taught by Jesus was not enough for the church. Quickly it moved toward an orthodoxy in which it demanded a confession of faith in Jesus, the use of Sacraments and a complex legalistic system of religious doctrines and practices. Now, however, thanks to nineteenth-century scholarship, the church was being liberated from this intolerable burden and the simple religion of Jesus was being recovered in its pristine purity.

It should be noted that Weiss, Wrede, and Wernle all belonged to the *religionsgeschichtliche* (history of religion) school, of which Bultmann was to be a distinguished representative in the second generation. This movement which was to influence both Old and New Testament scholarship began in the 1880's with a circle of young scholars in Göttingen who reacted against certain features of Ritschl's theology and demanded a more thoroughly scientific investigation of the phenomena of religion, both in the Biblical records and beyond them.[14] The founders were Albert Eichhorn, Gunkel, Wrede, and Bousset, although they in turn looked back to such men as Wellhausen and Duhm as belonging with them. They desired a purely historical conception of the Bible free from all dogmatic considerations, their assumption being that a theological concern must inevitably interfere with the scientific character of any investigation and distort its conclusions. They were also dissatisfied with a literary criticism that left unexplored the history of the traditions embodied in the literature. Two changes of focus in the last quarter of the nineteenth century that influenced them strongly were the widening of the scope of religious interest from the Biblical records to the religious phenomena both in the world surrounding the Bible and in the whole history of human civilization, and the exploration of the complex social forces in history.

Close upon the heels of the founders came Johannes Weiss, Wernle, Heitmüller, Weinel, and Troeltsch, and then, in the second generation, Gressmann, Hans Schmidt, and Mowinckel in Old Testament and such men as Dibelius and Bultmann in New Testament. Form criticism in the New Testament and tradition criticism in the Old Testament were parallel developments. There was a special interest in the exploration of eschatological concepts in both Testaments and in Jewish literature. Gunkel and Gressmann set the whole of Old Testament eschatology in a new light, and Weiss and Bousset forced the recognition of the character and importance of Jewish eschatology in the ministry of Jesus and the early church. Where Ritschl had interpreted the New Testament directly against the background of the Old Testament and had neglected the significance of late Judaism, the new school concentrated upon building out the Jewish and Hellenistic religious background between 200 B.C. and A.D. 200, against which the origin of Christianity had to be interpreted. Its tendency was by reaction to neglect the importance of the Old Testament for the interpretation of the New and to make too much of the Jewish and Hellenistic parallels to New Testament ideas and practices. There were wide variations of viewpoint within the school, and the school exerted an influence upon scholars who would have disclaimed any adherence to it, yet it came to represent a scholarly tradition of a particular color and with presuppositions which weighted the scales in a particular direction, such as an extreme skepticism about what can be known concerning Jesus or the assumption that the conceptualities in which the New Testament gospel is expressed can be viewed in detachment from the essence of the gospel itself. The basic characteristic, however, which gave the movement its strong appeal and its great value was the scrupulous integrity of its historical scholarship and its willingness to follow the facts no matter how disturbing the consequences might be for established viewpoints.

Chapter III

TWO DEVOTED LIBERALS

In Marburg, where both Barth and Bultmann finished their schooling, the leading journal of liberal thought had its home. *Die christliche Welt* (*The Christian World*) [1] had been founded in 1886 by Martin Rade, one of the most brilliant students of Harnack and a genial theologian who somehow managed to enlist the cooperation not only of a wide range of liberal scholars but also of some who were of a more conservative viewpoint. He had formed an association called " The Friends of *Die christliche Welt* " to provide a broad basis of support for his journal, enlisting in it pastors and laymen as well as scholars. Each year this association met in some rural or urban center to hear papers that dealt with the live theological issues of the time and to discuss the policy of the journal. Rade prided himself that most progressive developments in German theology came out of this circle. When Barth, Gogarten, and Bultmann later began to strike out on a course that seemed to negate the standpoint of liberalism, he consoled himself that even this strange product had had its beginnings under the shadow of *Die christliche Welt*.[2] For a whole year Barth served as assistant editor of the journal, and Bultmann, too, during his early years in Marburg was a close associate. Both of them attended the annual conferences of " The Friends of *Die christliche Welt* " for years to come. From this fact we can infer the milieu in which they were most at home as they finished their university education.

Bultmann upon graduation went directly on with his New Testament studies to prepare himself for a life of teaching. Barth, after his year as an editor, became an assistant pastor in Geneva, where he remained for two years, but his writings show that he was already deep in the study of systematic theology. This divergence of interest will throw the focus of our study more on Barth in this chapter, since while Bultmann was writing articles of a more technical and only slightly theological character in order to establish himself in the New Testament faculty, Barth was actively participating in the life of the church and grappling with the problems of interpreting the Christian faith with integrity in the world of modern culture. But neither of them had begun to move out of the liberal theological realm in which they had been educated. Barth has documented the fact that by 1910 he had attached himself to the prevailing tendency among younger followers of Albrecht Ritschl but " not without a certain alienation in view of the issue of this school in the philosophy of religion of Ernst Troeltsch, in which I found myself disappointed in regard to what interested me in theology, although for the time being I did not see a better way before me." [3] He had Herrmann's support in his unwillingness to go all the way with Troeltsch in his science of religion. Bultmann as a New Testament scholar was much more deeply involved in the *religionsgeschichtliche* (history of religion) school, and, if we may judge by slightly later evidence, less critical than Barth of its claims and program as a historical science, but there are signs that he too agreed with Herrmann that religion as the inner reality of man's relation with God is unavailable to any science for description and analysis. It is important to recognize, however, that both men began their careers as convinced liberal theologians who, although they were in disagreement with some tendencies of liberal scholarship, saw no viable alternative upon the horizon. Barth, by the time he was twenty-eight had written two major theological articles for journals within the perspective of this school, sufficient in their competence to mark him as a coming leader in it. In short, he was a theologian of the Neo-Protestantism (the liberalized Protestantism of the nineteenth and early twentieth centuries) which a few years later he was to attack with such vigor. The importance of this is that the theology of Neo-Protestantism was never for him, as for some of its critics, an interpretation of Christianity that he had known only in other men. It was the theology by which he himself had once lived and preached and taught.[4] When he criticized Schleiermacher, he could never forget in the midst of the criticisms that in his youth Schleiermacher had provided the ground on which he stood theologically. Though he could not continue to stand there, he remained grateful for what Schleiermacher had done for him and for others in the past.

1. BARTH'S EARLIEST PUBLICATIONS

Barth's first publication of any size was an article on "Modern Theology and Work for the Kingdom of God," [5] written in 1909 when he was on the point of becoming a pastor in Geneva. While attending a student conference he was asked why so few graduates of universities where the theology was markedly liberal enlisted for service in foreign missions, in comparison with graduates of conservative schools such as those in Halle and Greifswald. The same question might have been asked in America at any time during the first half of this century when the preponderance of volunteers for foreign service were conservative in theology. Barth widened the question to read: Why does modern theology make the entire practical work of the ministry more difficult to face? He found the answer in the slowness of the liberal student in arriving at a tenable faith that would provide a basis for action, and he set forth two reasons for this slowness. First was the demand of liberal theology that a man should think for himself with integrity, calling true only what he himself sees to be true, proving all things, finding his salvation on his own. It was impossible for him to take over a religious code or standpoint ready-made. Second was the exposure by historical science of the relativity of all that has happened in history, including the historical phenomena documented in Scripture. No longer could one make historical events or a historical person or a historical creed into an absolute, identifying them directly with the truth of God and escaping thereby from all insecurity. The conservative student, by his readiness to give his assent to a traditional formulation of faith and his absolutizing of either the Bible, the Jesus of history, or the creed, or perhaps of all three together, put his uncertainties behind him and was ready for action. But, for the liberal student, this would mean the loss of his integrity and the end of all honest thought.

The problem with which Barth was wrestling here was how to combine an evangelical faith with scientific theological investigation which would make use of the best equipment and the best knowledge available. He had no sympathy with some who solved the problem readily as they entered the pastorate by turning their backs on the academic world, throwing overboard the whole complex of modern theological issues and adapting themselves to their practical situation by conformity with whatever might happen to be the respectable religious standpoint. They called this " being realistic," but for students of Harnack and Herrmann it was unthinkable. The scientific method in theology had already become a necessity of their very being, a matter of ethical integrity. They could not close the door at any point against historical investigation, even though the historian exposed ruthlessly the relative nature of all religious phenomena and reduced Jesus to the stature of a founder of religion like any other. Then, when historians had laid bare a more or less exact picture of the Christian past, leaving no illusions about the relativity of it all, the Christian was left with the task of appropriating for himself whatever was essential in the concepts and experience of the past. In history there are only generally valid facts while religion knows only individual values. " Religion is for us experience in an intensely individual form," Barth writes. " The essence of modern theology is religious individualism." Even the conservative von Hofmann was in agreement with Schleiermacher that the individual Christian consciousness was the basis of Christian knowledge. Truth is not truth until it is reality in the experience of each man. The impulse of the man who realizes his ethical impotence and the slenderness of his inner grasp of truth is to seek a power in the tradition or life of the church to which he can submit himself as a shortcut to faith. But faith by its nature demands personal experience, and " we feel it a duty to take full and clear account of the relation of this experience to the general cultural consciousness on its scientific side." The process that began with the scientific investigation of the Christian past had to end with " the absolutely inner act of faith which is inaccessible to all adequate intellectual formulation " and yet which must be in harmony with the cultural advances of modern man. A student required many years to think his way through such a complicated process and he might be tempted to be ashamed of the incoherence that was part of its cost, but, once committed to its presuppositions, there could be no drawing back. There was no theological alternative for a really honest Christian.

The same general theme of " The Christian Faith and History " [6] was developed on a larger canvas a year later in 1910 (a 41-page essay which was not published until 1912). This essay is specially valuable and worth outlining in detail because of the evidence it gives of how competently Barth was wrestling with major theological issues at the age of twenty-four and how his thinking, already deeply rooted in the Schleiermacher-Herrmann tradition, was groping out beyond it to reconcile the reality of a life-transforming revelation of God in Jesus Christ with the sober realities disclosed by the scientific investigation of the past. The central problem of theology at this time for Barth was the relation of the present experience of God — the inner life of the Christian, his obedience, his peace — to the whole history of religion in the past. How was continuity to be established between the concepts in which faith found its formulation in the past and those which it required in the present? The problem was posed for Barth by the two most important theological movements during the years 1870 to 1910. The " history of religion " school had shown that supernatural factors such as revelation and miracle cannot be established historically, with the consequence that " God disappeared out of history " (3) and both faith and dogmatics, insofar as they tried to base them-

selves on anything historical, lost their object. But this happened because
the scientist of religion set himself outside the sphere where revelation is
a reality and the uniquely theological problem appears. The school of
Ritschl, however, insisted that theology must seek its object in a historical
revelation and especially in the picture of Christ preserved in the church
of Christ, a revelation whose content for Ritschl seemed to be a selection
of New Testament and Reformation ideas. Therefore the problem was to
devise a methodology that could get at "the actual origin and existence
of Christian experience of God in history" and show "the relation of
faith to history as it exists in the actual Christian consciousness" (4).

First, then, faith is defined on the basis of psychological observation as
"experience of God, direct consciousness of the presence and activity of
the superhuman, supernatural and therefore absolutely transcendent life-
power" (5). By it the individual is lifted to the transindividual, to an experience of God in which there is no time, past and future being one with
the present. But faith is also a social fact and as such a historical phenomenon. It exists only in a community of persons, a community that has
continuity in history. For the Christian, the experience of God is conditioned and determined by the fact that the personality of Jesus has been
present in this historical community. Faith, therefore, has in it two elements, one a reality in history and one that transcends history. In this definition Schleiermacher and Ritschl joined hands, the former in his locating
of faith in an immediate experience of the divine and the latter in his
widening of its context in the historical tradition of the church.

With this definition operating as a criterion, Barth then reviewed the
history of faith, beginning with Paul. Paul's faith certainly depended in
some measure upon the church's tradition, but the Spirit had to reveal
Christ to him so that the knowledge residing in tradition became a knowledge that was his own. The Catholic Church tried to safeguard the knowledge of Christ, first by the canon of Scripture, then with a bishop who was
the authoritative interpreter of Scripture, then with its dogmas as a rule
of faith, its presupposition being that Christ is known in the church past,
present, and future. But the safeguards usurped the authority of Christ
himself and obscured the nature of faith. Luther and Calvin tried to return to the simplicity of Paul, Calvin being more Christocentric than Luther, but they retained the external supports for faith that Catholicism
had erected in the canon of Scripture and the confessions, and, though
they first defined faith as nothing other than fiducia or trust, they paved
the way for the post-Reformation development in which intellect and will
became separated and faith became the means of appropriating the rational word of God and with it salvation. Orthodoxy thought it was bring-

ing men to faith when it presented to them the " saving facts " — Christ
as true God and true man, who came to earth to save sinners, reconciling
them to God by his blood on the cross — and regarded their acceptance of
these facts as acceptance of the truth, but actually it was destroying men's
integrity in leading them to call something truth that was not truth for
them, securing a naïve assent largely out of ignorance. Even convinced assent dare not be confused with the faith that justifies. Such assent leads on
the one hand to a fleshly security and on the other to uncertainty about
personal salvation. It is like Luther in the cloister, struggling to make himself believe more firmly.

A new development began with the Enlightenment which challenged
and dissolved the external supports for faith one by one and made man in
every realm seek the ultimate authority for truth in his own consciousness.
There began a development in which science, morals, and art each discovered its own laws, not in traditions from the past but in the present
consciousness of man. It was inevitable that, parallel with this in religion,
consciousness should assert its autonomy, negating the authority not only
of a church hierarchy but also of the Scriptures and the creeds. For a time
this revolution resulted in hopeless confusion, but eventually Schleiermacher brought order out of chaos and pointed the way forward. He
penetrated to the root of religion in a determination of feeling or self-
consciousness in which self-certainty and God-certainty are one. This living center of reality is below the level of thought and action, a realm like
the Platonic Ideas, the source of all thoughts and decisions, yet itself neither thought nor decision but direct, unanalyzable, irrational, personal-
individual aliveness. It is " the peace of God, which passes all understanding " and which must not be confused with the ideological concepts in
which faith expresses itself and presents itself to the understanding. Schleiermacher could say: " I lie on the bosom of the infinite world. . . . I am
in this moment its soul. . . . It is in this moment my body." The eternal
content of existence manifests itself in the human consciousness, the infinite in the finite. Barth's judgment at this time was that this new formulation of faith was the Romantic way of saying what Paul and the Reformers had said in other terms, so that in Schleiermacher the great
succession was renewed!

On the question how this faith arises in man he continued to follow
Schleiermacher. It does not just exist of itself. It is an event, a happening
(in German, Geschichte), occasioned in the lower religions by the impact
of nature on man, but by the impact of society on him in the higher religions. " The creative principle through which faith comes to be is love,
is the personal inner experience of pure self-surrender and pure commu-

nity" (55). What makes it Christian faith is that Christ is mediated to us by a chain of witnesses. We live in the historical community that had its origin in him and between him and us stand a wide variety of witnesses. Francis of Assisi and Bodelschwingh may be mediators alongside Paul and Augustine and Luther. Michelangelo, Bach, Mozart, Beethoven, Goethe, and a host of others may be those who "paint Christ before our eyes." But faith is not present until he is "Christ in us," and without that immediacy of faith Christ remains for us a figure of mythology, a fragment of historical knowledge. Only faith discerns the divine activity in him (57). "Where faith is not present and one has no use for mythological thinking, a critical rationalism is the only possibility." Barth quoted Angelus Silesius: "If Christ is born a thousand times at Bethlehem and not in you, you remain eternally lost. The cross at Golgotha cannot save you from evil where it is not raised up in you. I say, it does nothing for you that Christ is risen when you still lie in sin and in the bonds of death." Christ has to be known from within ourselves, but the Christ in us is also *Christus extra nos,* the Christ of history. "The effective history is the faith which is effected" (58).

When we ask what it is in Jesus Christ that makes him the factor in history through which God effects man's salvation, Barth's answer comes directly from Herrmann, "In Jesus we see an inner condition of life attained which deserves the name *justitia* (righteousness) for it is self-denying obedience in love without reservation, and therefore *the* perfect actualisation of the *a priori* determining of man" (60). This obedience is the fountain of grace "which, transcending all criticism and indifferent to historical affirmation or denial, 'shines and glistens in the gospels' (quote from Goethe)." "If we have religion at all, we have it because from the religion of Jesus through all kinds of channels the substance is given us. 'Jesus' faith is the revelation' (quote of Haering)." But this revelation which he constitutes for us and in us is not accessible to science. The science of religion can assist clarification concerning the revelation, setting the human witnesses before us, discerning "the picture which the believers have made of God's revelation for themselves, the reflection of the experienced miracle, the witness to the glory of Christ that they have seen," (69) but the miracle of revelation itself is beyond the grasp of any scientific methodology. Revelation is a seeing and appropriating of "immediate life."

Here, then, is a Barth, emancipated from orthodoxy largely by Schleiermacher, confirmed by Herrmann in his determination to find the content of Christian faith in Jesus Christ, agreeing with Ritschl that this content reaches modern man only through a definite historical tradition, refusing to let the science of religion deny him the right to speak of a revelation and action of God, and at the same time recognizing freely the revolution demanded in Christian thinking by man's new understanding of himself in modern culture. Already he had made a tolerable synthesis of the major progressive theological movements of the age. This would be the theology behind his preaching and teaching during his two years in Geneva and the theology with which he began his ministry in Safenwil.

In 1914 Barth published another substantial article, on the problem of attributing personality to God.[7] The influence of Schleiermacher is again evident. Religious experience in which one is conscious of a life that he has in immediate communion with God is seen to be the inner fortress of religion, a reality below the level of all intellectual formulations but to which the formulations must do full justice. Experience is the source of all religious statements. But he could not agree with Schleiermacher's mild antipathy to the idea of personality in God. Communion with God in prayer seemed to him to demand a " Thou " who could respond to man's " I." At one point Barth mentions Hermann Kutter, whose primary theme was the rediscovery of the living personal God, and it may well be that Barth's concern with the theological problem was inspired by his early contact with Kutter. The problem, as he saw it elaborated in the contemporary theology, was that only the transcendent dimensions of the self could be applied to God, the limited individuality of man in his becoming himself having to be set aside. But this withheld from God the character of an active Subject which the experience of communion demands and made him a complex of abstract qualities. Yet an individual " I " who is endless in time and space is unthinkable. Becoming is impossible in God. Our dilemma, therefore, is that we have to hold together two elements in the nature of God which we are unable to combine in our thought.

Our religious experience Barth describes as a " life from God " which is given us through our connection with history and is an inner conditioning by history. In it we have God and on the basis of it we can speak of God. But he confines his attention to the experience that is " a life from God and in God " awakened by the gospel of Jesus, and endeavors to show how the very nature of this experience points to both transcendental absolutes and personal subjectivity in God. It is interesting that he expects New Testament scholars to disapprove of his procedure in approaching the New Testament gospel with a modern theological problem, but this does not hinder him from positing a continuity between New Testament religion and our twentieth-century religion and insisting on the right of the systematic theologian to seek answers to his dilemmas in the Biblical text. In the gospel he finds a double concern, on the one hand with the person or self of man and on the other hand with the more impersonal Kingdom of God which dwarfs the "I" of man. We learn that we are not here to save our souls but to give God the glory in the coming of his Kingdom. Self is lost in a reality that is far beyond the self. Golgotha represents the sacrifice of personality for the sake of the Kingdom. Thus the tension of these two elements in Christian experience corresponds to the tension of the two elements in God and warns against either of them being allowed to cancel out the other.

The essay shows Barth still firmly rooted in the school of Schleiermacher and Ritschl, though not uncritical. The living center of his faith is an experience of God, and the task of theology is to find the most adequate contemporary conceptual expression for it, without for one moment forgetting which is primary and which secondary. For such a viewpoint, the old doctrinal controversies were an aberration of the past. Readers of Barth's later writings who are puzzled by his warm affection for a Schleiermacher whose theological era he claims is coming to an end need to learn what Barth at twenty-eight owed to Schleiermacher. In a letter to Barth in October, 1921, Thurneysen, looking back, reminds him of the evening rendezvous in Thurneysen's home in Leutwil when for the first time they dared to say aloud to each other that they could no longer share the faith of Schleiermacher. But the process of extrication was to take many years. The roots went deep. The mention of Kutter is significant, for it points to the relation with the Swiss religious socialist leaders Kutter and Ragaz, which was to play a part in the rebellion of these years against the all-pervasive cultural Christianity of the time. But perhaps most significant of all is the first sign of a bringing together of New Testament exposition and the problems of systematic theology, for this was eventually to lead to a dogmatics based on exegesis of Scripture in contrast to the more philosophically oriented dogmatics.

2. An Early Sample of Bultmann's Thought

In this same period Bultmann published two articles [8] but they are of a character that makes it impossible to infer much from them concerning his theological position. The first, in 1910, is a comparison of the style of the Pauline preaching with that of the Cynic-Stoic diatribe. The second, in 1912, is on "The Religious Element in the Ethical Teachings of Epictetus and the New Testament." By these publications he was mounting the academic ladder, achieving a lectureship at Marburg in 1912 and a professorship at Breslau in 1916. The two essays deal with New Testament subjects, but in the context of comparative religion, and indicate his attachment to the " history of religion " school in New Testament scholarship. As we have already seen, this was the school in which scientific historical methodology was pressed to its most radical extreme, the religious phenomena of the Old and New Testaments were constantly placed against the background of contemporary non-Biblical religions, and a tendency to depreciate the uniqueness of Christianity at certain points was balanced by a seemingly scientific demonstration of its superiority to the other religions.

The essay on Epictetus and the New Testament was occasioned by a recent book of which Bultmann was critical. He begins with a general description of Epictetus' ethic, which had as its goal a life in harmony with nature. Nature was conceived as both rational and social, with emphasis upon the former. That man has knowledge of goodness, beauty, happiness, usefulness, and their opposites was taken for granted. By this knowledge he was expected to regulate his life, but many things stood outside his control, so that the area of control had to be defined narrowly as the inner life. He had to be free of the passions such as anger and hatred. The whole ethic took a largely negative form: to deny oneself and endure whatever happened. Honor, riches, and all such worldly achievements were to be surrendered as enslavements, since one had to be free from even the desire for whatever lay outside his control. The inescapable was to be endured. The whole ideal of life was passive, resulting in a man's withdrawing into himself. No creative conquest of nature or formation of a community was possible upon the basis of it.

Bultmann then turns to the theology of Epictetus. Though the Greek deities were nonexistent for him, he did not attack the official religion but counseled participation in it. He spoke of " the divine," but mostly of " the god " or " the gods." The order of nature to which man submits is directed by God, and man cannot know his own nature without knowing God. Man is God's son, sharing his reason with God, though his body is the body of a beast. He can never be alone without God and is intended as a child of God to be like him. As God's creature man should be ashamed to dishonor God. His life should be one of obedience to him and as an obedient son he is free from fear of all earthly powers. The world, ordered by God, has harmony in all its parts and provides what is needful for all. Neither animals nor men need worry where they shall find their food. God has equipped man with the resources to meet every possible situation. Therefore, thankfulness should be man's constant attitude. Epictetus' piety, unlike that of the Stoics who merely endure whatever life brings of good or evil, "spreads a sunny joyfulness, warmth and peace about itself."

The parallels with the New Testament are obvious. Man is God's child, whose true nature is to be like his father. God the Father cares for lilies and men alike that they may be free from care. A man must be obedient to God even in the smallest things in life. He must trust God in good and evil days alike. In his communion with God he is lifted above earth's sorrows and freed from the fear of death, so that he is content whether he has much or little. But Bultmann warns that the parallels are deceptive. Although the terms that are used are similar, their meaning is quite different in the two instances. The difference appears when the basic theology is brought to light. For Epictetus, man's relation to God as a son to a father is not personal but, rather, is a fixed order. There is no idea of grace or revelation, since God's reason is already present in man. An attitude of humility or childlike openness toward God is out of place. God's gifts can be taken for granted and do not need to be awaited. God is little more than a personification of man's highest ethical thoughts. There is no living God who directs nature and history and guides peoples and individuals. Everything that happens does so by unchangeable laws, so that God is in this aspect a personification of what happens. There is no meaning in speaking of a care of such a God for his creatures. And this determinism neutralizes ethical freedom. In such an order the will of man is not free to act but only to refrain from acting. There can be no mastering of nature. The most a man can do is to will whatever happens. Life is paralyzed. Nature and history are fixed in their course and have no goal toward which they are moving. The historical dynamic of Christianity is totally lacking. Neither man in general nor man as an individual has any destiny before him. The most truly religious moment in Epictetus is his rejoicing in the creation, but this is pantheistic and is not to be confused with the Christian's gratitude to God, which is primarily gratitude for what God himself is to him.

So far the essay has been a routine exercise in comparative religion, but when Bultmann begins to press beyond the concepts to their source, we hear a few things that are significant for future developments. First, he points out the limitation of historical method, that it cannot take account of revelation or supernatural realities but must confine its attention to the human psyche. This does not mean that it denies the existence of revelation but only that revelation is beyond the scope of its investigation. Here we see the influence of Herrmann with his insistence that man's life in God is of such a nature that it eludes the observation of the historical scientist. The historian, therefore, must take as his final task the analysis of the psychology of history. He cannot get beyond the human psyche. Thus, in investigating the source of the differences in concept between Epictetus and the New Testament, we have reached the limit of historical investigation when we have exposed a difference in "personality-consciousness" (which was later to be called man's "self-understanding").

Here the Christian is distinguished by his consciousness of sin and guilt while Epictetus knows nothing of guilt, but only weakness and error. The Christian is called to repent of what he is that by grace and forgiveness he may become his true self, but for Epictetus no such becoming is necessary, since man is already in possession of his true nature in the divine logos. He has merely to reflect on the true way of life, to remember what he already knows, to correct his errors and overcome his weakness. His ideal is attainable, though it may require a struggle. There is no radical alienation from God or from his own true self to be overcome. He does not have to become anything essentially different from what he is. But for this reason neither he nor humanity is going anywhere. There is no new being in prospect for him, no *Heilsgeschichte,* no movement of history toward a goal, no leaving behind of an old world to find a new one as in Christianity. Providence in history brings nothing new. The relation of man with God is static and unchanging. Man is driven in upon himself and in his self-protectiveness has little concern for society. The circle of life is drawn very narrowly, and life itself has lost all sense of mysterious heights and depths.

In summing up, Bultmann expresses admiration for Epictetus' unified, firmly established personality, which is greater than his doctrine. The comparison, however, has served chiefly to bring out what is characteristic in Christianity. He ends by asking two questions: whether the similarities in ethical ideas would serve as a point of contact for Christians in their approach to Stoics, and whether the elements of a living religion, present in Christianity but lacking in Stoicism, provide an adequate explanation of why the New Testament religion conquered.

From this essay we get a very limited view of Bultmann's theology in the prewar period. He belongs in the most progressive echelon of the "history of religion" school in New Testament scholarship. He is committed to a scientific methodology that will expose the facts of man's history ruthlessly without considering whether or not the facts may be embarrassing to the church. The church ultimately will be served only by the full acknowledgment of whatever is true. But he disagrees with Harnack and other historians in their claim that historical science can expose the essence of religion or the essence of Christianity. The historian has limitations, and a failure to recognize them carries him astray in his conclusions. Perhaps the comparison of the New Testament with Epictetus has more theological import than appears on the surface. The pantheistic immanentalism of Epictetus was not far from the surface in some liberal theologians of the time. In fact, much of the contemporary theology was more Greek than Christian in its basic concepts of God and man. Bultmann's essay therefore shows a sharpened theological awareness for what was distinctive and unique in the Christian gospel. But there is no suggestion at any point that he was ill at ease in the theological milieu of Marburg in 1900–1914. There are some sentences in a sermon of 1917 [9] which suggest that he looked back on that period as one of almost idyllic security and satisfaction — " hours of carefree joy with our friends, . . . hours of pure, unalloyed joy in work and creation, of devotion to the precious powers of spiritual life, of pure enjoyment in the ripe fruits of human creativity." He might perhaps have added: hours of unbroken confidence that the triumphs of Western civilization were paralleled by the triumphs of Christian intelligence in all the areas of theological scholarship.

Chapter IV

THE BEGINNINGS OF REVOLT, 1913–1917

MANY FALSE IDEAS have long been current concerning the origin of the theological revolution that is connected with the names of Barth and Bultmann. One of the commonest has been that it was a postwar phenomenon engendered by the atmosphere of crisis in which men lived for a few years after seeing their world torn apart by the war of 1914–1918. Bishop Stephen Neill [1] reports that it all began when with the outbreak of war in 1914 Barth found himself in the embarrassing dilemma of having nothing to preach and was forced to read his Bible in a new way. Others have attributed the fresh beginning in theological thinking to the influence of Kierkegaard's philosophy, his existentialism providing the basis for a reconsideration of the meaning of the gospel.

Barth himself has negated the exaggeration of Kierkegaard's influence upon him in an address delivered in Copenhagen in 1963 on the occasion of his receiving the Sonning Prize.[2] He told how in 1909 he bought a book of Kierkegaard's, "The Instant," but it made little impression on him, he was so preoccupied at the time with the theology of Harnack, Herrmann, and *Die christliche Welt,* and then with Christian socialism. Not until 1919 did Kierkegaard enter his thought world seriously, "but from that time onwards he appeared in an important role in my literary utterances." Soon after 1922, however, Barth recognized serious dangers in the influence of Kierkegaard and, while grateful for what he had learned from him, became more and more critical of existentialist developments in theology.

No one can ignore the effect of the war upon the thinking of both Barth and Bultmann.[3] We shall find abundant evidence for that. But the influence was exerted during and not just after the war, and, at least so far as Barth was concerned, merely accelerated and extended a revolt that had begun before the outbreak of the war. The theology of Neo-Protestantism, with its harmonization of Christianity with bourgeois civilization, had begun to crumble for him before ever the war began, and he was already wrestling in his preaching and teaching in the parish with the problem of what the Scriptures had to say to the desperate need of modern man. It was because the Scriptures had begun to come open to him in a new way that the war from its beginning represented for him the collapse of the cultural and theological structures of the nineteenth century, a judgment of God upon an order of life that in its pride and complacency had been unaware of the seriousness of its sickness. Therefore, Bishop Neill has the cart before the horse. The war did not find Barth with nothing to preach. Already he was immersed in the Scriptures and for that reason had some understanding of the deeper significance of the catastrophe when the war came.

1. Influences That Came with Thurneysen

In 1911, Barth began a ten-year pastorate in Safenwil, an industrial town in the Aargau region of eastern Switzerland. Two years later Eduard Thurneysen became pastor in Leutwil in a neighboring valley, but with a mountain between, and there began an intimate and unique sharing of life and thought between these two men which has continued unbroken through all the years until the present day. More than once Barth has stated that Thurneysen, far from being a theological satellite of his, provided the impetus which set him working in a new direction in theology and has constantly helped him correct his course across the years.[4] They had to travel on foot between their towns in order to talk together. Sometimes they met each other halfway. There were no phones, so when they could not meet, they sent postcards and letters. But the discussion between them never ceased, concerning plans for sermons and then the sermons themselves when they had been preached, concerning their theological studies, concerning the problems of congregational work, then beyond that the problems of the church at large and the progress of events in the world far beyond their valleys.

Thurneysen introduced Barth to new streams of thought which at once made him begin to set in question much that he had taken for granted. Through Thurneysen he came in contact with Christoph Blumhardt of Bad Boll and Hermann Kutter of Zurich, and began to see the theological significance of the novels of Dostoevsky. Blumhardt is perhaps the most important of the three. Little known in America, he exerted a profound influence upon a wide range of religious leaders in Europe. The Swiss religious socialists, Kutter and Ragaz, and Brunner as well as Thurneysen and Barth, owed much to him, but many others in Germany who went quite different directions claimed to have found their inspiration from him.

There were two Blumhardts, father and son.[5] The father, Johann Christoph, pastor in Möttlingen from 1838 to 1852, began a notable ministry of healing as a consequence of his experience with a deranged girl in his congregation (1842–1843). He became convinced that she constituted a modern instance of demon possession, and calling upon the power of Christ to liberate her from the evil spirit, saw her restored to health and a sound mind. Word of the event spread, a revival broke out, and people came swarming to him from near and far. Many received healing, and eventually in 1852 he moved to Bad Boll, where he established a center to which people might come for the restoration of both physical and spiritual health. His motto was " Jesus Is Conqueror," and his ruling conviction was that Jesus Christ has the same power today to overcome the ills of men that he had both before and after his death in New Testament times. Beginning as a Pietist, Blumhardt moved out from Pietism to emphasize not so much the conversion of the soul as the liberation of man from all the forces of evil through the inbreaking of God's Kingdom. A new age begins to dawn as men once more receive the Holy Spirit. He lived in constant expectation of the Last Day when Christ would return, but this generated no quietistic attitude but, rather, a passionate protest against everything in the world's present life that brought suffering to man. In the name of Jesus he took up the battle against the powers of darkness. His concern was for the whole life of man, not just his soul but also his body and all that entered into his life, and not just that the man should be forgiven and healed but that in his forgiveness and healing God should be glorified.

The son, also named Christoph, joined his father in Bad Boll in 1869 and eventually took over the leadership in the institution. Like the father, he broke with Pietism, teaching men to focus all their expectation upon what God himself would do and to put no trust in pious practices of their own. They both found in Pietism an unhealthy concern of men about *their* relation with God, in contrast to the Scriptures in which the entire concern is with *God's* relation to man. They shrank from attempting to convert men lest the men should be converted merely to the Blumhardt point of view rather than to God. They were unwilling to encourage men in an individualistic concentration upon their own salvation rather than upon the coming of God's Kingdom on earth. The younger Blumhardt lived until 1919 and, for a man who made no pretense of being a theologian, exerted a remarkable influence upon the development of twentieth-century theology. The central element in his life and thought was a simple yet all-powerful belief in the possibility of God's acting in the midst of life today to transform the human situation. All that was needful was a faith that would be an unconditional openness to him. The great barrier to the coming of the Kingdom was the egotism of man, his determination to be his own master, his refusal to let God touch the central place of decision in his life. Blumhardt taught men to expect God's action, no longer to worship a distant God but to wait in confidence for God to show himself the same God whose mighty acts were the subject of the Scriptures.

There is a passage in one of the Barth-Thurneysen letters which states that the point at which they began to rethink their theology was with the doctrine of the Holy Spirit.[6] A reading of their early sermons furnishes the best commentary upon this. They begin not with man and man's experience (as Barth did in the earlier period) but with God. The direction of their thinking is no longer from man to God but from God to man. God is not a mysterious X which has to be presupposed in order to make sense of the complexities of religious phenomena in the life of man but is the first word that has to be spoken if all the other words are to have any meaning. Not man but God is the primary reality, the first certainty. The question mark is placed not against God but against man. This they learned from Blumhardt, to begin with God, and this was the startling reversal in their thinking as they proceeded to draw out theological implications in a way that Blumhardt would never have dreamed of doing. Modern theology, with its foundations in man's religious experience, they saw to be a colossal attempt to build a bridge from man to God, to find a bridgehead in man on the basis of which a relation could be established with God. But this approach was possible only when one ignored the claim of the gospel that in Jesus Christ and in the sending of the Holy Spirit, God has already opened the way of access to himself for man. Many who read the Barth-Thurneysen sermons in the thirties will remember how suddenly they were made aware of the man-centeredness of their own thinking and preaching. Unconsciously they had always begun with man. Actually, it was a consequence of the whole religious and cultural milieu out of which they came or in which they were still deeply embedded. They spoke much more readily of man's predicament, man's sin, man's faith, man's religious experience, man's problems of conduct, man's beliefs, than of God, of who God is and what he has done, is doing, or will do for the redemption of man. Therefore, it came as a shock, an awakening shock, to read sermons that were much more concerned with God's thoughts concerning us than with our thoughts concerning God, man, and all things. Revelation as a past and yet still present reality had become the starting point for theology, rather than religious experience. The Holy Spirit was the name for the living God in the event of self-revelation in the present moment.

From Blumhardt came also a new understanding of the place of eschatology in Christian faith. Long before Albert Schweitzer and Johannes Weiss compelled scholars to recognize the intensely eschatological expectation in which both Jesus and the early Christians lived, the Blumhardts in Bad Boll had recaptured in actual life the eschatological dimension of the New Testament faith. For Schweitzer, Weiss, and others, it remained merely an aspect of Jewish ideology that had persisted in early Christianity, a distinctly Jewish anticipation of the approaching end of the world that gave to the Christian movement in its first stages a somewhat hysterical character, a phenomenon somewhat embarrassing for Christians of the present day to remember and that they certainly would not want to reproduce. (One remembers the more recent embarrassment and estrangement of many American Christians when the World Council of Churches took the " Christian Hope," i.e., eschatology, for the theme of its 1954 assembly in Evanston.) For the Blumhardts, however, eschatology was essential to faith, giving it a perspective that it could gain in no other way. The Kingdom of God had to be proclaimed as both present and future, breaking in upon the life of man now, yet meeting a determined resistance at every point in man's life so that there could be no complacency about its present progress and no identification of it with the spiritual and cultural achievements of modern man. The present situation had constantly to be seen as an era between the victory of Christ in his cross and resurrection and the coming victory when his sovereignty over the world would be complete. In this time between the times we are in the midst of a life-and-death struggle between God and the forces of evil. The decisive battle has already been fought and won for us, and the risen Lord moves through history as " the Conqueror," but there are battles still to be fought and the Christian fights them with confidence in the final victory which has been promised. He is saved from all utopianism by the knowledge that the present is not yet and cannot be the time of full redemption, and he cannot despair even in the darkest hour because he knows that the final victory must belong to Christ. *Warten und eilen!* (Wait and hasten!) was the watchword of Blumhardt and became that of Barth. The victory from which he comes and the victory that is his goal together give the Christian patience to wait for what God is yet to do but at the same time impel him to press on toward the goal. He is content to await God's time, yet is filled with the impatience of God himself that his Kingdom should come.

A third aspect of Blumhardt's faith was his strong sense of political responsibility. He was free of the quietism and otherworldliness of Pietism. The place of the Kingdom's coming was not just an inner realm of the soul but the world where men lived, with all its questionable political and economic structures. The evil to be conquered was social as well as individual in its manifestation and was particularly evident in the grinding poverty of the industrial masses. Blumhardt not only became a socialist but joined the Social Democratic political party, the party of the workers. Since that party had become strongly antireligious, mainly because of the hostility of so many churchmen to the interests of the workingman, his action was most unpopular in the church. For six years he served as an elected member of the Württemberg parliament representing the Social Democrats. There is a direct line which can be drawn from this to the action of Barth in joining the Social Democratic Party in 1915, in giving leadership to a strike of factory workers in Safenwil in 1917 and in having at one time been tempted to become a trade-union organizer. The same line continues in his resistance to Hitler and Nazism in the thirties.

Hermann Kutter and Leonhard Ragaz, Swiss disciples of Blumhardt, were the founders of the " Religious Socialist " movement in Switzerland and Germany. The workers, awakened by the writings of Marx and others, and scornful of a church that had so long ignored their plight, had given their Social Democratic Party a strongly antireligious character. Adolf Stöcker, the Berlin court preacher, had initiated the " Christian Social " movement with the aim of winning the workers away from social democracy but had become increasingly conservative and nationalistic in his program. Friedrich Naumann has founded an " Evangelical Social " movement with a more liberal viewpoint but with the same aim of counteracting the influence of the Social Democrats and drawing the workers back to the church. Kutter and Ragaz disclaimed all such objectives. For them the starting point was a recognition that the power of God was at work in the revolutionary socialist movement of the workers. Kutter asserted that " the living God is manifesting his Kingdom in the social movement which is today permeating the whole world, and which finds its most imposing expression in the German Social Democracy." To draw men out of that movement and back into a church that was satisfied with its dogmas and ceremonies would be to remove them from where God is present and active to a locale where he is absent. Kutter countered the prevalent condemnation of Social Democrats as atheists by pointing out how they, in spite of their professed unbelief, matched Jesus' description of the " blessed " in the Sermon on the Mount: They " hunger and thirst after righteous conditions . . . are advocates of mercy . . . hate what is common, base and greedy . . . are despised and persecuted . . . lay up for themselves no treasures on earth and declare war on money-getting . . . open their whole hearts to the poor and oppressed." [7] According to the New Testament standard of judgment, Kutter found the godly church people godless and the godless Social Democrats the true servants of God's Kingdom.

It is not surprising that Kutter as minister of the cathedral in Zurich emptied it of its bourgeois conservatives and then refilled it with a quite different congregation. For him everything hinged on the simple truth of the Bible: "God lives," so simple, that nearly everyone fails to see it. The Bible is diametrically opposed to our Christianity. "What we have in the person of Jesus before our eyes is the experiencing of the Father. . . . He and the Father are one. . . . What he did was the work of the Father" (25, 26). The difference between Jesus and us is that "He had God and we have not." We have only a lifeless idea of God. But we could have God if we would have him as the revolution-making God that he is. And "he who has God worries not, simply because he cannot worry. There are no questions, no uncertainties, no mysteries to vex his soul, any more than they could trouble the play of the sunbeam. All is play because there is only one reality — God." Therefore, the one task of the preacher is to proclaim God, the living God. One can see where Kutter and Barth would later have to part company. For the proclaimer of God to become involved in theological disputation was to lose his vocation, so far as Kutter was concerned.

Ragaz was even more antagonistic to the institutional church and to involvement in theology. He was pastor of the cathedral in Basel and then professor of theology in Zurich, but more and more he was seized with the conviction that following Christ meant casting in his lot with the poor in the fullest sense. He was burdened by his possessions and social position and wanted to become a factory worker. By 1911 he began to break with Kutter, offended at his view that the one thing necessary was to proclaim God and that only the pastors could do this rightly. Also, from 1914 on, Kutter was strongly for Germany in the war, whereas Ragaz wanted Germany and German militarism to be defeated. Ragaz was influenced by Tolstoy and was attracted by anarchism for a time. In Zurich he met Trotsky through helping improve a translation of one of his writings but was later shocked by Trotsky's resort to force. He worked hard to keep German Social Democrats from going over to Communism and the Third International. Ragaz was not happy as a theologian. Theological teaching seemed to cripple him inwardly. He became convinced that both theology and the church were obstacles in the way of the coming of the Kingdom, and as a consequence resigned his professorship in Zurich finally in 1921. He was the first in Switzerland to make a careful study of Kierkegaard, and it was Kierkegaard more than any other influence that made him restless in the church. "If Kierkegaard meant the great No in my life, Blumhardt meant the great Yes." [8] Yet both men in some measure combined No and Yes.

Thurneysen, responding to an address by Ragaz at a conference of Swiss pastors in 1927,[9] described how he himself and Barth began as religious socialists in the days before 1914. "We were both at first religious socialists like many others, as one had to be at that time if the mightiest call of the age, the call of the social need and social task and the voices of those who put that call into words, had awakened one out of the deep slumber that encompassed the church." Combined with this was the movement for abstinence. They saw in the two movements the advance of God's Kingdom. Then came the war which they recognized as a massive judgment upon the bourgeois Christianity of the past. But as the war continued it became God's judgment not only on bourgeois Christianity but also upon the whole religious socialist ideology. Socialism in Europe became largely nationalistic. It had professed to lead the way to a new world but its claims were no longer credible. A great gap opened up in life to which all the solutions devised by men were too small. Yet this disillusionment and break with religious socialism " never meant any questioning of the justice and bitter necessity of the political and industrial socialistic workers' movement." Only the illusions, such as the equation of the movement with the coming of God's Kingdom, and the ideology were stripped away. The Bible, which had begun to speak to them in a new way, captured their full attention now and pointed them to what alone would fill the gap. " We read it with the eyes of the ship-wrecked for whom everything has gone overboard," and in it they heard the word of forgiveness, the word of the Kingdom that comes not from men but from God. Ragaz had emphasized the realities of man's situation, but they now saw the necessity that the word of God which men had ceased to hear should be brought into relation with those realities, since only in such a meeting was there hope of reformation.

It was Thurneysen who also brought Dostoevsky into the picture. In 1921 he was to sum up his estimate of the theological significance of the Russian novelist in a booklet [10] that Barth found unusually effective in shaking students loose from their cultural Christianity. But before 1914, for both Thurneysen and Barth, Dostoevsky had combined with Blumhardt and Kutter to set a question mark against nineteenth-century theology. From his Russian observation point he had looked with remarkable penetration into the soul of nineteenth-century European man, cutting through the veneer of his civilization and holding up a mirror to him in which he might see for himself the radical contradictions of his existence. His power to disturb his readers lay in his knowledge of man, his recognition of the mysterious depths of man's being, and his freedom from the illusions with which men ordinarily conceal those depths from themselves. He probed ruthlessly into the problem of man and at its bottom he found the infinite pretensions of the human self, its rebellion against the limitations of humanity and its passion to be God. Western civilization he saw as the attempt of a deluded humanity to build a Tower of Babel up to heaven, to master heaven itself with its cultural and religious achievement. And the church he saw as an essential part of this blasphemous structure, a human attempt to satisfy the hunger and thirst for God that drives men to seek their life from a source beyond all things human. The Grand Inquisitor who had to protect the established religious order against the disrupting influence of Jesus represented more than the Roman Church. What man cannot endure is that a question mark should be set against his entire existence. He wants to possess God within himself so that he can domesticate Him. But in doing this he loses God, and man without God is a man without a future and without meaning or purpose in either the external or the internal events of his life, but also a man who by his very nature must break out in some way or other against such an existence. Hence the succession of strange characters in the world of Dostoevsky's novels, just as David and Saul, Judas and Simon Peter, are strange in the Bible, but strange only at a distance, for as they come closer they become revelations in every age of the man who cannot get free from God. But the novelist's last word was not of a humanity that drives itself mad in its hunger for God but rather of the possibility of resurrection, the promise of a humanity aware of its limitations and aware that the center of its existence must always be beyond itself in God.

The exposure of the explosive contradictions between Christianity and Western culture was the beginning of a liberation from the old cultural Christianity for Thurneysen and Barth. The confusion or merging of cultural values with religious faith was not the exclusive achievement of any one school of theology. It is not that anyone chose or chooses to effect the union but, rather, it is the unconscious outcome of men being born and nurtured in both a religious faith and a culture. Each becomes integral to man's existence, by their values giving meaning to life, so that it is intolerable to think that there is any essential contradiction between them. Western civilization, which seemed to be the product of Christian influences, was thus given the status of a Christian civilization and came to be called "Christendom." Beyond the Christian church lay this semi-Christian world, a very comforting thought. Missionaries to the world beyond Christendom took for granted that they were representatives of both the Christian faith and this so-called Christian civilization. There were Christian countries and non-Christian countries. In 1966 it is not difficult to recognize these assumptions as dangerous self-righteous illusions. A civilization that has produced two world wars in a half century and has looked on helplessly at the murder of six million Jews is sick. But here were men who already had that insight before 1914! It lay at the very root of the process of rethinking that began then for Thurneysen and Barth. The achievement is all the more notable when one considers how extensively Western civilization in its American form as the "American way of life" continues even today to be identified with Christianity by many people and that even a Reformed theologian such as Brunner could still operate with the concept of Christendom and make the future of Christianity dependent upon the preservation of Western civilization.[11]

2. The New World in the Bible

More decisive than any of these influences was Barth's rediscovery of the Scriptures, or rather of the word of God in Scripture. Thurneysen describes how he took his office as a preacher seriously. "He sat down before the Bible each day of the week and in his own new way ploughed it like a farmer who goes out into his fields in the early morning and makes furrow after furrow. . . . Karl Barth stands before us already in this early period as a reader and expositor of Scripture. The tablets of Holy Scripture are erected before him and the books of the expositors from Calvin through the biblicists and all the way to the modern critical biblical interpretation lie open in his hands. Both then and now this has been the source from which his whole theology has come. . . . That the springs of the Bible should flow afresh in our time is the great concern that here is central, and indeed the sole concern."[12] In his lecture on "The New World in the Bible"[13] Barth himself has told how he felt like an explorer discovering a new continent as the Bible came open to him in a new way. The startling and astounding thing was that this continent seemed to have been hidden from even the ablest Biblical scholars and theologians that he had known. Certainly his theological education had not exposed it to him. A theology with its focus upon religion and religious experience had had no eyes or ears for the apprehension of revelation, for a word among the words of Scripture that was not just a word about religion or about

God but a word in which God himself takes the initiative, comes upon the scene and establishes his authority in human affairs. It was an awesome responsibility that in his preaching a mere man should be charged to let this word sound forth into the life of his people. The service of the Blumhardts, Kutter, and Dostoevsky to Barth was that they opened his eyes to see in Scripture what had not been there for him before.

How far all these influences had reached by September 4, 1914, we cannot say exactly, but we know that on that day one theological era came to a decisive end for Barth and another era began. War had been under way for one month when a manifesto appeared in Rade's *Die christliche Welt,* signed by a whole array of German theologians, to give a religious validation to the Kaiser's war. On the manifesto were the signatures of Barth's most respected teachers. In a letter to Thurneysen that day he wrote: "The unconditional truths of the gospel are simply suspended for the time being and in the meantime a German war-theology is put to work. . . . Here is sufficient proof that the 'truths' were nothing more than a surface varnish and not an inmost possession of this *Christliche Welt* Christianity. It is truly sad. Marburg and German civilisation have lost something in my eyes by this breakdown, and indeed forever." Elsewhere he has written: "Disillusioned by their conduct, I perceived that I should not be able any longer to accept their ethics and dogmatics, their biblical exegesis, their interpretation of history, that at least for me the theology of the nineteenth century had no future." [14] A failure in ethics revealed to him a bankruptcy in theology. But he was able to see it only because already for him forces had been at work shaking the theological structure in which he had been living and laying bare ominous cracks in its foundations.

3. BULTMANN IN 1917

When we turn to the Bultmann of this period, we find much scantier evidence of his development — one sermon and one scholarly article — but it is sufficient to indicate the general direction in which his mind was moving and that he, too, was in transition from an old world to a new. Whether there was ever a break with nineteenth-century liberalism has been questioned. Bultmann himself asserts that his aim has been to combine the contributions of liberalism with those of the "dialectical theology," [15] but the accusation has been made by Ethelbert Stauffer that he merely continues the liberal tradition in a revised form. Geraint V. Jones has repeated this claim in the *Expository Times* for July, 1956, enumerating five points that seem to him to support it: the concern to express the Christian faith in the thought forms of modern man, the total rejection of miracle and the supernatural on the basis of a world governed by natural law, the rejection of any authority for Scripture as a whole, the rejection of any doctrine of the atonement, and the rejection of a Christology based on what Jesus Christ is in himself rather than on what he is for us. There is a measure of truth in this indictment and the details could be extended even farther. There are many points at which Bultmann's views on issues in New Testament scholarship and on theological questions are a continuation of older traditions. In his refusal to regard the Old Testament as Christian Scripture he is in line with his teacher Harnack. In his denial that Jesus regarded himself, or in his lifetime was regarded by his disciples, as the Messiah, he follows the line marked out by Wrede in his work on the Messianic secret in Mark's Gospel. But too much can be made of this. Every theologian stands in some measure of continuity with the work of those who preceded him. The most that can be said of Bultmann is that the break with the past was not nearly so radical for him as for Barth, but that does not mean that no break occurred. Bultmann in the nineteen twenties considered himself a participant in a massive revolt against the past, and no one living in that time would have questioned the fact. Our task is to probe the character of his revolt.

In 1917 Bultmann preached a sermon in Marburg on " The Hidden and Revealed God." [16] We must not read more into this sermon than is there, but it does leave with the reader the impression of a mind and spirit of great integrity struggling in the midst of the confusion and tragedy of war to find his way out of an old religious construction that had collapsed about him and to take a few hesitating steps toward a reconstruction. It is not so much that he chose to leave the old world as that it left him, that it had disappeared as one of the casualties of war. He looks back on it with a certain nostalgia as a world in which he could work at the tasks of scholarship undisturbed, in " devotion to the precious powers of spiritual life " and " pure enjoyment in the ripe fruits of human creativity." Religion and culture, both at a high level of refinement, were there to be enjoyed. But now in wartime what he calls " new powers of life " which demand the sacrifice of " everything precious and worthy of life " have claimed their rights, and life itself has become a riddle and a mystery. Man peers into it seeking some unifying meaning in it all, but he is not sure whether he is looking into the depths of God or the depths of Satan. His passionate hunger is " to see God in this confusion of forces." His mistake in the past has been that he has pictured God too small. God is only to be known as " a hidden and mysterious God, full of contradictions and riddles." Because this is God's nature, there is an infinite dimension to religious experience and a man is inspired to approach life with reverence and humility. He can never have a finished and static answer to the question of God, because the reality of God is always far beyond the grasp of his mind and frequently contradicts what he thinks he knows. " What unfolds itself within such contradictions is the riches of an infinite creativity." Thus, God must be found present even in the war and its horrors, and not just as a God who seeks to drive men to repentance by such devastating experiences but as One who is revealing himself in a new way. The war is before all else a time of divine revelation. " An old and illusory concept of God has fallen to pieces. . . . We stood in God's presence naked and alone; never before have we been so permitted to gaze into the depths of God. . . . Never before has God expected something so grand from the race of men. . . . We see a sense of sacrifice and a heroism that wreaths even the humblest brow with a crown of glory. . . . We have learned to pose questions to destiny in a completely new and more profound sense." Man " like God, can accept death and destruction into his work so that life may grow out of them." This is the hidden wisdom of God " that is able to bring all the demonic powers of darkness into its plan of salvation." Then finally the crucified Christ is seen as the embodiment of this supreme wisdom which comes to its triumph in a tragic death.

Several things are very clear when this sermon is seen against the background of prewar liberal theology. For Bultmann, the various forms of orthodox theology had ever been excluded because of their dedication to compromise. " In them we could have had only an innerly broken existence." [17] The demand of liberalism for integrity of thought and research even though it should seem to endanger men's souls, leading them into serious doubts, was for him inescapable. But liberalism had lost the ability to speak clearly of God and of God's revelation of himself in the midst of the events of time. Theologically, liberalism was exposed as hopelessly bankrupt when tested in the furnace of a world war. " We want an infinite *revelation* of God," Bultmann says,[18] and he underlines the word " revelation." " Revelation " was a word that had become an embarrassment to the scientists of religion in whose midst Bultmann had come to maturity, especially if " revelation " was understood in the Biblical sense of the self-revelation of a personal God in which he himself comes to man to transform man's life and give new meaning to his experience. Religion rather than revelation was the word on which all things turned for them. But what Bultmann not only wants but asserts as a reality of wartime experience is revelation. The hunger for God is such that it cannot be satisfied unless "he gives us a part of his being, his Spirit, that opens our eyes." This is grace, the gift of God himself to us, "a fulness of life that streams in upon us, completely as a gift." A number of new emphases are evident here. God is God and not just man spoken of in a heightened tone. God, even when he is revealed, remains hidden from the mind of man, so that no man and no theology can claim more than a broken knowledge of him. Revelation is not communication of knowledge about God but communication of grace in which God in some sense gives himself to man. This grace brings not only new life but a new understanding of the unity of meaning in the whole of life.

When we ask how this revelation takes place, the answer seems to be that it is experienced as man lays himself open with reverence and humility to all the mysterious and contradictory forces of life. This reverence and humility in man's approach to life is even called "the bridge that leads from man to God"! Moreover, it is the contemplation of "a greatness in mankind such as we never dreamed of," man's capacity for unbelievable sacrifice "that reveals to us the forces of God in man." [19] If we seemed before to be moving away from immanentalism and a man-centered theology, here we are back in a thinking that starts from man's experience and builds a bridge from man to God. It is striking that in the whole discussion on revelation there is no mention of Jesus Christ. The cross comes in at the end in two sentences as the supreme symbol of the truth that has been revealed in the experience of war. The wartime revelation is not made dependent in any way upon the hearing of the word of the cross. This becomes distinctly puzzling and all the more striking when we note how insistent Bultmann has been across the years that the decisive, liberating, and life-transforming revelation of God to man is in the proclamation of the crucified and risen Christ. When Fritz Buri and Schubert Ogden have accused him of theological inconsistency in assigning this absolutely unique and indispensable revelatory significance to the word of God and have called for a dekerygmatizing as well as a demythologizing of the gospel, he has resolutely stood his ground and refused to budge. In fact, in many of his writings he seems by his emphasis upon justification by faith alone to be attempting to destroy any possibility of a bridge from man to God. Only in the kerygmatic word does God break through upon man and give him a future. Is this conception, then, of the "how" of revelation which we find present in 1917 to be regarded as a residue of the prewar theology that was soon to disappear as Bultmann worked out the implications of his theology more thoroughly?

In order to answer this question we have to reach forward to an article written in 1963,[20] provoked by the discussion of Bishop Robinson's book

Honest to God. There are remarkable parallels at some points between the article of 1963 and the sermon of 1917. In 1917, the depths in the life of this world and in the life of man are revealed as the very depths of God. In 1963 this is spelled out more plainly: modern man no longer can conceive of another world transcending this world. " The transcendent is not to be sought, nor can it be found, above and beyond the world, but only in the midst of this world." This is what Bultmann, together with Tillich, Ebeling, and Robinson, is determined to assert. Christian faith speaks of " a revelation and means by it an action of God as an event which is not visible to the objectifying thought of reason, an event which as revelation does not communicate doctrines but concerns the existence of man, or better: makes it possible for him to understand himself as borne by the transcendent power of God." All of that he could have said, and did say in other words, in 1917. But how in 1963 is the revelation said to occur? We are told that we must hold ourselves open for encounters with God in the changing situations of our life, " encounters which will change us and let us become ever new. . . . What is required of us is selflessness, not as a method of moral conduct, but as the readiness no longer to hold to our old self but to receive our authentic self ever afresh. This readiness can be a questioning one, but it can also be a fully conscious one. For God can melt us, surprising us, where we did not expect it." The discussion is then brought to an end with a reference to Matt. 25:31-46, which teaches us that we meet God in confrontation with the needy brother. Again, as in 1917, there is a concluding reference to the New Testament but no indication of any necessary part that the New Testament witness plays in the occurrence of the revelation. Man's openness to God in the changing situations of life seems to be the essential factor, an openness in which he does not protect himself against the claim of his neighbor upon him.

There can be no criticism of the two emphases that revelation takes place in the midst of the changing situations of our life and that confrontation with the neighbor is inseparable from confrontation with God. But are openness to life and to the neighbor sufficient to lay us open to God? Is it not strange that Bultmann should leave this impression without being conscious that it is the very thing Buri and Ogden would want him to say in accusing him of inconsistency in his usual doctrine of a unique kerygmatic revelation? Perhaps we should conclude that deeply rooted in Bultmann's religious experience there are two conceptions of the " how " of revelation that he has never recognized as inconsistent and so has never resolved the contradiction between them.

Also in 1917, Bultmann published an article on " The Meaning of Es-

chatology for the Religion of the New Testament." [21] It appeared in an
issue of the *Zeitschrift für Theologie und Kirche* which was specially in
honor of Herrmann's seventieth birthday. The influence of Herrmann,
and of Schleiermacher behind Herrmann, is evident in what Bultmann
has to say of religion. The essence of religion is man's relation to the
transcendent, to a divine world, to God. The relation comes into being
" through experiences which are given to man beyond reason and nature,
which overpower him, to which he gives himself freely, and which he
calls revelation or grace, in which he knows himself not creative as in
other regions of culture but simply dependent." Each religious experience
is new, original, independent, and therefore does not naturally become a
link in a historical sequence. One cannot speak of development in religion. The nature of religion places it beyond the reach of the historian,
since he has no methodology that can reach beyond the human to take
account of a relation with a divine world. His developmental concept, applicable as it is to the phenomena of religion, does not apply to its essence.
Two things are most significant here. We meet again a description of man
experiencing revelation or grace in religion, and it is clearly the essence of
religious experience in general without any reference whatever to Christianity or Jesus Christ. We also meet a sharp distinction between the essence of religion and the external and ideological phenomena in which religion finds its expression in a particular age, a distinction that was
eventually to be the basis of Bultmann's project of demythologizing. But
to see the latter clearly we must examine what he had to say concerning
New Testament eschatology.

First, Bultmann took his stand with Johannes Weiss and Windisch in
recognizing that the consciousness of living in the last times was characteristic of the whole of early Christianity and must be the comprehensive
motif of a New Testament theology. In this the Christian church was the
daughter of late Judaism and carried to fulfillment its eschatological ideas
and moods together with those of the John the Baptist movement. " The
eschatological consciousness gave Jesus his task." He called his people to
repentance in preparation for the Last Day. So near was it that its powers
were already present. Bultmann considered it possible but not certain that
Jesus' trip to Jerusalem in the last week of his ministry was in expectation that the end was about to come and that his cleansing of the Temple
was to make it ready for the new age of the Kingdom. Certainly the early
Christian community considered itself to be the chosen Israel of the Last
Day. Its missionary preaching beyond Palestine was eschatological, and so
also was Paul's thought and preaching. This orientation persisted even
into the Gentile congregations. The eschatology provided a spur to ethical

action and inspired a readiness for sacrifice, but along with other factors it led to a separation of the Kingdom from the world and an antagonism to culture. In Paul it produced a negative attitude toward marriage. And yet all of this eschatological framework was simply a kind of temporary Jewish envelope that enclosed the essence of the new religion. The eschatological ideology is not of itself religious. " The eschatological consciousness is only the psychical condition of an epoch or group " and as such is no more essential to religion than art or science. It is only the emotional context in which religion originates. As a psychic phenomenon it belongs within the realm of the purely human and is open to historical investigation and description.

The general contours of the Bultmann of 1917 begin to be evident. He is a painstaking scientist of religious phenomena, trained in the " history of religion " school and prepared to follow his quarry into the remotest corners of man's psychic consciousness, but aware as few of his colleagues were aware that historical science has severe limitations in the realm of religion. The essence of religion in which the whole being of man is laid open to God is not accessible to either observation or evaluation. When Bultmann speaks of this essence of religion, his personal involvement is plain. This intangible experience of revelation or grace is the burning center of his own existence, but he uses a terminology in expressing himself that is closer to Schleiermacher's mystical language than to his own later kerygmatic interpretation of revelation. Nevertheless, the factors are already present that were to produce both Bultmann the severely scientific historian and Bultmann the theologian, the two not wholly separated but with a clear line of distinction drawn between the territories in which they were to operate. A change is under way, hardly a revolution as yet, but at least a transition, and provoked not so much by any rediscovery of revelation in Scripture as by an experience of revelation in the tragedy of wartime. But the content of the revelation, however conceived, was distinctly Biblical and Christian, no mere synonym for man's apprehensions of truth and meaning in the universe, but the self-revelation of a personal God who in revealing himself gives something of himself that brings newness of life and new self-understanding to man.

CHAPTER V

OPEN REBELLION, 1917–1920

FRIEDRICH GOGARTEN, a German Lutheran like Bultmann, who was later to be his theological companion, struck the keynote of the next period in an article entitled " Between the Times "[1] which he published in 1920! The title of the article was in 1923 to become the title of the new theological journal published under the joint auspices of Barth, Thurneysen, and Gogarten. Gogarten spoke for all those who felt that they stood between an old world that was dead and a new one that was not yet born. Barth, on reading the article, sent Gogarten a greeting and, after a visit with him four months later, wrote jubilantly to Thurneysen, " Here is a dreadnought on our side and against our adversaries." The article was addressed directly to the representatives of the old theological world, to the men who had been the teachers of Barth and Gogarten. It announced to them that somehow all their theological phrases had a hollow sound for the new generation. Words that once had seemed full of meaning were now empty and powerless. They were the language of a world that was now dead. Those who felt this were not lighthearted rebels against their seniors. On the contrary, it was a sorrow to them that it should be so and that they should no longer be able to hear what their theological fathers were saying. The simple fact was that in spite of all they had learned from them that was interesting and instructive, the one word that it was now necessary to hear was missing. In this time between the times there was more to be learned from Nietzsche and Kierkegaard, Master Eckhard and Lao Tse, than from these former theological instructors. He then turned their own principle of the historical relativity of all things against them. Theologies participate in this relativity. Why, then, should anyone take offense when the new generation pronounces the theology of the prewar era and of the nineteenth century a relative human construction that has had its day, has made its contribution, and should now be allowed to die? The question that has become most urgent is whether there is any longer anyone who can really think and speak of God. " We know that he has never hidden himself from the simple. But we have all been so deeply involved in the human that we have thereby lost God. . . . There is no thought in us any longer that reaches to God. None of our thoughts reach beyond the human sphere; not one. We know that now, and, in knowing it, we are as though we had never known anything. . . . We can no longer deceive ourselves and confuse the human with the divine." There is to be no more talk of the divine elements in culture and civilization. Culture is a perishable human phenomenon. But with this critical recognition the ground is cleared and the way open at last to pose the question of God afresh. Revisions of the old order are not sufficient. What is now required is not new constructions but repentance. What the future is to be is not yet clear but it *is* clear that men must turn away from a world that is dead to become open to what God will bring.

1. BARTH AND THURNEYSEN IN THE LATER YEARS OF THE WAR

The letters of Barth that begin September, 1914, are valuable in showing how far he and Thurneysen had progressed by 1917.[2] Already in 1914 they were passionate religious socialists, studying the Bible intensively with their people, focusing the hopes of men on the coming of the Kingdom in their preaching, cooperating with the Social Democrats in their endeavors to secure justice for the workingman, and trying to find their way toward a new theology in all their thinking together. Their sharp polemic against the old order both in theology and in the church establishment had brought accusations of uncharitableness as early as the summer of 1915 and they were conscious of a " cause " that appeared ever greater and truer, much too big for them. " The ' program ' is gigantic in every respect " (33). By the summer of 1916 they are talking of a coming time when they will " strike the great blow against the theologians " (36), but it is still far distant and requires a lengthy preparation. " The decisive strokes for which we now prepare cannot come for another ten years." Actually, it was to be only three years. In June, 1916, Barth wrote of " such a daring position as we so greatly desire to establish " and proposed taking up more extensive theological and philosophical studies again. He was already making extracts from Kant. Then in July, 1916, he began to work at a commentary on Romans and by the end of October had finished the third chapter. As he consulted all the commentaries from the Reformers to the latest critical ones he discovered the writings of the nineteenth-century conservatives such as J. T. Beck and Tholuck who had tried to combine historical scholarship with an evangelical orthodoxy that insisted on the revelation of God in Scripture. The work went slowly: a year later he was not yet finished with Rom., ch. 5!

An address on "The Righteousness of God"[3] delivered in January, 1916, shows how strong the influence of Kant and Herrmann remained and yet how the Pauline doctrine of God's righteousness was becoming central. Herrmann, building on Kant, had found in the human conscience an awareness of the righteous will of God in which God himself is revealed. So also for Barth, conscience was "the only place between heaven and earth in which God's righteousness is manifest." Men, looking about them and within themselves, see an evil will at work in the world, a capricious and self-seeking will that creates disorder and distress, the "fiendishness of business competition and world war . . . economic tyranny above and the slave spirit below." Life would be impossible if conscience did not reveal another will and the possibility of another world. The temptation of men is to make peace with the unrighteous world and to accept the inevitability of its being a hell. The Biblical prophets, however, make men's consciences articulate and rouse in them the longing for God's righteousness. But how have men responded to this trumpet voice of conscience? They have tried to meet its demands and so to still the voice by various forms of human righteousness, a moral superiority for themselves and their families that leaves the world's unrighteousness untouched, a legal and political order that protects them but leaves the world's will unchanged, a religion that provides a place of serenity and safety apart from the evil world where they no longer even think about "the critical event that ought to happen." In the pursuit of all these forms of human righteousness men have built for themselves a Tower of Babel and have set up a god of their own devising as though he were the Christian God. This false god has as "his worshippers all the distinguished European and American apostles of civilisation, welfare and progress." But now in wartime the tower has begun to crumble and the man-made god has been exposed as dead. Here at last is the possibility of a new beginning. Conscience must be let speak to the end, without being drowned out by our morality, culture, and religion, until God's will appears before us as the Wholly Other before which we bend in humility and yet at the same time with a childlike joyousness "that God is so much greater than we thought," and that so much more is to be expected for our world than we knew. And now the Bible enters the picture more directly. "In the Bible this humility and this joy are called — faith." When we let God speak within, God works in us and the new world begins. Faith generates "a new spirit out of which

grows a new world. . . . Life receives its meaning again. . . . Morality
and culture, state and nation, even religion and the church now become
possible," for the Kingdom of God begins to come on earth. It hardly need
be pointed out that conscience still occupies the place here that the word
of God in Scripture was shortly to take over.

There is a sermon from 1916 entitled "The Pastor Who Pleases the
People" which was printed without Barth's knowledge [4] and which reflects graphically the situation in Safenwil. Taking Ezek. 13:1-16 as his
text, he asserted that nine tenths of his congregation wished him to be
a false prophet, expressing the mind not of God but of the "decent"
people. They want their church to be at peace with the school, the factory, and all the institutions of the community. They believe in heaven
and hell but only as distant entities, not as present realities in the homes,
the church, the factory, and the hearts of the people of Safenwil. But
they must realize that for them to have a Christian pastor in their village
is to have always a disturbance in their life. The Bible cannot come open
before them without creating a dangerous disturbance. It disturbs their
pastor even more than it does them. They think he is speaking against
them, but he is also speaking against himself. He would like to live in
comfort and peace as much as they would, but how can he if he remains
a faithful minister of the word of Scripture? Sometimes they try to get
free of their unrest by finding faults in their pastor and his wife or by
regarding the tensions they now feel in their life with each other as mere
quarreling, but they should recognize that they stand between the Spirit
of God and the spirit of Mammon. Some among them think to still their
unrest by "standing by the pastor" and opposing the others, but they
too must be shaken by God. The issue is not "for or against the pastor"
but "for or against God."

But how is the pastor so sure of the will of God? He knows it — "from
my conscience and the Bible." The will of God means a new life on the
basis of justice, faithfulness, fellowship, truth. The present structure of
man's life is a Tower of Babel without God. The Bible discloses the
new life in its coming. Jesus is the conqueror who destroys the old life
and brings the new as through him God takes possession of men's wills.
The greatest obstacle to God in the bringing of his new world is an unfaithful pastor. People who want a false prophet are saying No to God's
will and are choosing the old life against the new. They may do away
with their pastor and turn the church into a gymnasium or a factory, or
they may share their pastor's unrest and go God's way, but they cannot
go a middle way between these two. One can read between the lines the
tense situation in Safenwil created not just by Barth's preaching but also

by his activity on behalf of social justice in the life of the community.

Several times in 1916 and 1917 Barth and Thurneysen discussed publishing a volume of sermons jointly, partly to meet the accusation that
they offered their hearers theological stones while their opponents provided good homemade bread. Finally, in 1917 the sermons appeared. Fit-
tingly the last two chapters were tributes to the Blumhardts by both men.
Their primary aim in the publication was "to seek men who together
with us are disturbed by the *hiddenness* of God in the present world and
church and are made glad by his yet greater *readiness* to become one who
breaks through all barriers." The 1917 edition contained Barth's address
on " The Strange New World in the Bible " [5] which later was transferred
to his first volume of essays and no longer appeared in the second edition
of the sermons (1928). Before looking at the sermons, we need to examine this address.

The emphasis is strongly upon the word of God in Scripture as the
place where God's sovereignty, God's righteousness, God's Kingdom (the
terms are used synonymously) is revealed, but there is still a large place
left for conscience. It can be said at the very end that the longing for
God's new world is present in all men. " We all know that." An optimistic view of what all men really want still prevails. But the uniqueness
of the Bible as the record of the inbreaking of another world, the world
of God, upon our world comes to strong recognition. From the beginning, men such as Abraham, Moses, and the prophets perceive it as a disturbing promise, a command, a call, which makes them reach out far
beyond themselves. In the Bible flows a river that carries us away from
ourselves to the sea. The Bible contains a history of men and ideas that
is not too satisfactory as history, but within it there is another history
that confronts the historian with questions to which his reason can find
no answer — why Israel survived its servitude in Egypt, why Jeremiah
withstood the whole nation in the hour of its disaster, why men's lives
were transformed by the word of Jesus. The only answer is that God lives
and speaks and acts. " A new world projects itself into our old, ordinary
world." In this new world God is sovereign, and the decisive question is
whether we accept or reject his sovereignty. To accept it is to have in us
the faith that is the seed out of which the new world grows. The Bible
is not a book of religion telling us how to think rightly about God but
a revelation of God's thoughts about us, the story of how he has sought
and found the way to us. It is not the history of man but the history of
God. Its content is the living God himself. And now Barth remembers the
conservatives, Beck and Tholuck, whom he has been reading, men who
influenced his father, and he comments that " our grandfathers, after all,

were right when they struggled so desperately in behalf of the truth that there is revelation in the Bible and not religion only." The covenant concept of which he was to make so much use later also appears here. It is in the word of God in Scripture that God makes his covenant with us and has sealed it once and for all in Jesus Christ.

Perhaps it was because his thinking seemed to be bringing him into the proximity of nineteenth-century conservatives that Barth took pains to distinguish Biblical faith from pietism. The Bible aims not just at the saving of individual souls, either now or for the hereafter, but at the redemption of the world. God is the Father here and now. " He will not allow life to be split into a ' here ' and a ' beyond.' He will not leave to death the task of freeing us from sin and sorrow. . . . He has caused eternity to dawn in place of time, or rather upon time." This is the meaning of the word becoming flesh in Jesus Christ. Christ has become the mediator for the whole world, not just for my soul. " He is the redeemer of the groaning creation about us. . . . The events of the Bible are the beginning, the glorious beginning of a new *world*." The Spirit is not just an inner experience but " must break forth from quiet hearts into the world outside," creating " new men, new families, new relationships, new politics." " The Holy Spirit establishes the righteousness of heaven in the midst of the unrighteousness of earth."

When we turn to the book of sermons,[6] which are from both Barth and Thurneysen without identification, we find that the two addresses given in 1916 are pretty much summaries of the contents of the sermons. They center not so much on Jesus Christ as upon the Kingdom of God, the new world for which men everywhere hunger and thirst and which would even now be breaking in upon them if they would learn to wait for it in the openness of faith. The world is an empty watercourse waiting for the water to come. Men live surrounded by the forces of death and siding with death because they have not yet heard the word of life. They think themselves and their world creatures of fate and take religion to be submission to fate as though good and evil, war and peace, came inevitably. But Christ has broken through the wall on our behalf and revealed that God is Lord of the world. God is where mercy and love are, and where God is, men do not accept the cruel blows of fate but fight against them. The keynote of the sermons definitely is: " Hope in God," and they are consistently joyous proclamation of the coming of the Kingdom. This is important to note, since in some quarters there has been the impression, created by the fact that most readers began with the " Romans " of 1922, that in his early ministry and writing Barth was largely negative, emphasizing the judgment of God, the No of God, to man. But in his Good Friday sermon he speaks of how on such a day worshipers are likely to hear only how man crucifies Christ ever afresh. The accusation may be true enough, but it is not the right starting point. It drives men away with its angry No to men. First, they should hear how on Golgotha, Christ wiped out the accusation, so that Good Friday should be a day of joy. Jesus did not scold men's sins even at the cross but brought to them in himself a new world, the time of the new covenant, the time of freedom, joy, love, life, the Yes of God. " Why should we be against ourselves when God is for us? " In line with this he speaks of the futility of moralistic preaching. "The more there is of moralism and ideals, the more untruth and lovelessness." What prevents God's breaking in upon us is our stubborn assertion of our own rightness and righteousness. We comfort ourselves with our great knowledge, our high office, our moral and spiritual superiority and as a consequence reach a dead point with God. We are not willing to confess the hunger and thirst for God that is hidden deep within us.

These sermons speak more cautiously of the knowledge which every man has of God than did the earlier writings. "There is a hidden depth in every man where all the truths of the Bible are true indeed also for him. But unfortunately he hardly knows it or does not know it at all." The Spirit is needed to open our eyes to the truth. The Bible speaks to us of what we do not have, the living world of the living God. It can only invite us in and give us the key. It can only point to Christ but cannot bring him alive among us. The Spirit must come and open the door. Then, somewhat surprisingly, we are told that the Spirit waits for us not only in sermons, Sacraments, and prayers but also behind " worldly " books and behind human ideas and ideals in which men seek a better world. There are movements of the Spirit to be traced in the outreach of the masses for justice " in the social movement of our time or even in the Russian revolution."[7] This last quotation must be guarded from misunderstanding by Thurneysen's later assertion that during the war he and Barth finally broke with religious socialism and recognized as an illusion the identification of the revolutionary socialist movement with the coming of the Kingdom as heralded by Kutter and Ragaz. It may be worth noting also that apart from two sermons on psalms, the preaching at this time was concentrated wholly on the New Testament.

In one of the sermons there is a passage that speaks of the hunger for a new age as the prime characteristic of the time. "We are all different from our fathers in that we note a strange unrest in and around us which does not let itself be stilled any longer by any means but rather grows steadily and swells like a gigantic flood. . . . We look longingly for a new thinking and action which would really bring us liberation." This expresses itself socially, educationally, in popular revolts, in the Russian revolution, in a new spirit present in the churches. God waits for us to open the door to this new age. He has sent Jesus into our darkness to help us open it. Jesus' oneness with the Father in his earthly life is the source of his strength, and as we see him, " we want to share this marvellous gift and enter with him into the kingdom of the Father." In the preface to the 1919 commentary on Romans [8] Barth speaks of this longing as likely to make the men of his time ready for a fresh understanding of Paul, recognizing in his questions their own questions, so that ceasing to be spectators of Paul, they may find in his answers the new thinking which they seek.

2. THE REDISCOVERY OF PAUL

In order to appreciate Barth's statement that he wrote his commentary on Romans in 1916–1918 with the joy of an explorer in new territory, we need to remember what leading New Testament scholars had been making of Paul. We have already seen something of this in the work of four leading scholars. The practice had become very general of discarding a large number of elements in Paul that were objectionable to a liberal theology as merely temporary expressions of a timeless gospel. Wernle [9] objected to the Pauline depreciation of the earthly lifework of Jesus, the entitling of Jesus as God's Son, reconciliation through the blood of Christ, the typology of Christ and Adam, the Pauline use of Scripture, the doctrine of a double predestination, the baptismal sacramentarianism, and the attitude to authority. Paul was trimmed of his " temporary " features to fit the mind of the new day. Not only at this point did Barth rebel but also against the conception of exegesis as it had become generally established in Biblical scholarship. He was willing to grant the indispensability of linguistic, literary, and historical investigations, but these seemed to him to be only preparatory and to stop short of the real task, which was to let the ultimate content of the text as a revelation of God to man be heard ever afresh in the life of humanity. The exegete therefore should not consider his work finished with the historical achievement of interpreting the text in its original situation, leaving its contemporary significance to the department of practical theology. He must be theologian as well as historian, but even as a historian he should be engaged in a constant dialogue between the wisdom of yesterday and the wisdom of tomorrow. The commentary on Romans was thus an experiment in a new

form of exegesis which was to have far-reaching hermeneutical significance, and in support of such a venture Barth drew upon a wide range
of resources: Calvin's commentary of 1539, Bengel's *Gnomon* of 1742,
Rieger's *Betrachtungen über das N.T.* of 1828, Godet's commentary of
1881, Beck's of 1886, and Schlatter's of 1887. Other works used were Lietz-
mann's commentary of 1906 and Zahn's of 1910; Kutter's *Righteousness*
of 1905, as well as his articles on Romans in the periodical *Kirchenfreund,*
1894; also an unpublished lecture book of Barth's father, Fritz Barth. Four
centuries of commentaries were consulted.

Whoever approaches the "Romans" of 1919 having first read the revision of 1922 rather than the sermons and addresses of the preceding period is at once struck and astonished by the note of jubilation that is
characteristic of it. Having struggled through the tortured language and
the puzzling paradoxes of 1922, he finds himself fairly swept along by the
passionate enthusiasm with which Barth writes of the advance of the new
age which began with the incarnation, has continued ever since and is
even now ready to break through upon the world with mighty power.
A translation of the earlier commentary into English would in 1934 (and
would still today) have made more friends for Barth in the English-
speaking world than did the later one. Its whole way of thinking is more
congenial to an evangelical liberalism. Jesus' resurrection from the dead
is seen as inaugurating a new aeon of the Spirit for the whole world. He
was the "hinge of history." With him began a new human race, an international people of God. But the event reaches beyond man; it is cosmic
in its significance, restoring the world to its true order and establishing
a life-process in the midst of history by which the world's corruption is
overcome. The organic unity of God, man, and world is recovered in
Christ. By faith, men today are able to participate in the life-process, and
God no longer sees them as members of a fallen world. A direct relation
with God has been regained. God's truth has come to earth. The righteousness of God in Christ has become the righteousness of men, his obedience their obedience, and they have a knowledge of God in which they are
bowed before the innermost being of God (10). The new creation is not
just a future possibility; it is a historical event in Jesus Christ and the life-
process begun in history by him is *real* history in distinction from the unreal life of the old aeon of sin and death which preceded his resurrection
and still continues where men reject the new age. By implication the latter is unreal history. The sin of man is that he chooses to remain in an
unreal world with an unreal history in which God is necessarily hidden
from him and the meaning of life is confused.

Considerable attention is given to the description of the old world of

sin and death. In it man is not under grace but under law, and law is
equated with both religion and idealism. Blind to God because of his sin,
he is constantly asking what to believe and what to do (184). He makes
his human problem central, trying to find the right religion, the right
church, the right form of conduct, and in it all to make God his helper.
He hungers and thirsts " for dogmatics and ethics." He wants to become
a religious personality and to foment a new church or a new religious
movement. The ethical problem belongs to this world which is without
grace, for in the new world of grace that one enters when he is in Christ
he is possessed by a life that is the fulfillment of what men sought to
achieve by their religion or ideals. The Old Testament is not allowed to
stand alone as the promise of a new age. Barth speaks of " the truth of
God once written by the prophets of Israel, by Plato and their like " (420),
the latter taking in a broad sweep of idealists, Social Democrats, and
a mankind that far beyond the church hungers for the new age. The
voice of conscience speaks as loudly outside the church as inside. The great
questions break through among men in the street as well as among men
in the church. But conscience is now set on the same level with religion
and ideals, with only a negative function. They cannot bring any man to
God or open the door into the world of grace, but they can lay open the
impassable gulf between God and man, exposing the unfulfilled character of man's life even at its best (64). Conscience tells man what he is not.
The law accuses him in his unrighteousness. Idealism makes him aware
how far he falls short of his true destiny. Religion reveals to him his dilemma between an old world that is impossible and an unknown and
unthinkable new one. In short, they are the instruments of God's judgment upon the old world, the media by which he says No to it and
thereby prepares men to hear the Yes of the gospel. While this would
seem to be a purely negative function which would be transcended and
made irrelevant by the coming of the new age, they nevertheless retain
a certain positive significance as pointers toward the order of life which
Christ alone can create. All religion and idealism is relativized by Christ,
so that it has nothing of which to boast. But Christ does not destroy them;
rather, he validates them in a new context by fulfilling them. Moses, Plato,
Kant, and Fichte thus stand in a line (186), all of them being prophets
of God's righteousness, i.e., God's Kingdom. Throughout the past there
have been times when men have become homesick for the world they
have lost, and, their evil being restrained, the awareness of God has become
clearer for them, so that they make up " a history between God and man
which is like a red thread through world history " and which gives promise of the coming day. Unfortunately, however, instead of taking up the

prophetic task, men became Pharisees, making God's gifts the basis of human pride and divisiveness (26).

From within the *real* history that began with Christ a new understanding of the whole of history becomes possible. Immersed in unreal history in which God is hidden, man can make nothing of the events, but the knowledge of God that Christ brings discloses the mystery of what God is doing in history, and the temporal, this-worldly developments are seen as expressions of an eternal movement in the Beyond (338). Each incomplete event takes on new meaning in the context of the whole. God is at work in both faith and unbelief, taking even man's resistance to him up into his greater purpose. This transforms our understanding of predestination. God's election is primary. Rejection is secondary in God's purpose. No man is permanently rejected. The complete rejection of a man or of an epoch has never occurred (321). Always in the rejection there is hidden at the same time a divine election. "There is something divine that accompanies all the movements of history and human life." A time that seems to be one of rejection is meant to be a prelude to a new obedience. God's concern is with the whole world and not just with a number of individuals. Religious individualism conceals the focus and dimensions of his purpose. Thus just as Israel's rejection of Christ was seen by Paul to be accompanied by the opening of a door to the Gentiles, so the present stubborn blindness of the church to God is being used by him to make plain " that the world as such and not some specially sacred region in it is the field, the area, in which the kingdom of God is to come " (328), and to ensure that the message of the righteousness of God which goes forward without the church and in spite of the church may be the more freely proclaimed.

In the commentary, criticism of the church is severe but not indiscriminate. A line of distinction is drawn between true church and false church. Men cannot rightly see the line, but God recognizes the true battlers in whom the continuity of his purpose is preserved. Where Christians go about to establish their own righteousness, the church becomes the grave of Biblical truth and identical with the Jewish church of Rom., chs. 9 to 11 (268). The sickness of the church is a zeal for religion that issues in a devotion to all manner of religious projects, such as the production of a dictionary of " religion " (the *Religion in Geschichte und Gegenwart* of 1909), and the extension of European and American religion and civilization to remote regions of the world. Religion rather than the transformation of the world has been made all-important. But not for one moment did such criticisms encourage desertion of the church. Ragaz, disillusioned with the church, might give up his office as minister and professor, but not Barth. To be in Christ was to wait, in the midst of God's judgment upon the church, for the true church, purified by judgment, to appear. Thurneysen as a young pastor was about to leave the church when Christoph Blumhardt set him the task of being the church in the midst of a blind and unfaithful church.

A notable feature of the commentary was the extremely sharp polemic against pietism. It engaged in combat against the old pietism on the one side and the old liberalism on the other. The pietists turned man's gaze too much inward upon himself, preoccupied him with the salvation of his own soul, and made fear and trembling rather than joy the mood of his life (120). The intensity of the pietist's struggle for an inner revolution shows an absence of grace. It is under law and under God's wrath, not under grace, that a man is so divided against himself and torn between the extremes of bliss and despair. Under grace he knows the joy and freedom of reconciliation. In Christ one is free from himself and so free to live. Barth can even speak of "the inferno of pietism in which the demons do their work" (216). "The Holy Spirit in us is no subjective experience concealed in mystic darkness but is the objective truth that has disclosed itself to us. . . . It is our life-basis, not our experience" (114). There is no such thing as salvation of the individual, of the soul. Salvation is only in Christ (13). This does not mean no salvation for the individual but that he has his salvation only as God's purpose for the world, which is disclosed in Christ, encompasses his life. The body of Christ is an organism in which each member has his life in subordination to the purpose of God which is at work in the whole. Individualism, whether pietistic or romantic, is the source of evil. Our action in love for our neighbor must be determined by how we can best serve the movement of God's grace in him and for him.

3. The Political Life of the Christian

"As Christians you have nothing to do with the power state" (377). The power state exists in the region of God's wrath, in alienation from God, and controls evil by evil. The political realm is saturated with evil. "That Christians have nothing to do with monarchy, capitalism, militarism, patriotism, free-thinking, is so self-evident that I do not even need to mention it" (381). Their entire concern is with the coming Kingdom which only Christ can bring, with "the *absolute* revolution which comes from God so that he leaves the whole realm of the penultimate to the process of dissolution." But the Christian does not stand apart from political and economic affairs. He lets " the healing unrest that is set in his heart by God deepen, grow stronger, and augment the generally rising flood of the divine which one day will of itself break through the dams." Christians must take their full responsibility in political life and Barth expects them to find their place on the extreme left. But there must be no " Christian politics," no " religious socialism," for these invite confusion and defeat. Our task is simply to do our duty in the realm of God's wrath. Let there be " strike, general strike and street fighting if it must be, but no religious justification or glorification of it. . . . Military service as soldier or officer, if it must be, but on *no* condition as military chaplain. . . . Social democratic but not religious-socialist" (390). Nevertheless, he looks with hope toward the hour " when the now expiring glow of the Marxist dogma will blaze forth anew as world-truth, when the socialistic church will experience its resurrection in a world that has become socialist " (332).

The comprehensive schema of the work has a strongly Platonic element in it, merged with the Pauline. The world in which man finds himself is recognized by him to be a fallen world. Nature and man have their origin and being in God and so reveal him (14). The creative reason resides also in man. A man does not get free of his origin. The concept of God is given him as directly as his own being and to deny God is to deny his own being. But this seed of direct knowledge of God is suppressed in him before it brings its harvest and it issues in a subjective natural religiosity which produces various forms of idolatry, especially the deification of self. Blind to his divine origin, fallen man identifies God with the powers that impinge upon his life. The knowledge of God that Paul communicates to him, therefore, is really, with Plato, a reminding him of a knowledge that is hidden in him, and to recover his knowledge of God is to find his way out of an unreal world into the real or ideal world. Man in his unreal world remembers his origin but cannot find his way back to it. He remains a prisoner of death. But in Christ the seed of life, of reality, of the new age is planted in the midst of the old world and holds in it the promise of the eventual restoration of all things to their original order. God is at work in the life of the world and of mankind, effecting their deliverance out of bondage into freedom, out of brokenness into wholeness, out of death into life. The eventual victory of God is assured by the triumph of the new life over death in the resurrection of Jesus Christ.

What morality and piety could not do, God has done " through the real deed of inaugurating a messianic, divine-earthly history. In Christ humanity is turned once more to God and thereby the basis is laid for the restoration of all that has been lost " (8). " In this one man there has again appeared on earth the original, direct, normal relation of man to God. . . . In him, God can again show himself as he is to man and recognize himself in the likeness of the man. The righteousness of God which was in Christ is the secret of the power of his resurrection." " Our concern, thus, is our knowledge of God which is realized in Christ in which God comes near to us, not objectively, but directly and creatively, in which we not only see but *are* seen, not only understand but *are* understood, not only grasp but are *grasped*." God has not waited for us to come to him but has come to us in history, so that we are confronted inescapably by the decision for or against him. Faith is a responding with a human Yes to God's Yes to man in Christ, that is, to the grace which is the possibility of a new era of righteousness on earth. To say No to God is to sink back into the unreality of the old world of sin and death.

The commentary was published in Bern with the help of a subsidy and in May, 1919, Barth could speak of the " good press " that it had received, even the conservatives liking it. But of the one thousand copies printed only six hundred were sold. It was later transferred to the Chr. Kaiser publishing house in Munich through the interest of Georg Merz, and the remaining copies were quickly distributed in Germany. In the fall of 1920 the publisher wished to bring out a second edition, but late in October the book suddenly became unacceptable to its author. He refused to have it reprinted and began at once a rewriting in which he was literally to leave hardly one stone upon another. It should be remembered, however, that it was on the basis of the 1919 " Romans " that he was appointed to his professorship in Göttingen in 1921.

4. THE END OF A PERIOD

The thinking of Barth in this period is further illumined by an address on " the Christian's place in society " [10] which he delivered at a religious-socialist conference at Tambach in September of 1919. It belongs so distinctly to this 1917–1920 period that, being printed in a volume of essays which appeared long after 1922, it must have created serious confusion in the minds of those who tried to coordinate it with what they had read in the " Romans " of 1922. This conference introduced Barth to a German constituency. Before this he was known only in Switzerland. The one hope for a society that so plainly is on the wrong road is " Christ in us," Barth told them. The movement of God in history, which was a reality first in Christ, continues in us insofar as by faith we are in Christ and he in us. There can be no narrowness in defining those who are in

Christ. They are not to be identified simply as church people. "The community of Christ is a building open on every side, for Christ died for all — even for the folk outside" (274). Plato is at one with Paul and the prophets in "the mighty sense of reality" (286), the awareness of the real world of God which moves steadily toward its consummation. Life is what Plato and the prophets long for, and life which has the promise of ultimate victory over all unrighteousness is what the resurrection of Jesus Christ reveals. But when one tries to describe this life which is God at work in the world and in man's consciousness, what appears is static rather than dynamic, a motionless bird rather than the bird in flight (the first occurrence of this significant metaphor). To focus upon man's consciousness or experience of God, as theology has done, is to start at the wrong end of things and to have them hopelessly reversed. Man's experience is always ambiguous. For man, God is the Wholly Other, not to be confused with anything in himself, the transcendent God. But in the light of accusations that the "early Barth" so emphasized the transcendence of God as to make any relation with man impossible, it is interesting to hear him saying that "the separation of the two cannot be ultimate. . . . There *must still* be a way from there to here" (287), and insisting that both the natural and social world, even in their alienation from God, must be affirmed as God's creation. Neither the world nor any man in it can escape from a relation with the Creator who is also the Redeemer. This affirmation is consistently present in Barth's writings from the earliest to the latest.

Barth uses the Hegelian pattern of synthesis, thesis, and antithesis to interpret the relation to each other of the original Creation, the fallen world, and the coming Kingdom. The original divine order of Creation is the synthesis. The world as we know it is the thesis, and the coming Kingdom which sets the whole established order in question is the antithesis. Both the thesis and the antithesis have their origin in the synthesis. The world as it is must be affirmed as God's creation, even to the extent of accepting Hegel's dictum of the rationality of all that is. There is an original grace in the created order in both the natural and the social world. For this reason, the world as it is produces for Jesus analogies of the Kingdom, and Socrates found in men a general original knowledge of the meaning and aim of life (301). Socrates was astonished at this, and his astonishment was worship of God the Creator. The fallen world has hidden within it the marks and the pattern of its origin. This is true not only of the soul but also of society. "The new from above is at the same time the oldest thing in existence, forgotten and buried." Because we believe in God the Creator and affirm his creation in this way, "we shall maintain toward the world, toward men and ourselves, a grateful, happy, understanding patience. . . . We can permit ourselves to be more romantic than the romanticists and more humanistic than the humanists" (301). Only from the standpoint of an antithesis (Kingdom) which has its roots in the synthesis (Creation) can one accept the thesis (the existing world) so calmly (303). However, Platonism, German idealism, and a socialism that knows only the Kingdom which sets the whole world in question, all inevitably lead to a denial of life. A Biblical faith, on the contrary, combines affirmation and denial, not balancing the one with the other but following God's movement from the thesis through the antithesis to the ultimate synthesis or victory (310). What must be grasped is that the same God is both the attacker and the defender of society. Creator and Redeemer are one. At present we are more conscious of the attack, of God's No than of his Yes, though the Yes is prior to the No. "We are engaged in life's revolt against the powers of death that enclose it" (291). "What prevents us from looking at the resurrection itself, from acquiring God in consciousness, from experiencing him in history?" The God who is at work in history can awaken us to himself so that he is alive in us (296). Most significant here is the concept of analogies of the divine order, concealed in the Creation and visible only to faith.

5. First Signs of a New Way of Thinking

In April, 1920, Barth gave an address to a student conference in Aarau, Switzerland, on "Biblical Questions, Insights, and Vistas,"[11] which signals the end of this first period of revolt. It strikes many of the now familiar notes but also some quite new ones: the knowledge of God, however hidden, belongs to our created being, so that all men are inside and not outside the Bible's answer (52); the soul's origin is in a unity with God that can never quite be forgotten; theology and church chiefly narcotize the question of God, but some men such as Kant and Overbeck, who are not accounted religious, veritably lived the question; the Bible is witness to God, but religion, not content to be a witness, seeks to take God under its management and becomes an obstruction; the interest of both Testaments is not in the building of the church but in its destruction, and in the new Jerusalem there is no church; the church exists for the coming of the Kingdom *in the world*; the Yes of God to man in grace precedes his No of judgment but the Yes can be heard only within the No, and the grace received only when one has bowed under the judgment; election has to be understood as God's call which sets each man before the decision between life and death so that he has to respond ever anew in freedom, and the rejection in one moment may be succeeded by the faith of election in the next. But notably absent here is the recently dominant theme of the new world that broke into history with Jesus' resurrection and became the real history of man.

A much soberer and more subdued note is struck, particularly in the second half of the address. Soon we hear the names of Overbeck and Kierkegaard and the word " dialectic" and begin to recognize the transition that is under way, a transition that is to occupy our attention in the next chapter. The gulf between God and man is seen to be much deeper than was recognized before. The new world of God lies " beyond human thought." The truth of God is hidden in the original synthesis from which arise the Yes and No which men hear, so that Christian thinking is a dialectic which moves between Yes and No, and since the truth cannot be known directly, " biblical dogmatics are fundamentally the suspension of all dogmatics " (73). The emphasis now is upon death rather than upon life, following Overbeck's " wisdom of death." " Life comes from *death*. Death is the source of all " (80). " The only source for the real, the immediate revelation of God, is *death*. . . . He (Christ) brought *life* to light out of *death*." God's revelation to Job was " only a revelation of the ultimate and absolute mysteriousness and darkness of all natural existence " (79). " The work of Christ . . . is a type of obedience that leads him straight toward death " (80). There is no revelation any longer in history but only on the boundary of history where history comes to an end. The new world lies beyond history. Faith is not participation in a new life-process in history but " a venture into eternity," and there is no faith possible for any man until he has heard God's sentence of death upon his world. " Let us not fail to see that the people of our times stand in anxiety and need *before* the closed wall of death, hardly aware in any way of the new world that may be waiting behind it " (85).

God's No to man is this sentence of death upon the totality of human life. There is no place in time where man can put down his foot and find a secure basis for life. In his religions he thinks he has found such a basis in himself or in something in his world and produces a variety of idolatries. For that reason, " Jesus simply had nothing to do with religion " (88). Because the source of man's life is beyond death in eternity, he remains ever a wanderer in time. But there *is* eternity. God does say Yes to man. Beyond judgment there is grace. " He who makes the patriarchs strangers and pilgrims, allowing them no rest, is also their shield and their exceeding great reward " (87). " Resurrection . . . means the sovereignty of God " (88). The resurrection of Christ and his Second Coming are the same. It is " an event which, though it is the only real happening *in,* is not a real happening *of* history " (90). It gives significance to time but for that very reason is not part of a temporal corruptible order. There is no continuity between the old world and the new world. The coming of the Kingdom is sheer miracle. Since Barth's mind was already moving in this new direction in April, 1920, it is not surprising that he began to rewrite his " Romans " before the end of October.

6. BULTMANN BETWEEN 1917 AND 1920

We turn now to Bultmann to see what evidence there is of theological development between 1917 and 1920. During these years he was hard at work on the " History of the Synoptic Tradition," [12] the summary of his research in form criticism which he published in 1921, and the first publication that we have to consider, " The Question of the Messianic Consciousness of Jesus and the Confession of Peter," [13] belongs in that context. First we should note that form criticism for Bultmann was a purely scientific method of literary analysis, free of theological presuppositions. By distinguishing the formal characteristics of each literary unit in the Gospels and determining the order in which these forms developed, it was thought to be possible to place each in the historical context in which it originated and thereby trace with considerable accuracy the growth of the Gospel tradition in the early church. However, since the analysis of the forms depended greatly upon a reconstruction of the various stages in the early church's life while at the same time the reconstruction of those stages depended upon the analysis of the literature, there was more than a little subjective element in the process and certainly the conclusions could not fail to be influenced in some degree by the theological standpoint of the scholar. For instance, when the form of a unit showed the marks of the early Jewish-Christian church, did this mean that the unit *originated* in the Jewish-Christian church or merely that a valid report of an incident in the life of Jesus was given this form as it was told in the Jewish-Christian church? Bultmann tends usually toward the former conclusion, reducing radically, though not by any means totally, the amount of historical evidence in the New Testament concerning Jesus and his teachings. One may question whether this radical skepticism concerning what can be known about Jesus had its origin in his scientific analysis or in a theological conviction that the Christian faith, because it is faith in God, dare not be made to rest on anything that can be called historical.

The essay on Peter's confession in Matt., ch. 16, builds on the earlier work of Wilhelm Wrede,[14] who undertook to prove that the whole conception of the Messianic secret in Mark's Gospel is a construct of the author and therefore without value as evidence that either Jesus or his disciples thought of him as the Messiah during his lifetime. The Messianic faith was born in the visionary experiences of the risen Lord, and even then it was not a faith that he had been the Messiah but only that he was the Messiah-designate who would appear as the Messiah at some time in the future. Against this background, Matt. 16:17-19 is analyzed by Bultmann and characteristics are found that place it in the earliest church — Aramaisms, rabbinic concepts, the position of Peter. The conclusion therefore is reached that the story originated in the early Jerusalem congregation. The possibility of its having originated in an actual incident is denied on the basis that Jesus' question is artificial, since he knew quite well what men, including the disciples, were saying about him. The Jesus of the story therefore represents the risen Christ, and the disciples are the church. The words of the heavenly Lord are placed in the mouth of the earthly Jesus as in Matt. 18:15-20 and John 20:22 ff. The essay shows little concerning Bultmann's theology but serves as an illustration of how his form criticism reduced Jesus to a figure somewhere between a Jewish rabbi and a prophet.

The next essay, on "Ethical and Mystical Religion in Early Christianity," in 1920,[15] originally an address at a conference attended also by Barth, was even more emphatic about the figure of Jesus. In the earliest Palestinian tradition, that is, for the first disciples, we hear, Jesus was an eschatological preacher of repentance like John the Baptist, a prophet of the coming Kingdom, a rabbi, a teacher of wisdom. No unified story of Jesus' life existed. There was no cult of any kind and no invoking of Jesus as Lord. He and his teachings were remembered but in the context of a Jewish sect in which ethical fulfillment of the will of God was the way of salvation. A Christian church had not yet come into being. It was the Hellenistic church that first constructed a life of Jesus such as we find in the Gospels, basing it not on the Palestinian tradition so much as on the Gnostic myth of the Son of God who descends from heaven, works marvels on earth for man's redemption, dies, rises again, and returns to heaven. Christianity now emerges as the cult of the Lord-Christ, and salvation is a life that men have in oneness with this Lord. The religion is mystical rather than ethical in character. God is conceived as supernatural being, spirit, life, light, truth, the immortal in antithesis to the material, dark, dead being of the world. The reality of God is grasped in remarkable inner experiences rather than in his actions in history, experiences that lift a man beyond the world into a realm where the Lord of the cult dispenses the gifts of a supernatural world. This mythical Lord-Christ is combined with the Jesus of Nazareth of the Palestinian tradition by the Hellenistic church, but at a later stage, as in John's Gospel, the myth gets the upper hand of history and the Palestinian material is almost completely suppressed. Paul was a Hellenistic Jew who entered directly into the cult of Hellenistic Christianity, Palestinian Christianity having no influence upon him. His conversion was an ecstatic experience of communion with the Lord of the cult, so that mysticism was at the very center of the Pauline piety. In this whole reconstruction of the stages in early Christianity, Bultmann was following very closely the proposals of Wilhelm Bousset in his *Kyrios Christos* of 1913.[16] It is to be noted also that when he speaks of "the liberal theology" he adds, "with which I too count myself associated." Bousset had drawn an almost entirely new picture of the early developments, making a deep cleft between Jesus and Paul, but finding the real break at the point of transition from Palestinian to Hellenistic Christianity. It is in line with this that Bultmann consistently places Jesus in the period of the Jewish preparation for Christianity and insists, as he does in this essay, that Christianity as an independent historical reality, outgrowing the Jewish sect, begins at the Hellenistic stage.

Behind this entire construction is the conception of the Christian religion as being constituted by a divine revelation which becomes its intangible inner essence and in its various stages clothes itself in a temporary conceptuality. First, it wears purely Jewish ethical and eschatological clothing. Then in the Greek world it puts on Hellenistic clothing, mystical and mythological in character. The conceptual expression is a transitory, human-historical phenomenon that must on no account be absolutized. It is dispensable. But one dare not cast it aside lightly as nineteenth-century liberalism tended to do. Rather, one must find a new contemporary conceptuality to replace the old one, making sure that the essence is not lost in the transition. An illustration of a transference of this kind Bultmann found in the New Testament itself where the Johannine and the Pauline literature reinterpret the futurist eschatology of Jewish Christianity, placing the Kingdom which conceals the ultimate goal and meaning of man's life no longer at the end of time but above time and ready to break in with each successive moment. Already, then, in 1920 the ground was laid for the projects of demythologizing and existential interpretation which were not officially launched until 1941.

Bultmann, in the second half of his article, drew a parallel between the first and the twentieth century. He saw in his own time a similar transition from an ethical to a mystical Christianity, from an ethical Ritschli-

anism to a recrudescence of mystical Paulinism. The latter refers to Barth's
1919 " Romans." Historical criticism was misused by liberalism in the past
when it was expected to provide a historical basis for piety. Its function is
only to clarify and purify the spiritual content of consciousness, that is,
to help men distinguish between the transitory and the abiding elements
in religion, between history and revelation. Liberalism, fastening upon
what it conceived to be the Jesus of history, made an ethical Jewish Christianity the criterion and tried to strip away the Hellenistic elements as
accretions, blind to the fact that no historically conditioned form of the
past can be normative. But now Karl Barth in his commentary on Romans has produced a repristination of the Christ-myth of Paul, which is
just another form of the same error. No expression of Christianity in any
period of the past dare be absolutized. "One cannot artificially renew
a cultus and myth of former times, nor can one artificially create a new
one" (740). The best one can do is to lop off radically whatever has become antiquated and false and build in whatever is convincingly valid
until priestly or prophetic spirits can effect a new creation. Bultmann does
not commit himself too firmly in what direction he himself wishes to go
for the future. That it is an age of transition he knows, but he can describe it in such general terms as " a change in our era's feeling for life."
It is to be noted specially that he has a high respect for myth and cult
such as the Hellenistic age produced, " which could be the unique expression for the living, eternal, superhistorical element of a religion "
(739). That his later interest was to be focused in Pauline and Johannine
Christianity rather than in the Synoptic Gospels already begins to show
itself. Also, it is to be remembered that though he denied any Messianic
consciousness to Jesus, the Hellenistic apprehension of Jesus Christ as
Lord contained within it for him an insight into ultimate truth which
gave Christianity its basis. Yet he describes his era in 1920 as uncertain
whether vital religion for it is ethical or mystical. As a religious community it is not sure where lies the revelation of God, where the reality
of God is to be experienced. (We are reminded of his own ambiguity on
this point in 1917.)

Since the essence of religion in distinction from its temporary conceptual expressions is so important for Bultmann, we are anxious to know
how he defines it. Here he shows the influence of Schleiermacher, and
also of Rudolf Otto, under whom he studied in Marburg and who from
1921 on was to be his colleague there. The reality of religion is found in
the experience of the Wholly Other, before whom a man knows himself
impure in a way that is different from being judged by ethical reason. He
experiences a living reality to which he submits and he feels himself borne

up by it so that he is fulfilled in his being rather than merely fulfilling certain ethical demands. "In the stillness of the Wholly Other he can rediscover purity, his own self." And this new life is not his ethical achievement but the gift of the Wholly Other. Here and elsewhere when we come upon such statements about the essence of religion, they take on definitely a confessional character. They are not cold statements of scientific conclusions reached by the analysis of religious phenomena but are confessions of faith in the reality of divine revelation, but always with an obscurity about the "how" of the revelation. He makes very clear, however, that he has no intention of developing a real mysticism. The present tendency to mysticism he interprets as only the manifestation of a desire for religious life. The real mystic experiences God, not in his inner history of struggle and growth in obedience to the good but only in the cessation of struggle and the sinking of all action, even of the good, into silence or ecstasy. On the contrary, says Bultmann, a man is religious not because he has had certain psychic experiences or participates in a cultus or believes in a myth but only because he can speak of a revelation of God in which he has found God as a reality that masters him and blesses him, disclosing to him the meaning of his life (743).

The criticism of what seemed to be an absolutizing of the Christ-myth of Paul by Barth was accompanied by a significant word of praise for Barth's religious critique of culture. The point at which Bultmann and Barth first came together was thus the repudiation of cultural Protestantism, which to both of them was an erection of cultural values into idols. But they were soon to be equally agreed in their antagonism to the whole "Jesus of history" tradition. Barth was to applaud heartily Bultmann's demonstration that it was impossible to construct from the New Testament records a historical figure who could be made the object of faith. Both were attracted at this time by Otto's expression "the Wholly Other" to emphasize the transcendence of God, but Bultmann was much closer than Barth to Otto in his continuity with Schleiermacher.

Barth published a reply to Bultmann in *Die christliche Welt* in June [17] in which he told how, following the address, he and Bultmann argued long into the night, apparently about the possibility of drawing from the New Testament a unified picture of Jesus. Barth had, after long search, come upon a satisfactory picture in Weinel's interpretation only to have it shattered by Bultmann's demonstration of the disunity of the New Testament on the subject. But he was not yet willing to surrender. In the course of the argument he had hit upon an analogy that seemed to him to suggest a possible answer. A medieval book on alchemy with an account of a chemical experiment is discovered, but many parts are missing. The last two lines are torn away on one page. The next page, which contains the synthesis, is illegible because of ink having been spilled over it, so that only a few lines can be read. But the third page contains the outcome of the chemical synthesis complete. For hundreds of years chemical science tries to restore the missing lines, but only in the last half of the nineteenth century does it succeed in discovering a synthesis that corresponds to the one described. Does not this experiment actually restore the content of the fragmentary record? So also in regard to the fragmentary New Testament record, cannot a modern experiment with the faith that is described in the New Testament make good what is missing in the documents? The experiment is the basic religious experience, "I am in thee and thou art all!" Out of the eternal comes a Presence that penetrates the "I" of man like an axle in a wheel and has the power "to bring a rhythm into the whole chaos of subjective experience in that it lets what belongs to the 'I' (*das Ichhafte*) be caught into the rotation of the spiritual cosmos. Out of that comes a new objective order and valuation of all things in our personal experience, and all ethical expressions of life lose their demanding character since they flow directly, necessarily, naturally, inevitably, out of the newly-won center with the immediacy of the spokes of the wheel. Whoever surveys the fragments of the synoptic *and* Johannine tradition in the context of the comprehensive (*überindividuellen*) rhythm which has been achieved in personal experience (experiment) finds the given elements expanding and ordering themselves into a unified, centralized picture of Jesus. On this basis one could regard all the results of biblical research not only with philological and historical interest but also with personal ease of mind." What is most interesting here is the proposal that the Christian's experience of God in the present has an important and indispensable part to play in interpreting the content of the New Testament, a suggestion which would be shocking to the scientific exegetes of 1920 but which has played a major role in the more recent discussions of hermeneutical principles. It also throws a clear light on how Barth arrived at the "picture of Jesus Christ" that was to be increasingly central to his theology.

A second essay by Bultmann in 1920, on "Religion and Culture,"[18] makes it certain that as yet there had been for him no such break with Schleiermacher as Barth had experienced some years earlier. He is content still to define religion as Schleiermacher did, as "the feeling of absolute dependence" which is "only possible where one meets a power which brings his inner being to its freest fulfilment so that, freed and relaxed, he flings himself in its arms — submitting himself in free surrender" (435). In contrast to the autonomous creativity of man in all the spheres of culture, religion is passive receptivity and is not in its essence an objective describable phenomenon available to scientific investigation. Religion is an ineffable experience of ultimate reality that brings life to its fulfillment. "The meaning and power of this divine life is experienced as a *Beyond*, as beyond nature and culture alike" (452). "Real religion is present only in the moments of experience." Most of man's religious life is passed in longing for what lies beyond nature and culture. Only in the experience of the Beyond can he find wholeness of self.

That statement will be misunderstood unless one adds at once that, for Bultmann, culture too is essential to the self of man. Without culture, man's life is empty of content. Culture belongs wholly to this world, a product of man's reason, a relative human construction. In primitive society, cultural activities such as astronomy, medicine, literature, history, art, drama, and music, all originated in the religious cult, but in their self-development through the centuries they have, one after the other, had to emancipate themselves from religion and assert their own autonomy, that is, their right to follow the inner logic of their nature. Both in Greece and in eighteenth-century Europe, ethics as an aspect of human culture had to secure its independence as a function of the rational will of man. But this was no loss to the Christian religion; on the contrary, it assists a necessary clarification. "One cannot say too emphatically that early Christianity was a specifically religious movement, not an ethical one. It introduced no new ethical ideals" (421). There was nothing unique in the Christian command of love. It was Stoicism and not Christianity that handled such ethical questions as law, social relations (slavery), and the relation of the sexes. "Culture is the methodical unfolding of the human reason in its three aspects: the theoretical, the practical and the aesthetic. Thus the *activity* of the human spirit is essential for them: it builds the three worlds of culture: science, law and ethics, art" (435). Culture proceeds autonomously according to its own laws. What is right in it is determined not by any external authority but from within. Religion has its own sphere in the experience of the individual and is neutral toward the creations of culture, leaving them to find their own rational course. This means that it is neutral not only to art and science but also to ethics. Ethics belongs in the realm of culture that is under the direction of reason. Again Schleiermacher is quoted: religion should accompany action like music rather than the action arise out of religion. The idea that religion should lead to action can issue only in confusion. Then comes the striking but logical conclusion that "it is quite self-evident that religion is a private matter and has nothing to do with the state" (437). The two realms of religion and culture are as sharply divided as Luther's two kingdoms, perhaps more sharply. The most illuminating commentary on this position of 1920 is the recent pronouncement of Bultmann in the German controversy on the use of nuclear power: that the church should not interfere in such a matter but should leave it to the state authorities which alone have all the facts at their disposal on the basis of which an intelligent decision can be made.[19]

Religion and culture are thus two spheres of man's life which stand in isolation and contrast to each other. Both are necessary to his wholeness. But the temptation of man is to seek his fulfillment in the sphere of culture alone. Because religion eludes his rational investigation he leaves it out of account and finds himself frustrated in his culture. The nineteenth century confused its history of the external manifestations of religion with a history of religion itself which, because of the nature of religion as a relation with the Beyond, can never be written. In this confusion, religion was taken to be just one aspect of culture, and culture, having incorporated religion into itself, became a colossal idolatry. Postwar social democracy in Germany strengthened this tendency to idolize culture and to let religion in its unique nature become lost. But what use to man was the whole of culture if he lost his own soul? Now, however, culture itself was breaking up and " only a religious rebirth can save us " (453).

The concept of the Beyond which emerges here (replacing the Wholly Other) was to be crucial for Bultmann's thought for years to come, and at the same time it is very easily misunderstood. How central it has been for him is indicated by the title of his book of sermons " This World and the Beyond." And when we realize that for him the eschatological reality is the Beyond, we see that the title of his Gifford Lectures, " History and Eschatology " is actually synonymous with the title of the sermon volume. What makes the word " Beyond " so open to misunderstanding is that it suggests another world transcending this one, a conception of reality that Bultmann has consistently denied. He and Gogarten, who has seconded him in this, have insisted that the traditional metaphysical conception of a transcendent world must be abandoned once and for all. All that exists is comprehended within our one world. God is to be found, not in another realm beyond history, but in the midst of the forces that constitute man's history, or, as Bishop Robinson puts it, interpreting Bultmann, not in the heights but in the depths. It may be difficult to see how this differs from the immanentalism of nineteenth-century liberalism, and already it has encouraged a revival of that immanentalism. But Bultmann keeps insisting that the Beyond which is a reality only in the experiences of the individual is transcendent and is never to be confused with anything in man, in history, or in human culture, since it is God himself coming to man for his redemption. Only when we take seriously the dual nature of reality for Bultmann, the coexistence and yet the radical separation of the two realms of religion and culture, and that the work of a historian belongs wholly in the rational world of culture do we begin to understand the sharp separation between Bultmann the historian and Bultmann the theologian. The Lutheran Bultmann here stands far apart from the Reformed Barth for whom the sovereignty of God would not permit the separation of any area of life from the scope of God's ultimate rule.

CHAPTER VI

A CHANGE OF COURSE, 1920–1922

IN THE SUMMER of 1920, Barth was reading Overbeck and Kierkegaard and drawing from them highly explosive theological extracts that were literally to blast his 1919 " Romans " apart before the year was out. He must have been at work on Overbeck during the preceding winter, since in June, 1920, he published a pamphlet about him entitled " The Inner Situation of Christianity " which was later reprinted in his second volume of essays.[1] Perhaps it was his contact with the thought of Overbeck that opened his eyes in November, 1919, to an " ultimate wisdom " in I Cor., ch. 15, whose effect was like " shocks from an electric eel," [2] and in May, 1920, to the content of II Corinthians " which sweeps over me like a torrent." [3] He began work on II Corinthians each day with " a little private morning devotion from Kierkegaard." [4] He was also reading Nietzsche and in June spent a whole week on Nietzsche's beginnings.

1. OVERBECK

Franz Overbeck was professor of New Testament and ancient church history in Basel, 1870–1897. During his lifetime he was regarded as a curiosity, a professor of theology for whom eighteen hundred years in the history of Christianity had been a false development and the theology and church of his time so totally corrupt that they would not have long to live. Such negativity, and the close friendship with Nietzsche in Basel into which he was drawn by their common antagonism to the existing order, caused him to be labeled an agnostic or even an unbeliever by a Protestantism that had an unshaken confidence in both its theological and its practical achievements. He died in 1905, and it was not until his disciple Bernoulli published fragments of his theological writings in 1919 in the volume " Christianity and Culture " and Barth reviewed the volume in a pamphlet the following year that he began to receive recognition.

Overbeck counted himself a disciple of F. C. Baur in historical methodology but rejected both Baur's Hegelianism and his reconstruction of early church history. Overbeck's aim was to write a history of the church that would be completely objective, with all illusions stripped away, a bare presentation of the facts, in short, what he called " a profane church history." In the past the church's history had been seen through religious or theological spectacles, which gave it a coloration different from the remainder of human history. This was self-deception. The church must have the courage to face the facts. And now when Overbeck applied his method, he made two discoveries that were far ahead of his time and should have gained him considerable recognition. By his analysis of literary forms he was a progenitor of form criticism, and long before Johannes Weiss and Schweitzer, he recognized the intensely eschatological character of early Christianity. From his analysis of the literary forms in the New Testament, the apostolic fathers, and the patristic writings, he found that the first two had a form that was unique, a new creation, while the third adopted the forms of profane world literature. This suggested to him a uniqueness of life in the apostolic period which was lost as the church made itself at home in the world. Then, from his examination of the New Testament records, he concluded that the constitutive elements in early Christianity were an expectation of the world's end and a corresponding attitude of world denial. In its beginnings, Christianity was a life from another world that stood in radical contradiction to everything in this world. Overbeck invented the category of *Urgeschichte* (primal history) to describe this life of the early Christians which was *in* history but not *of* it, in fact which constituted a complete break with history. They lived wholly from beyond history. With the abandonment of its eschatological faith, the church became a historical entity, subject to the ordinary historical forces and therefore an absurdity, a self-contradictory phenomenon. Christianity, therefore, from the time of the patristic apologists has been a self-deception and its theology an attempt to justify its betrayal of itself to the world. He detected in the book of The Acts and in Justin Martyr the beginnings of a postapostolic degeneration. The theology and Christianity of his own time, with its total absence of eschatological perspective and its confident affirmation of man, his history, his culture, and his religious achievements, seemed to him to represent the most extreme form of that degeneration. He expected its quiet dissolution in the future.

Barth discovered in Overbeck a companion for Blumhardt. The two stood "back to back . . . Blumhardt as the forward-looking, hopeful Overbeck, Overbeck as the backward-looking critical Blumhardt." [5] Both alike by their grasping the eschatological character of New Testament faith were made aware of the radical antithesis between the life of faith initiated by Jesus Christ and the ordinary life of man in history. The new creation was not a revision of history but the possibility of a new existence from God that would mean the end of history as men had known it. The death on the cross was the meeting point between the new creation and the world of man, and the whole of human history had to be understood in the light of the judgment of death that was thereby stamped upon it. The old world does not have in it the possibility of developing from within itself the new world that alone has the promise of fulfillment for man. Barth drew out the implications of this as Overbeck did not. The old world must die if the new world is to be born. The resurrection life becomes a possibility only beyond the sign of death. Only when this antithesis between the two worlds is clearly seen does the Christian faith take on its full revolutionary character. The Christian cannot compromise with the old world, using his faith merely to make life tolerable in a world that is doomed. As a citizen of God's Kingdom he has to live in perpetual revolt against that world. And he has to recognize his own Christian religion in all its history as deeply involved in the corruptions of history.

Barth warned his readers that Overbeck's book was dangerous for them. It would shake them out of their false religious and theological securities and set them in motion, leaving them nowhere to rest ever in history. All, all, even the most impressive Christian constructions, were relativized by the eschatological perspective. The whole of man's history, including the history of the church, lay in a region between *Urgeschichte,* the miraculous heaven-sent era to which the New Testament bears witness, and the new creation beyond the end of history. There could be no resting place, no stopping place, anywhere in between. The understanding reader hears himself called away from all the fleshpots of Egypt to venture forth into the wilderness. To become a Christian theologian, therefore, is not to find or to construct a theology in which the mind and spirit can come to rest but, rather, to recognize all such human bases of security as idolatry and to be perpetually launching out into an unknown future.

Overbeck seemed to be in some doubt himself whether he should be considered a skeptic or a believer. His disciple Bernoulli inclined to the former judgment, but Barth insisted on the latter and posed the alternatives as "happy, loving doubter" or "critical enthusiast." The No of Overbeck to the world, he saw to be the reverse side of Blumhardt's Yes and to presuppose the Yes, whether Overbeck in his lifetime recognized it or not. Overbeck and the Socrates of the *Phaedo* were "heathen proclaimers of the resurrection of whom it is said: Such faith have I not found in Israel." There is no evidence that Overbeck envisaged the possibility of a new theology or a new day for Christianity beyond the decline and death of its present form, but he was himself a new kind of theologian and he suggested what might be when he said that "only a heroic Christianity which finds its basis in itself in antithesis to every age can escape the fate of Jesuitical perversion." [6]

Overbeck set Barth in motion. He destroyed the schema of the two ages in history that dominated the 1919 "Romans." No longer could the new creation be described as a new world which broke into history in Jesus Christ and became a life process, a new stream of "real" history in which the Christian participates by faith. All human history, Christian or non-Christian, stands under the sign of death and judgment. And yet the reality of the new life for man that had been revealed in Jesus Christ and was the goal of human existence had to be affirmed in its primary significance as God's Yes to man, not just as a future possibility but as a reality in the midst of history. How could it be said to be in history and yet not subject to the forces of history? To meet this problem Barth adopted Overbeck's category of *Urgeschichte,* a history within history which, because it is determined not by human forces but by the action of God, eludes historical description and explanation. But Barth combined Overbeck with Blumhardt, criticism with hope, negation of the old world with affirmation of the new, and saw all history as an era between the times, between *Urgeschichte* and Parousia. As never before he grasped the mortality of all things in the present world and found in death "the iron broom which sweeps away the lies which burden our earthly life." [7] But at the same time there appeared to him more clearly than ever the certainty of the coming of God's new world in the hope and promise of which a man must live confidently and joyfully in each moment of his life. Barth tells how, listening to Ernst Troeltsch in 1910, he had felt that the outlook for Christianity as constituted in the modern world was a dim one, but now with Overbeck he began to question whether by its nature it could ever have any prospect in history, whether its entrance into history must not always be its betrayal and death. He was now able to accept Troeltsch's relativizing of all history without despair. Here he was affirming a radical disjunction between this world and the Beyond, between man's world and God's world. In this disjunction there was the danger of an otherworldliness and a negation of culture. But blocking this was his faith that the world even at the peak of its unfaithfulness remained God's world with

God at work in all of its life. No longer was there any room, however, for even the slightest vestige of the old liberal idea of a revelation of God in history. There would seem to be a parallel here with Bultmann's sharp separation between the two worlds of religion and culture, assigning religion to an inner world inaccessible to science, and with the source of its life in God, and culture to an outer world that is under the direction of man's reason. But Bultmann's two worlds are really just two separate aspects of the one world of man. His life is in two compartments that are neatly separated from each other and balanced against each other, both being equally necessary to the completion of his existence. Contrary to this, Barth's two worlds negate each other. This world continues the present order of its existence in rebellion against God and must be conquered and brought under God's sovereignty if man is to be redeemed. His culture, his reason, and all elements in his life participate in his sinful rebellion and must participate also in his redemption.

2. KIERKEGAARD

The influence of Overbeck was combined during 1919 and 1920 with that of Kierkegaard. Since there have been such misapprehensions concerning the significance of Kierkegaard for Barth, some writers finding the origin of his distinctive theology in Kierkegaard, it is important to note how late the Danish philosopher entered the picture and how his influence was related to that of others. Perhaps what has led to the overrating of the influence has been the highly visible effect of Kierkegaard's dialectic and terminology on the language and general forms of expression in the 1922 "Romans." That they vanished from Barth's writings almost as suddenly as they entered has rarely been noticed. Actually, in the revolutionizing of Barth's thinking in 1920, Overbeck had much more responsibility than Kierkegaard, but this passes unnoticed, since so few persons know anything of Overbeck or take the trouble to compare the 1919 "Romans" with the 1922 "Romans."

Barth himself set down the record in 1963 concerning his relation to Kierkegaard.[8] In 1909 he bought "The Instant" but it made little impression and led to no extended interest. "By 1916 a number of us of the younger generation had set out to introduce, with hesitating steps, a better theology than that of the 19th century and of the turn of the century — better in the sense that in it God, in his unique position over against man, and especially religious man, might clearly be given that honor which we believed we found him to have in the Bible." The shift was from a man-centered to a God-centered theology. This preceded the influence of Kierkegaard. Kutter provided a stimulus for emphasis upon God as the ground and object of faith, but this was achieved only gradually. " The first edition of my ' Romans' itself lacked much in this respect." He names Dostoevsky, the Blumhardts, Overbeck, Plato, and Kierkegaard as important influences, but not the Reformers. " The Reformers of the 16th century did not yet evoke much response in us." What, then, was the contribution of Kierkegaard in the period between the two editions of Romans? First was his critique of " speculation which blurred the infinite qualitative difference between God and man." Note that the existence of such an infinite difference was not learned from Kierkegaard. It was from the Scriptures that Barth first drew his emphasis " God is God and man is man," and it was by his reading of the Scriptures that he had been emancipated from the old immanentalism. But the distinction had remained somewhat blurred by elements of speculation that persisted from an earlier stage of development. Now, Kierkegaard with his incisive critique of Hegelian speculation cleared the air and let the distinction stand forth in its sharpest form. Second, he cut through an aesthetic forgetfulness of the absolute claims of the gospel and set in the forefront the need for personal decision in response to those claims. Third, he warned against the danger in interpreting Scripture, of surrounding it with explanations that make its message innocuous. Fourth, in his attack upon Christendom he undercut " all the too pretentious and at the same time too cheap christianism and churchiness of prevalent theology, from which we ourselves were not as yet quite free." Kierkegaard was the herald of a really new day. He relegated not only Hegel but a whole world of thought to the past.

Barth provided also a critique of Kierkegaard in 1963. In giving full play to the costliness of discipleship, Kierkegaard made the definition of a Christian much too gloomy. He was too individualistic, with no place in his thought for the people of God, the Christian congregation, the church. He agreed with Augustine and Scholasticism against Luther and Calvin that love of self precedes love of the neighbor. " Did not a new anthropocentric system announce itself in Kierkegaard's theoretical groundwork — one quite opposed to that at which we aimed? He was bound much more closely to the 19th century than his enthusiasts were willing to believe in 1920. In fact, he fortified a man-centered Christianity immensely and the anthropocentric reaction in mid-20th century theology springs from his existential dialectic." " We may perhaps raise the historically pointed question whether his teaching was not itself the highest, most consistent and most thoroughly reflective completion of Pietism, which in the 18th century along with rationalism laid the foundations of that christianism and churchiness which the pious portrayed, which Kierkegaard opposed so passionately, and which we forty years ago set out to oppose anew by invoking his name among our allies." "I consider him to be a teacher into whose school every theologian must go once. Woe to him who has missed it!" But let him not remain in it or return to it. He must go on from it, letting it be the pinch of spice in his theology. Barth comments that after 1922 express references to Kierkegaard became ever fewer in his own writings, but Kierkegaard's "peculiar tone" remained as an undertone. What Barth had to learn from other sources was, first, that the gospel is *glad* news; second, that it is news which the *congregation* must pass on to the whole *world;* and third, that the news is from *on high.* Far from building directly on Kierkegaard, Barth in the 1920's, having stirred men to read Kierkegaard by his 1922 "Romans," was himself mainly concerned to disentangle himself from certain strong elements in the philosopher's influence that seemed to him to lead theology back into the nineteenth century rather than forward into a new age.

It is not difficult to understand why Kierkegaard should have had a strong appeal at this time for both Barth and Bultmann. They were in rebellion against the bourgeois appropriation of Christianity as the religious reinforcement of its cultural values, a synthesis that could be achieved only by ignoring the revolutionary elements in the gospel and its offensiveness to the natural man, and they recognized in Kierkegaard a distinguished predecessor in this rebellion. He had involved himself in public controversy and most likely shortened his life in his protest against a naturalization of Christianity that meant the neutralizing of its offensive thrust. The clergy, he had said, should win men to a real faith by deterring them from such compromises and exposing to them the full contradiction between the gospel and their present existence. Also, Barth and Bultmann had been challenging the ability of historical scholarship to penetrate beyond the human phenomena, either in the records concerning Jesus Christ or in the Bible as a whole, to the divine reality that alone elicits in man the total response of faith and can be recognized as the object and ground of faith. But here was the Dane, nearly a century earlier, insisting that since history can never give more than approximate knowledge, it can never be expected to provide a basis for faith; indeed, that to attempt to establish such a historical basis is to substitute knowledge of facts for faith in God, a form of human security for the risk that is always involved in the decision of faith. The Christ remains unknown to the historian no matter how much information he assembles concerning Jesus, for he can be revealed only to a faith that is open to involvement in discipleship. Barth had been developing a new approach to Scripture as a whole that was in line with this, criticizing the Biblical scholars for their spectator attitudes as historical exegetes and for thinking their task finished when they had merely set the text in its original ancient context. The crucial task was to let the ancient text become contemporary with the twentieth-century reader so that the word of God that was heard in it then might be heard in it now. But here was Kierkegaard talking of reading Scripture with the heart as though it were a love letter addressed to the reader, to be heard and responded to by him rather than analyzed and explained in an objective fashion. Barth's eschatological perspective, which relativized all achievements in time, including those of Christian faith and knowledge, so that the Christian could find no stopping place in history, found an echo also in Kierkegaard's teaching that one is always in process of becoming a Christian and can never count himself to have arrived. These parallels are sufficient to warn us against attributing to Kierkegaard's influence what was merely strengthened, clarified, or confirmed by it, and to make us take seriously Barth's insistence that his use of Kierkegaard's philosophical terminology in the 1922 "Romans" was no more than a borrowing of language to express Biblical truth, so that the peculiar terminology could be stripped away if necessary without making any change in the underlying thought. Two highly important elements, however, for which certainly Kierkegaard has considerable responsibility and which require special attention, are the conception of God as Unknown and the consequent introduction of dialectic, both of which will be considered as we deal with the "Romans" of 1922.

3. GOGARTEN

A figure who belongs in the picture for both Barth and Bultmann at this point but who is frequently left out of consideration is Friedrich Gogarten, the Lutheran pastor in Stelzendorf in Germany whose blast "Between the Times" we have already heard. With a strongly philosophical interest in theological questions, he was drawn into association with Barth and Bultmann by his militant rejection of the whole idealistic framework of prewar theology. In 1920, Bultmann, when he commented unfavorably on what seemed to him a too wholesale and too uncritical adoption of Pauline theology by Barth, spoke with strong approval of a book published by Gogarten in 1917.[9] In October, 1920, it was directly following a visit of Gogarten with Barth that the latter became conscious that his "Romans" had to be completely rewritten. Philosophically, Gogarten began with Fichte and in 1914 had published a book on "Fichte as Religious

Thinker." The development of his theology had taken a very different course from that of either of the other two. Luther had been the chief source of theological stimulus for him, emancipating him from the idealistic tradition and eventually making him see in it the primary perversion of modern theological and secular thinking.

Gogarten was soon to find common cause much more with Bultmann than with Barth and he was later to be a major force in the thinking of some of the post-Bultmannians such as Fuchs and Ebeling, but from the beginning there were tensions in his relation with Barth. His interest seemed to Barth more philosophically than theologically centered. His conception of himself as having a special mission to the literary public, the people of culture, seemed more than a trifle pretentious. And his eagerness for a frontal attack on the old nineteenth-century theology and philosophy seemed to betray an underestimate of the dimensions of the theological situation and of the resources necessary for such an attack. In February, 1922, Barth wrote to Thurneysen: " I remain somewhat sceptical about Gogarten's presentation of things. . . . [He] would like to push forward to an ethic in which he would find a basis directly for class, vocation, family, etc." [10] This was the beginning of a doctrine of orders of creation which was later to have serious consequences. In July, 1922, the separation became even more evident at the annual conference of the " Friends of *Die christliche Welt*." Barth reported that he had to keep quiet when Gogarten talked or " we could easily have got in trouble with each other ' in front of the enemy.'. . . The Christological problem is dealt with and solved by him with the help of a speculative I-Thou philosophy. . . . Heaven only knows where that will lead." Yet in 1923, Barth combined with Gogarten in the launching of the journal *Between the Times,* and the two considered themselves representatives of one theological movement. In 1933, Barth asserted that the alliance was based on a misunderstanding. We can only conclude that from the beginning it had been an uneasy alliance and that the theological differences between the two, though recognized, were actually deeper than either of them knew at the time. But in antithesis to the assessment of the situation in 1920–1923 which pictures Barth, Bultmann, and Gogarten in the closest agreement, it must be emphasized that already in that period the differences were present which during the next ten years were steadily to send them in diverse directions. Gogarten's ethic, which provided a basis directly for class, vocation, and family, was to grow into an ethic that provided the basis directly not only for a man's nation but specifically for German nationalism. In October, 1922, Thurneysen wrote to Barth, " We shall not easily let ourselves be led astray to take the little step backwards that shows itself in Gogarten's doctrine of the orders of sin." [11]

What, then, accounts for the temporary unity of these two men? They were united in their recognition of the necessity of a radical break with the theology of the nineteenth century, in their opposition to an idealistic immanentalism, in their hunger for a new inbreaking of the word of God which Christ alone can speak into the human situation, and in their awareness of the relativity of all things human, including the structures of Christian theology. Gogarten and Bultmann in 1920–1922 do not seem to have shared Barth's interest in Kierkegaard. H. C. Wolf in his book *Kierkegaard and Bultmann*[12] speaks of Kierkegaard being mediated to Bultmann, theologically through Barth and philosophically through Heidegger, but Barth himself holds that Kierkegaard reached Bultmann primarily through Heidegger and with a distinctly Heideggerian cast to his character.

4. THE "ROMANS" OF 1922

In assessing the factors that impelled him to rewrite his commentary on Romans, Barth puts them in the following order. First, he had gone deeper into Paul, particularly in an intensive study of I and II Corinthians. Second, Overbeck had challenged his earlier understanding of both history and eschatology, forcing him to include all history in Paul's world of sin and death, the age that is passing away, and to see the new age as promised so that man can live joyfully in the strength of the promise, yet never a reality in the midst of history except in that special form taken by the faith of Jesus and his disciples which Overbeck called *Urgeschichte*. Third, he had achieved a better understanding of Plato and Kant with the help of his brother, the Christian existentialist philosopher, Heinrich Barth. Then in fourth and fifth place come Kierkegaard and Dostoevsky. Sixth was the shock that he received, not from critical reviews of the 1919 "Romans," but from favorable ones. He was aghast at some of the theologians who found it possible to agree with him and realized that he must have concealed what he really intended if he had made such approbation feasible.

The "Romans" of 1922 represents not so much a revision of the 1919 commentary as a reaction against it. It is a turning point almost as sharp as the earlier one in 1914 and in the nature of things much more clearly documented. The 1919 "Romans," under the influence of conservative nineteenth-century theologians such as Beck, was dominated by a schema of sacred history (*Heilsgeschichte*). The stream of "real" history showed itself in a preparatory way in the Old Testament, and in figures such as Socrates and Plato, broke through into the world as a new creation in Jesus Christ, and from that point on became the life-process of an international people of God, not identical by any means with the church and sometimes manifesting itself most powerfully beyond the church (as in Democratic Socialism). By faith one became a participant in this stream of new creation in which the world and man were restored to their unity with God and began to move toward a future consummation. God, hidden in the old world of sin and death, was known to man in this new world of faith, so that one could speak confidently of what He was doing in history.

With one great sweep of the hand all of this disappears in 1922! The new world of God stands in absolute contradiction to the whole world of human history. No exception is made for Christians or the Christian church. Believers and unbelievers alike belong to the world which is under the sign of death and judgment. The arrogance of religion is in attempting to justify some men in separating themselves from their brothers under judgment. God has included all in sin that he may have mercy on all, but there is no mercy unless there is an unconditional acceptance of the judgment. Faith is before all else a recognition that all are sinners, without any possibility of new life in themselves and knowing only the hollow at the center of life which is the source of their helplessness. The new world begins beyond the boundary of this world, not as a future event beyond the last moment of time but as the boundary of each moment. In Jesus Christ it touched our world of death as a tangent touching a circle, touching and not entering history, but in touching it, bringing into being in history a life different from what had been known before. Where it touched, there was revelation of the certainty of God's world, which became the promise in the strength of which men could really live with confidence and hope from that moment forward. The resurrection of Jesus was the triumphant revelation of the divine world in which alone man's life is fulfilled. But no man enters that world in his earthly life. The man of faith lives on the boundary of it, with his life centered in the world beyond, and yet confessing to his dying day his involvement in the world of sin and death. In 1919, the Romans to whom Paul's letter was addressed were seen as " saints " who were " the hopeful beginning of a new human race," but in 1922 this was changed to " called to be saints " who in response to their call have a life of faith in which their rest is always their unrest and their unrest, their rest. The new life of the man in Christ is historically invisible. His life is never Kutter's " life in the reality of God," never an experience, but only a hope, an " eternally future reality." Historically and psychologically he knows himself to be still the old man in the old world. The man of faith is not righteous but is only *counted* righteous in *God's* sight. His righteousness is visible only to God, never to himself, so that every basis for self-righteousness is removed. All temptation of man to exalt or justify himself morally or spiritually or to fall a prey to the illusion that there is something divine about him is cut away.

Against this background we can better understand the insistence that God is " the Unknown." Here other influences were at work: Cohen, the neo-Kantian philosopher at Marburg for whom God was the hidden abyss and origin beyond the boundary of man's life, and Kierkegaard with his " infinite qualitative difference between time and eternity." Barth in his introduction to the " Romans " of 1922 (page xiii) confessed: " If I have a ' system,' it consists in holding before my eyes as persistently as possible in both its negative and its positive significance what Kierkegaard has called ' the infinite qualitative difference ' of time and eternity. ' God is in heaven and thou upon earth.' The relation of *this* God to *this* man, the relation of *this* man to *this* God, is for me the theme of the Bible and the sum of philosophy in one." In the 1919 " Romans " the hiddenness of God from man was due entirely to sin and was a phenomenon of the old world which was negated by grace so that in the life of faith God was known. Theology was a human possibility once the transition was made to the new world inaugurated by Christ in which sin and blindness are overcome. But, in 1922, sin rises up and hides God even from the man of faith! Since he remains a sinner, he remains blind to God. As a man of faith who stands on the boundary between this world and God's world he is distinguished by his recognition of God as the Unknown. The God who is unknown to him is the Origin of his life which he can never completely forget, the beginning and end, and so the source that lies beyond the boundaries of history. Barth can even speak of the Unknown God as the enemy, the overpowerer, the judge, death, which sets a considerable question mark against the unknownness of the Unknown.[18] This dictum was to prove not only a source of misunderstanding and confusion to readers of Barth but a position that he himself soon recognized as indefensible and misleading in its 1922 form, although in a revised form it has remained basic to his theological thinking. What he sought to overcome in 1922 was every claim of man to take possession of God either in his thinking, or in his experience, or in his conscious existence. The God who could be so possessed was no more than a projection of the human psyche and therefore an idol.

There are a number of factors which condition the statement that God is the Unknown. Barth can speak of the new world of God in the same terms, as unknown, and yet in the resurrection of Jesus that new world is revealed to faith so that it becomes the primary certainty of life. Moreover, the new world is also the world of man's origin which he can never completely forget. Faith knows sufficient of the unknown God to love him in his hiddenness. He is hidden in nature, in history, in the psyche of man, in the human existence of Jesus. His revelation is not to be identified with anything in the whole creation. This insistence has to be recognized as a reaction against theologies whose fundamental error was the identification of divine revelation with some element in man such as conscience or reason, or with history as a whole, or with a sacred history within history, or with the Bible itself, or with the Jesus of history, or with the inner life of Jesus. Nowhere is God to be known directly, not even in the Bible or in the figure of Jesus, and not even to faith. All our knowledge of God is *broken* knowledge, a seeing as in a glass darkly. Then, when we press Barth's statement that the Unknown God appears to man as his enemy, we find this means that his judgment upon all men, his No to man and his world, the great negation, is known. In 1919 the positive function of law, religion, and idealism (which were placed parallel) was to reveal God's No, laying bare the gulf between the ideal and the actual in man's life, confronting him with the contradiction between his world and God's world, and so beginning the movement out of the old world into the new. Religion and idealism, therefore, were a preparation for redemption, and in the new world of grace were not destroyed but were fulfilled, taking on a new character in the new context. In 1922 the No of God becomes more comprehensive. Religion, idealism, and law initiate no movement out of the old world. They belong to the world of death. Religion, including the most earnest forms of Christian religion, even the superpiety of a Kierkegaard, stands in antithesis to grace as death does to life. The No of God thunders in man's ears, particularly in the Christian gospel, and until he hears that No and lets himself and all his works, especially his religious works, be judged, he cannot hear the Yes of God to man, the saving Yes which has all of God's love and mercy in it and which is hidden in the No. God's Yes is inseparable from his No. It is its presupposition and is primary while the No is secondary. Grace precedes judgment. But not even a whisper of grace can be heard until the judgment is embraced unconditionally. There is no bridge from religion to grace, from even the most spiritually-minded man to God. Grace is sheer miracle, a new beginning, impossible on any human basis but possible by the power of God. Only when all these factors are kept in mind does it begin to be clear why God is called " the Unknown."

5. DIALECTIC AND URGESCHICHTE

The brokenness and indirectness of man's knowledge gives to Christian thinking the character of a dialectic. No simple direct statement about God or man is possible because the man who speaks stands on the borderline between two worlds that are in absolute contradiction to each other. In God the contradiction is resolved but only in God, never in the sphere that is open to man's knowledge. The synthesis lies beyond the thesis and the antithesis in what the philosopher calls the Origin and the theologian calls the Unknown God. Only the thesis and the antithesis can be known, not the synthesis, though it is the source and basis of all. Therefore, the thinking must move back and forth between the thesis and the antithesis, which seem contradictory and yet both of which contain elements of the one truth that is essential to man's life. The consequence is that the truth has frequently to take the form of paradox. Every statement that can be made is only a partial truth which, taken by itself, leads us astray by the element of untruth in it, so that it must be followed by another statement that will overcome its untruth, and so on ad infinitum. This is the best that can be done and the only honest form of thinking for a man whose world of sin and blindness is bounded by death, even though the gospel has given him confidence in a grace hidden in the judgment and a life that is more powerful than death.

The dialectic may be illustrated by what is said concerning the new man in Christ. In 1919 the new man knew himself to be a new man. The world of sin and death lay behind him as he now participated in the new historical stream of life initiated by Christ. He still had his battles with the old forces, but he was consciously a participant in the new age. But in 1922 he only stands on the threshold of the new age. The newness of his humanity is not visible to him but only to God. To himself he is still the unrighteous enemy of God, the sinner under sentence of death. He confesses his solidarity with a world that is lost in its sin. And yet in Christ he has been given hope of the new man. All his conduct is determined by that hope. He has a new self, his own true self, the existential " I," but it is hidden and intangible as yet, historically invisible, so that he dare not claim to be the new man. There are no Christians, only the possibility, the impossible possibility, of there being Christians, revealed in Jesus Christ. Thus when Barth interprets Paul's statement concerning Christians " having the Spirit " (Rom., ch. 8) he has to qualify each word. He does not wish to conceal that " we have heard the wind from heaven, have seen the new Jerusalem, have found the eternal decision, that we *are* ' in Christ Jesus,' " but if we emphasize " we " or " have," we are back in the region of religion rather than in the realm of grace. We have to qualify the " we " as " not we " and the " have " as " not have " in order to do justice to the inner contradiction in our self and in our " having " as it now exists. This at least suggests both the meaningfulness and the tortured character of the dialectic by which Barth sought to do justice to the brokenness of our knowledge.

It is not only God who is hidden but also Christ, the new man in Christ, the new world in Christ, and the whole church of God. The church, when it lets itself become engrossed in religion rather than with the purpose of God for the world, becomes the very peak and climax of the world's resistance to God. The church is truly the church of Christ only when it lets itself come under God's judgment, knows its rejection, and begins to pattern its actions after God's coming world. It is noteworthy that the sharp emphasis upon the blindness of the church in 1919 and the tendency to contrast that blindness with the sight of men beyond the church in the socialist movement becomes in 1922 an equal emphasis upon the blindness of church and world. The glowing hope for a socialist world disappears and in its place is a polemic against the revolutionist who thinks he can create the new world and in the endeavor becomes as much a tyrant as his predecessors. The true revolution is from God alone. But there is no softening toward the church. What is visible in the world as church must always be a highly questionable religious institution, torn within itself by the contradiction that permeates all things human. The true church, like the new man, is historically invisible, visible only to God, a miracle of grace. Yet the empirical church remains the place of witness to the unseen, where the gospel of judgment and grace is proclaimed and even the man who knows the human impossibility of the true church maintains his place in the institution that he may bear his witness to what is divinely possible.

The dismissal of *Heilsgeschichte* (sacred history) from within the bounds of history created the problem of how to describe the manifestations of the eternal world of God in the realm of time. To be *of* history was to be subject to the forces of history and involved in the processes of history. Therefore, such manifestations could not be historical in that sense, and yet unless they took place *in* history they could have no significance for man. To resolve the difficulty Barth seized upon Overbeck's category of *Urgeschichte* (primal history) to describe a realm beyond history and yet in history, sometimes also called the "unhistorical," in which movements, events, realities, have their being. What happens in *Urgeschichte* determines what happens in the realm of the historical. *Urgeschichte* is in a real sense a redefinition of *Heilsgeschichte,* removing it to a realm beyond the historically visible. The story of creation as history is of no interest, Barth says, but as an event in the realm of *Urgeschichte* the act of creation is fundamental to all life. The fall of man is called "supertemporal," being the fall of all men, their loss of their original unity with God. The historical Abraham, even if his history could be validly reconstructed, would not concern us, but the "unhistorical" Abraham does. The shift of terms could be confusing but it need not be. All point to a single realm beyond history and yet in history.

Jesus, like Abraham, is uninteresting historically, but the revelation of God in him, first of God's judgment, then of God's mercy in the judgment, makes him the center and source of all history. In him the origin of life itself is revealed, the original unity between God and man, the remembrance of which haunts all men. In him the world of God which bounds every moment of time breaks into time decisively. It remains hidden in the historical events as all *Urgeschichte* does but is disclosed to faith, in the cross as the judgment of the world and in the resurrection as the joyous proclamation of God's Yes to man. The resurrection, therefore, is not history but belongs in this realm above history. In order to hold apart the two worlds that meet in Jesus Christ and to prevent any mixing of the divine and the human even in him, while at the same time asserting the reality of the incarnation, Barth used the geometrical analogy of the tangent, which touches the circle and yet does not enter it, and by its use he laid himself open to the accusation of a docetic concept of Christ. What often has been ignored has been the concreteness of the event in history when God's world touched the circle and the firmness with which Barth insisted on the incarnation as the word becoming flesh. The section where he speaks of the incarnation seems to return to the undialectical, passionate directness of the 1919 "Romans," and also to go far beyond the earlier version in making the incarnation crucial, so much so, as we shall see, that Bultmann accused Barth of going much too far. The tangent was really meant to do more than merely *touch* the circle, for where it touches, "our world ceases to be historical, temporal, objective (*dinglich*) and directly visible." In short, *Urgeschichte* becomes reality in time. The world of God breaks into time and in the strength of that inbreaking the man who by faith is under grace "stands already in the *Urgeschichte* and End-history [where] God is all in all."

Barth drew upon Nietzsche as well as Overbeck in distinguishing a realm of the "unhistorical" or "primal history" beyond the historical. Nietzsche had said that a full explanation of historical events could not be found in history itself. The source of the events eluded man's observation and in the past when he tried to speak of such a source he resorted to mythical language. Great deeds are achieved by men through the existence of this mythical, unhistorical atmosphere which surrounds the historical. Strip away the mythical, and the source of great deeds is lost. Only the historian who is open to the unhistorical in the present can be aware of it in the past. For Barth, all the events of history are rooted and grounded in this unhistorical *Urgeschichte*. For that reason, the familiar world for both Jesus and Plato was full of analogies of the divine world. The new meaning revealed in Christ was the deepest truth of the old world, hidden so deeply in it, however, that the analogies became visible only in Christ and were never bridges out of the old world to God. God as the negation of all things mortal is also their true being, origin, creator. All men carry their eternal being in them as their unborn eternal future. Also, *Urgeschichte,* as the hidden origin of historical events, is their unity. Apart from it, the past is a chaos of antiquities. But *Urgeschichte* transcends the brokenness of time and makes events far separated in time contemporary with each other. We become contemporary with Abraham, with Jesus Christ, or with Paul, when by faith we are in some measure participants in the same hidden world which, because it is God's world, brings past, present, and future together into one.

Finally, the inadequacy of all human language has to be recognized. It can at best offer analogies that point beyond the seen into the unseen to describe the indescribable and to make men aware of the unknown God, the unknown man, the unknown humanity, the unknown world, which are ever breaking through all our conceptualities and forcing us to shape new ones. The reality on which our hopes are focused is not a static being but a dynamic coming, the movement of God behind all the life of our world and of each one of us, in which he is establishing his Kingdom. That is why Barth again and again speaks of the theologians as trying to paint a flying bird. The bird in movement is God in movement. The best the theologian can do is to recognize the difference between the bird in flight and the stationary bird on his canvas. He may even make it look as though it were flying, but when he is finished, the bird has already moved on. The sin of the theologians and of the church is that they think they have caught the bird in their picture and they settle down to be content with the image they have of it instead of following it in its flight. The theologian has to be ever ready to put behind him the pictures he has drawn in the past, and with his eye on the bird, do it all afresh. Faith means following God in his movement through history. That is why Barth to the very end of his life has always been making fresh beginnings and has never been ashamed to repaint the picture: three commentaries on Romans, two beginnings with the *Dogmatics,* and in the twelve volumes of the *Dogmatics* a constantly continuing movement of thought that through all changes has the unity of never losing its focus on the flying bird. At the end of his " Romans," he points out how Paul himself prepared the way for the liquidation of Paulinism in not asking his churches to adopt his point of view in all things but pointing them ever beyond himself to the works of God which no man can do more than serve with integrity in his own limited fashion.

6. BULTMANN'S CRITIQUE OF THE " ROMANS " OF 1922

Bultmann published an extended review of the 1922 " Romans " in *Die christliche Welt*[14] shortly after its appearance. His own major work on the form criticism of the Gospels had been published in 1921 and had established his reputation as a highly competent New Testament scholar and a ruthless pioneering critic. He now shocked the world of scholarship by the measure of approval that he gave to Barth's volume. It had set a question mark not only against the dominant theologies of the day but also against the established methodology in the historical exegesis of Scripture. Who was this Swiss pastor, now since 1921 a neophyte professor of systematic theology in Göttingen, who dared to challenge a structure that the world's greatest Biblical scholars had been slowly perfecting for two hundred years? Such presumption was infamous. But when a critical scholar of Bultmann's eminence dared to stand at least to some degree with Barth, it puzzled the world of scholarship and guaranteed the book a hearing. Bultmann agreed at a number of points with Barth's conception of exegesis: first, that every individual passage in a document must be interpreted in the light of the content of the document as a whole, and second, that the exegete can bring out the meaning of the text only if he himself has an inner relation to the subject matter of the text, i.e., that to attempt a purely objective exposition without theological presuppositions is absurd. He also agreed that Barth had grasped firmly the nature of faith for Paul in refusing to equate it with any form of religious experience or any human standpoint, in sweeping away everything that man may use as a basis of self-justification before God, and in restoring to faith its uniqueness as response to the reality of God. He even agreed that the exegete must achieve a personal closeness to his author that makes him almost forget that he is not himself the author of the text.

Yet Bultmann's distance from Barth was evident on every page of the review. Before the review appeared Barth heard from a Swiss student in Marburg that Bultmann had spent the last six hours of his course discussing the 1922 " Romans." He gave the course more the form of a study group and took " fearful pains " to understand Barth. The student reporting thought Bultmann had declared himself in agreement somewhat too quickly, and when he gave some details concerning Bultmann's comments, Barth's response was: " So there is still all manner of old leaven to be swept out even in Marburg." [15]

The Bultmann who speaks in the review shows little change from the Bultmann of the 1917–1920 essays. He gives forceful expression to his own convictions omitting so much in the " Romans " that does not interest him that his review becomes more an expression of his own mind than an indication of the nature of Barth's theology. "Religion" is the category within which his thinking still moves and the rebirth of religion in its uniqueness as response to a transcendent God is his paramount theological interest. Therefore, although Barth had insisted that all religion, even the most earnest and sincere, is the peak of man's self-justification and resistance to God, Bultmann begins by equating faith and religion and defining the purpose of Barth's book as "the demonstration of the independence and absoluteness of religion." In spite of Barth's open revolt against the whole tradition of Neo-Protestantism from Schleiermacher to Otto, Bultmann places him directly in line with these two men behind whom he sees the figure of Paul. The great succession is: Paul, Schleiermacher, Otto, Barth! It is clear that he is confusing his own lineage with that of Barth.

No attempt is made by Bultmann to compare the 1922 "Romans" with the earlier version. He merely remarks that the revision impressed him much more than the original and that he will leave the comparison to someone else. His concern is to test the Pauline character of the theological ideas. He begins with faith and here what impresses him is Barth's success in overcoming the tendency in contemporary theology to subjectivize faith. Bultmann, in line with Herrmann and Otto, had for some time been emphasizing the unique character of faith (or religion) as a life-encompassing, total response of man to the reality of God. Only God is able to evoke such a response and thereby bring man to self-fulfillment. Herrmann had led the way in protesting against all confusion of faith with cultural values. Now Barth, with his polemic against experience, against mysticism, against the historical visibility of faith, and against pantheism, has taken up the same battle, in some ways less effectively than Herrmann. But what seems to escape Bultmann in this evaluation is that Barth's polemic is directed not just against false forms of religion but against *all* religion. The relativizing of human religion for Bultmann stops short of the final step that would leave man standing in midair with nothing in his own experience on which to set his feet, not even his own most sincere and passionate response to reality. He misses the point of Barth's radical negation of religion because he fails to see how central eschatology is for Barth and that in defining faith Barth starts not from what faith means for man but from the other end of things, from the world of God which is everywhere pressing in upon us. The reality of that world is revealed in Christ in its antithesis to our entire human world so that faith is first of all the apprehension of it as God's judgment upon us and only then as God's transforming grace. This contrast between the two men comes out most sharply when Bultmann, in speaking of "the way of faith," and em-

phasizing the highly individual character of faith as each man's own response to God, insists that all one man can do for another is "to show him
what faith *means*." For Barth, faith, like the life of the new man in Christ,
is indescribable as a human phenomenon because to describe it one would
have to draw God himself down into a human formulation. But for Bultmann the problem is merely to distinguish true faith (religion) from false.
It is not accidental, therefore, that in the review we hear nothing of the
Unknown God, the unknown world, the unknown new man, or the unknown church. The impact of these conceptions upon Bultmann's understanding of the Beyond as the realm of primary reality which is completely concealed from man's knowledge and yet is the source of the
saving word which alone can bring him to the fulfillment of his life, seems
to have been later than 1922.

It is not surprising, then, that Bultmann objects to Barth's description
of faith as awareness of the hollow at the center of life (*Hohlraum*). What
Barth was trying to say was that, when a man examines his own experience and consciousness, what he finds is not the evidence of God's presence but the evidence of God's absence, the hollow in the human wheel
that awaits the axle of God. Not even the profoundest Christian experiences or achievements can fill that hollow. When they try to do so, they
become "the peak of sin." The hollow remains because man ever remains man, the sinner whose enmity toward God has to be overcome ever
anew by grace and forgiveness. But to Bultmann a faith that is not a reality in consciousness is an absurdity. A man does not merely believe that
he believes; he knows that he believes. Barth's whole dialectic of "I" and
"not I" is to Bultmann confusing and unnecessary. To pose it as a tension between two contradictory worlds is to make mysterious and obscure
what can be described very simply as the process by which a man moves
toward the fulfillment of his true self. Both the old self and the new self
are psychologically describable entities. (Later Bultmann was to posit the
competence of the philosopher to describe them.) True faith as a phenomenon of our consciousness is nothing other than obedience, submission,
self-offering. It is "a unique determination of our consciousness." One
comes to faith "by taking thought if and where in his life he meets the
reality to which he can — must — bow absolutely. Inner sincerity is the
only 'way' to faith, sincerity which does not evade the ultimate question
concerning the meaning of human existence, sincerity which is ready for
the sacrifice even of one's own I, ready to take the road to the 'king of the
dark chamber.' That reality can never be made visible and every man has
to make the decision for himself." There is little change here from his
earlier description of faith. He claims to be merely clarifying what Barth
left obscure and seems quite unaware of the radical hiatus between him-

self and Barth at this point. The contrast between Bultmann's individualism and Barth's social perspective is particularly striking.

The same approach continues in his consideration of *Urgeschichte* or the " unhistorical " in history. He accepts the insight that the events of history are determined in a realm deeper than the conscious and observable phenomena of history, but he identifies this realm, not as Barth does as a superhistorical divine realm beyond the processes of history, but as a deeper level in the human psyche. In science, art, and all man's activities his conscious achievements are the consequence of hidden forces that have been at work below the level of consciousness. Barth seems to him to be indulging in futile speculation when he projects this invisible inner realm as a hidden world beyond our world and attributes to it a reality of its own.

The student reporter from Marburg had said that the discussion of the " Romans " somehow ran aground on the question of Christology. Bultmann, like Barth, had already rebelled against Herrmann's location of the ultimate revelation of God in the " inner life of Jesus," in his holiness, moral integrity, and love, which was Herrmann's way of getting around the scholar's uncertainties about the historical Jesus. Bultmann's form-critical analysis of the traditions made him unwilling to sanction any reconstruction of the consciousness or inner life of Jesus. At that point his judgment as a historian accorded well with Barth's theological conviction that no history, not even the history of Jesus, can have direct revelatory significance. History is flesh, the flesh of a world of sin in which God is hidden. In faith we no longer know Christ after the flesh but after the Spirit. He has to be revealed to faith. But when Barth says that the years one to thirty are the years of revelation, Bultmann parts company with him decisively. " I confess that I simply do not understand him; here I can see only contradictions." To make these years of Jesus' life in history the one point in all time where the perpendicular of God's world intersects the horizontal line of man's world seems to deny the earlier assertion that nothing in Jesus' life or teaching or healing ministry makes him the Christ but only his death and resurrection. So also when Barth asserts that " it is Christ's obedience to God, his taking upon himself of man's sin, his form of the servant, that constitutes the revelation," Bultmann declares that he has no idea what this means. It seems to him that Barth has taken the Pauline myth to be a description of Jesus' life in time.

There has frequently been misunderstanding of both men at this point, so that it requires careful examination. It must not be assumed that both mean the same thing when they deny direct revelational significance to the human history of Jesus. The key to the difference between them is the word " direct." Barth was willing to agree with Bultmann that Jesus' history is essentially of no more importance than many other human histories, but only when the conditioning words " apart from revelation " were added. Rightly understood, then, he was saying no more than the New Testament records themselves show to have been the conviction of the early church — that except insofar as God was revealed in the human story of Jesus, the church had no interest in preserving the memory of it. For Bultmann, Jesus' life and ministry were only preparatory to the revelation of God in the kerygma of the early church. Not in the earthly life of Jesus and not even in his cross as an event in history, but only in the church's preaching of the cross, came the decisive moment in the birth of the gospel and the church. Jesus as a man belonged in the context of Judaism as a kind of prophet-rabbi. But for Barth the decisive moment was in the life, ministry, death, and resurrection of the *person* Jesus Christ. How he seemed to men was of no account. Who he was, was hidden in his outward historical form, but *hidden to be revealed to faith*. And the discernment of faith was that in his person the original unity of the whole creation was restored, the rift between God's world and man's world made by sin was overcome by grace, and God was once more at one with man. The human life of Jesus was not irrelevant to the revelation but on the contrary became the medium of the revelation through the action of the Spirit. This difference between the two men became ever clearer in their later writings. For the one, the incarnation could be only a myth signifying that Jesus was the bearer of the revelation from God, whereas for the other, it was the disclosure of the ultimate truth concerning God and man, concerning Creator and creation. For the one, " divine " and " human " were absolutely exclusive terms, the infinite qualitative difference between eternity and time, between God and man, making it an impossibility that God should become man. For the other, the infinite difference between God and man and the New Testament assertion that God became man in Jesus Christ were the two — seemingly but not actually antithetical — poles of one truth, between which the mind must move and to both of which it must hold firmly if it is not to lose the very foundation of truth itself.

Light on this issue may be shed by a passage in a later essay of Bultmann's [16] in which he characterizes the New Testament concept of God, the Holy Spirit, indwelling man as " mythological," since an autonomous human spirit cannot be penetrated by any alien spirit, even God's Spirit. He does not seem to take account of the possibility that " indwelling," while it suggests physical location and undoubtedly had that meaning for first-century man, may denote the interpenetration of two personal existences in intimate relation with each other. That Paul can use " Christ in me " and " I in Christ " interchangeably surely shows this. The incarnation of Jesus Christ and the indwelling of the Spirit in the Christian are therefore analogous, and the question is whether they are mythological expressions or testimony to the reality on the one hand of the perfect oneness of God with man in Jesus Christ and on the other of the broken yet promised oneness of God with all men through Jesus Christ.

Bultmann's final criticism of the "Romans" casts long shadows ahead. He is disappointed that Barth's discernment of the distance between all human language about the gospel and the gospel itself did not lead him to distinguish between the essential Pauline gospel and temporary elements in Pauline thought that obscure his gospel for later generations. According to this way of thinking, the rabbinic, Hellenistic, and Gnostic features of Paul's thought should have been stripped away to leave only what was of the Christian essence. Here again Bultmann, in common with Weiss, Wrede, and Jülicher, draws a sharp line between the human, historical, and transitory in Paul and the divine eternal essence. But Barth will have none of this.[17] The revelation is not to be heard by clearing away the temporary historical elements that make up the human person of Paul but by attentive listening to the witness of this concrete and complex historical person. To strip away the rabbinic, Hellenistic, and Gnostic features would be to lose the real Paul, the apostle, and to gain an abstraction, created by critical scholarship. Moreover, the rabbinic, Hellenistic, and Gnostic elements in his thought have a significance in the new context of his gospel quite different from what they had in their original usage. Bultmann feared that such an approach to Paul's writings came dangerously close to reviving in a new form the old literalistic doctrine of the inspiration of all Scripture. Barth feared that the attempt to separate the temporary expressions from the eternal content of Scripture could result only in a process like the peeling of an onion until one would be left with only a tiny distilled essence of doubtful validity.

7. POINTS OF UNITY

Such was the relation of the two men to each other in 1922. So great were the theological differences between them that it is hard to understand how they could think that they were allies in a common cause. They were perhaps more firmly united in regard to what they were against than in any constructive theological program. One has to remember that together they faced the angry opposition of almost the whole theological world. They were leaders of a revolt that challenged the validity of all the dominant theologies of their day. To a church that had come to base its confidence mainly on the Jesus of history in one way or another, they were both dangerous and radical skeptics who were robbing the church of its Jesus. And Christians, who had been taught by Harnack and others to be impatient of theological issues, to regard such doctrines as the incarnation and the Trinity as excess baggage that the church should cast overboard to lighten the ship for its journey, and to demand simplicity in all religious statements, were affronted by the complexity and what seemed to be the obscurity in the writings of these men. The two were united in their determination to break decisively with the past and were conscious that they were inaugurating a new theological age.

There were also a considerable number of points of positive agreement. They were agreed that the era of a purely historical exposition of Scripture that claimed to be achieving objectivity by divesting itself of theological presuppositions was at an end and that the Biblical scholar must be both historian and theologian to do justice to the text. It should not be forgotten that at that point they were pioneers in a revolution which during the past forty years has changed the whole face of Old and New Testament interpretation. They were agreed that the Bible as a collection of human historical records must be unconditionally open to critical investigation, unimpeded by any attempt to identify part or all of the history directly with the revelation of God, since the revelation must come to men ever afresh from beyond the historical plane. On how it comes and how it is related to the historical they differed. But they were agreed that it must come from beyond and that there must be no confusion of the " Beyond " of God with the " here " of man. In a world blinded by the illusion of divine immanence they stood together in defense of the transcendence of God and of a Pauline faith that takes seriously both the alienation of man from God and the all-importance of God's justifying act in Christ by which alone that alienation is overcome. With this measure of common ground uniting them, and finding themselves constantly under attack from the same quarters, it is not surprising that they overestimated their points of agreement and for a time allowed their points of difference to fall into the background. But the gulf was already apparent which was later to become so deep between them. They were like planets, each moving in its own orbit, which ran somewhat parallel for a time but were never united in one orbit and, when they still seemed close, were actually both on courses that were already carrying them apart.

8. SOME EXPLANATORY ESSAYS

Barth was greatly in demand as a conference speaker in 1922 and was constantly journeying to and fro. Three published addresses stem from

124 THE DIVIDED MIND OF MODERN THEOLOGY

this activity but they chiefly repeat in a different form what had been said in the 1922 " Romans." In speaking to ministers on the need and promise of Christian preaching and the task of the ministry in general,[18] he tended to underestimate the dimensions of his theological program and to represent himself not at all as the initiator of a new theological era but merely as a pastor who, in taking seriously his situation between the two riddles — the Bible on one side of him and the life of his people on the other — had been impelled to write a marginal note to all theology. His theology was no more than " a corrective, a pinch of spice." He tried to guard himself against misunderstandings of his emphasis in "Romans" upon the No, or judgment, of God by insisting that whenever the No of God is really heard, the Yes of God is heard within it. To come under God's judgment is to know his grace. "*This* condemnation is forgiveness. *This* death is life. *This* hell is heaven. *This* fearful God is a loving Father." [19] Theologians who have interpreted Barth's emphasis upon God's Yes to man in recent years as though it were a reversal from an earlier exclusive emphasis upon God's No might well take note of how in 1922, and before 1922, the No and the Yes were inseparable, and the Yes even then was seen as primary to the No, the judgment being itself a work of God's grace. In an era when men thought they could have grace without judgment, they had to be told that only sinners broken under God's judgment could hear his word of grace. But in an era when men see only judgment and despair of grace, the emphasis has to be shifted to the grace that is hidden in the judgment. He is concerned also in these addresses to clarify the nature of dialectic in his thinking, for it was this that had led to so many misunderstandings. Men failed to see that both the Yes and the No had to be held together since the truth lay beyond them and that he was constantly moving between the two. They took one side of the dialectic apart from the other and treated it as though it were intended to be the whole truth. Thus, the paradoxical statements produced by the dialectic were for them simply absurd contradictions rather than pointers to the truth. The truth lies at the center and "the genuine dialectician knows that this Center cannot be apprehended or beheld. . . . Our task is to interpret the Yes by the No and the No by the Yes without delaying more than a moment in either a fixed Yes or a fixed No." "Neither my affirmation nor my denial lays claim to being God's truth."

One address [20] was pointed to meet criticism of the "Romans," the criticism that ethics had been neglected. Again, there is little that goes beyond the "Romans," but the implications of the theology for ethics stand out with much greater clarity. The prosperous bourgeois prewar culture with its self-confident theology had possessed also a self-confident ethic, codified for it by the Ritschlian school. Troeltsch's ethic had been that of the new German economic civilization. But with the breakup of the old culture "the era of the old ethics is *gone* forever." Man's confidence and belief in himself has been shattered. Modern man therefore asks the ethical question with a passion that his predecessors did not know. His whole world is shaken and set in question when he asks, "What ought I to do?" Behind his question is his connection with "the One who regards him from the viewpoint of *eternity*." His world and everything in it is under the judgment of God. But the concept of the good that exposes the sickness of man and his world demands some form of millenarian hope, a goal for human history. Barth's own conception of the goal takes the definite form of the socialistic ideal: a community of righteousness with no paternalism, no exploitation, no oppression; true freedom without class discrimination; the abolition of nationalism, unrestrained power and war; a civilization of the spirit instead of a civilization of things; human values instead of property values; brotherhood in place of antagonism. But the more clearly the goal is envisaged, the more certain man is of his inability to achieve it, so that the problem of ethics, like the problem of the ministry or of the church or of theology, leaves man in an impasse.

Against the background of this statement of the problem Barth then develops what he holds to be the teaching of Paul, Luther, and Calvin. Man first of all finds himself under condemnation. But this is the narrow pass which leads to truth and to the redeeming answer. "We are to bend before the doom revealed in the problem of ethics. . . . It is through the inescapable severity of this doom that we come upon the reality of God." Only when we recognize our world as the realm of death do we begin to see the gulf between the creature and the Creator and beyond the gulf the deathless life of God that is our true portion. Within the realm of death, man's goals are corrupted by sin to the very end of his days so that the law must remain in force; yet within this realm "civilisation possesses its own true dignity . . . as a *witness, a quite earthly reflection,* of a lost and hidden order." Hidden within it are the marks of its divine origin. But having said this, Barth is swift to deny the concept of orders of creation (in which Gogarten was so interested), a hierarchy of functions in the natural order — parent, pastor, heaven-sent king — which are exempted from the scope of the all-encompassing judgment. All relations in life are infected with sin and all are in need of redemption. Man himself cannot think his way through to any solution of this ethical problem. If he could, then he would be able to build his own bridge to God. His only hope is the bridge that God himself has built in Jesus Christ. The answer to our dilemma is in revelation and faith.

CHAPTER VII

AGREEMENT AND DISAGREEMENT, 1923–1926

THE PECULIARITY of the years 1923 to 1926 is that, while at that time they were thought even by Barth and Bultmann themselves to be the period of their greatest solidarity with each other, it was during these years that new influences made themselves felt which were to widen and deepen the gulf that already separated them. In 1923, Martin Heidegger became professor of philosophy in Marburg and an association of Bultmann with him began which was to have far-reaching consequences for theology. Heidegger during this period was at work on his volume "Being and Time" which he was to publish in 1927. In 1923, Barth was immersing himself in the writings of Luther and Calvin and lecturing on Zwingli. In February, 1923, he sent Thurneysen four hundred pages of typed material on Calvin. Zwingli was a great disappointment to him. He felt compelled to rank him as a predecessor of modern Protestant theology and no longer was puzzled by Luther's anger at him. In September, 1923, Thurneysen urged him to develop a dogmatics of his own and throughout 1924 he was hard at it, in the process exploring the resources of his own Reformed tradition and finding undreamed-of treasures of wisdom in it. In November, 1923, Thurneysen remarked that until now they had been more Lutheran than Reformed but now a new Reformed era was beginning, marked by a subdued tone and an emphasis on the two-edged character of the word of God. Earlier, in the fall of 1922, Barth had made contact with a group of orthodox pastors in the northwest of Germany who had been shaped by the influence of Kohlbrügge [1] and with whom he was surprised to find that he had so much in common. Thus, while Heidegger was drawing Bultmann in one direction, the Reformers and representatives of an orthodox Reformed tradition were drawing Barth down a quite different path.

1. CONTROVERSY WITH HARNACK AND TILLICH

In 1923 the senior church historian, Adolf Harnack, and the young theologian of culture, Paul Tillich, both spoke out in criticism of Barth and his associates. Barth had at one time been a devoted student of Harnack but now found his former teacher harshly critical of his development. In April, 1920, when the two met in Basel, Harnack branded Barth " a Calvinist and intellectualist " who would eventually " found a sect and have inspirations." [2] He saw Barth as endangering the historical and scientific character of theology and undermining its position in the university communities. Unwilling to dignify the subject by examining it in a careful scholarly article, Harnack thought to dispose of it by formulating fifteen embarrassing questions which he published in *Die christliche Welt* [3] without naming Barth. To limit the capability of historical science was to destroy it. To set God's world in radical antithesis to man's world was to encourage flight from reality and the abandonment of ethics. To find no truth in Goethe's pantheism or Kant's idealism or to separate the experience of God from the experience of the good, true, and beautiful, was to embrace barbarism and atheism. The exclusion of reason must lead to some kind of Gnostic occultism. The real Christ would be exchanged for a dream figure.

Barth quickly published fifteen answers. His claim that the existing theology had been led into a neglect of its primary theme by its purely historical interest was no disparagement of critical and scientific historical work, he said, but only a recognition of its inability to compass the content of the gospel which in its essence is a relation between God and man. Barth set forth once more in brief compass the positions that he had been working out for ten years, showing at each step that they were the consequence of taking the content of Scripture seriously, and gently questioning the validity of Harnack's self-confident cultural Christianity. The claim of Harnack to be already in such sure possession of the truth of God and the love of God was simply incredible to Barth. The transition from man's old world of sin and blindness into God's great new world seemed to him to require nothing less than a new birth and more time than any man is ever likely to possess. We have to live in the promise of it, being saved by hope. He also pointed out that the most recent historical work on the Gospels no longer supported Harnack's assurance that the historian could produce an authentic picture of Jesus.

Harnack's response, which showed no intention of trying to understand what Barth was about, drew from Barth the suggestion that it would greatly aid the discussion if Harnack would read what he, Thurneysen, and Gogarten had been writing in recent years. What professed to be a defense of modern scientific theology was actually nothing more than a defense of Harnack's own particular brand of modern theology. It was surely not necessary for one to follow the dominant nineteenth-century pattern in order to be accounted scholarly. That would be rather hard on Paul, Luther, Calvin, and others. A false conception of theology as a purely historical discipline had divorced it from preaching and the life of the church. The task now was to recover the unity of theology and preaching. At the heart of the problem was a rethinking of the meaning of revelation. The concept of a unique revelation of God in Jesus Christ was surely no innovation but, rather, the inevitable consequence of taking the content of Scripture at its own valuation. To affirm such a revelation was to deny revelation in culture and nature, but, far from making the life of humanity meaningless, this brought men into the crisis which discloses both the depth of their predicament and the greatness of God's promise for them. To the charge that he was merely resurrecting a dead theology of the past, Barth answered, "We have to think *in* our time *for* our time"[4] and he could have added "in continuity with the Scriptures, the Reformation, and the best that we have learned from the nineteenth century."

Paul Tillich, then in Berlin, on a visit to Barth in 1922 had spoken of the 1922 "Romans" as one of the signs of a new "theonomous" period dawning in history, but in 1923 he published a critique.[5] What he approved in Barth and Gogarten was mainly that they had set theology in motion, but to him their concept of revelation was entirely too narrow. Where they found only the judgment of God, the No of God to man, in the existing order of the world, in culture and in conscience, he held that both grace and judgment are revealed together in the creation, though paradoxically to faith, and that the conscience of man is the locale of revelation. Also, where they affirmed a positive undialectical revelation of grace and truth at one point in history, in Jesus Christ, he denounced this as an absurdity, a binding of faith to a relative historical phenomenon which could produce only confusion and submission to a false authority. Jesus as a figure in history could be no more than a symbol of a much more all-pervasive reality. The ground of being, the unconditioned, is revealed to faith through all reality, so that what is needed is not a theology focused on the Biblical witness but a philosophy of religion that is able to take account of revelation in the full breadth of its manifestations but particularly as it evidences itself in the history of culture.

Barth, in answer, declared himself uninterested in a "frosty Unconditioned" behind the universe or in a philosophy or theology of culture.[6]

For him Tillich's revelation of grace and judgment in nature, culture, and the human spirit was entirely too facile and utterly incredible. Christian theology was based on a personal revelation of a personal God in the person of Jesus Christ. For Tillich's revelation, Christ, Scripture, Holy Spirit, and church were basically superfluous and came in only as symbols. Tillich, in a reply, justified this on the score that the symbols God, Scripture, and Christ had now become so encrusted with false meanings that a new terminology had to be found. In the exchange, Tillich had drawn comfort from the fact that Barth found in the existing order of the world analogies of the original unbroken divine order that constantly remind man of his Origin. Where for Barth the analogies were hidden and were revealed only in Christ, for Tillich they were evident to faith quite apart from Christ. There may have been a warning in this to Barth to guard himself more carefully than formerly in his use of philosophical parallels and terminology.

2. The Reformed Heritage

These controversies made clear to Barth the need for more careful definition of the doctrines of Christology, Scripture, and church. Two essays in 1923 show this new emphasis. Barth's study of Luther issued in a long essay on Luther's doctrine of the Eucharist[7] in which he demonstrated how close Luther was at first to the position later formulated by Calvin. Luther was concerned to guard against the Sacrament's being regarded as a good work of man or a sacrifice offered by him to God. It is God's action for man, and God acts in his word which is heard in the words of institution. The word of God added to the bread and wine makes them sacramental. Without the word they remain a body without a soul, letter without spirit, a sheath without a knife. On the question whether the laity should receive the cup, Luther could remain indifferent, since the one thing needful was for them to have the word. The bread and wine were signs confirming the word. Luther also emphasized that only faith could feed on the bread of God's word. Neither sacramental action nor the signs could of themselves be effective. He warned his people not to receive the Sacrament unless they came in faith and he even considered instituting an examination of communicants " as to the state of their hearts." He was driven to his later emphasis upon the " is " in " This is my body " only when it seemed to him that the central reality of the Sacrament as an actual feeding upon Christ in faith was seriously threatened. This interest of Barth in the doctrine of the Eucharist is significant mainly of the

movement in his thought from a strongly negative and critical attitude
to the church toward a positive appreciation of its centrality in God's ongoing work of grace and consequently in theology. A few years before, it
seemed almost as though he considered that the church had become irrelevant to what God was doing in the world. That this was not so was demonstrated by the earnestness with which he undertook all the tasks of its
ministry and refused to turn his back upon it as Ragaz and other Christian socialists had done. The church with all its failures and blindnesses
was still the place where, uniquely, witness had to be borne to God in the
midst of the world. But now with the death of all romanticism which
identified socialism with the inbreaking of God's Kingdom, he began to
look upon the church with somewhat different eyes.

The deepening appreciation of his Reformed heritage is even more evident in an address delivered in September, 1923, to the General Assembly
of the Alliance of Reformed Churches.[8] He had been asked to speak on
" The Doctrinal Task of the Reformed Churches." He began with an extract from an address delivered at an earlier meeting of the Alliance which
illustrated the widespread distaste for doctrinal discussion, the disparagement of it in contrast to practical concerns, and the fear of it as a source
of disunity. Exposing ruthlessly the doctrinal vacuum in the church which
let its preaching become inane and let its most earnest Reformed church-
manship become a spectacle of contradictions, he pointed the way back to
the source of the Reformed faith in the living word of God which has to
be heard ever afresh from Scripture and in the hearing calls the church
ever afresh to self-reformation. Therefore, the central doctrinal task he
saw to be a restatement of the Scripture principle, cutting through all confusion concerning Scripture and laying open for the future the one possible source of renewal in doctrine and life. " Reformed doctrine " is simply
what we must say when the Spirit of God has spoken to us through the
word of Scripture and has become the crisis of our existence. These words
remain human words but, spoken in the crisis, they are witness to God's
word. That word discloses the only possible basis for the life and preaching of the church. The confessions of the church point to it, but like all
else in the church they are humanly fallible and must ever be reformed.
Barth noted the difference here between Lutheran and Reformed, the Lutherans having made one confession the authoritative guide to the understanding of Scripture, while the Reformed fathers could see no one confession as final but left the door open to the necessity of new witness in
the future. He suggested that a new confession might well be the task
of a church that heard for its own day the promise and command of God's
word. Coming events cast their shadows before, not only in this sugges-

tion, but also when in his discussion of the difference between Lutheran and Reformed in Christology he hazarded the prediction that: " If the old discernment becomes new in us, we may reestablish for ourselves a theology of the second article, which is sadly lacking." There already is the theme of the Barmen Declaration of 1934 and of the twelve-volume *Dogmatics* on which publication began in 1932. Looking back, he detected a profound wisdom in the Reformed fathers who held, in opposition to Luther, that Christ remains hidden in both the Scriptures and the Lord's Supper until God reveals him to faith, and who thereby guarded the freedom of God in his own revelation. A direct identity of Christ with the elements in the Sacrament or with the words in the book would have the effect of making revelation "a piece of direct information, a religious fact," and of concealing what is all-important, that the word of God is not an entity apart from God but is God himself in his word.

3. SERVANTS OF THE WORD

Early in 1923 the journal *Zwischen den Zeiten* had been launched, with Barth, Thurneysen, and Gogarten cooperating as editors. Gogarten had wanted to call it " The Word," but Barth dismissed the suggestion as " unbearably presumptuous." " It would be better to call it ' The Ship of Fools.' . . . God knows it would never do in Germany that *we* should have the insolence to go marching out with ' The Word ' on our lips." As always, Barth sought to guard against the confusion of *any* human words with the word of God. Through the years he has been burdened with the accusation of the very presumption that he was most anxious to avoid — as though he were claiming to have captured the word of God in his theology. Nothing of his endeavors either in 1923 or at any later time can be understood until it is grasped firmly that for him both preaching and theology operate in a human sphere with human words in response to the divine word which is always beyond them. No man ever captures or possesses the word of God.

Late in 1923, Barth and Thurneysen published their second book of sermons, *Come Holy Spirit*,[9] again without giving any indication which of them was responsible for each sermon. It was a sign of their solidarity with each other, and the sermons were intended to show how their entire work in theology came to its focus and fruition in their preaching. Their claim had been that in their theology they were simply listening to Scripture on behalf of the man of their time and reporting what they heard, but their assertions were in such contradiction to what passed currently as religious truth, on the authority of the most distinguished Biblical and theological scholars, that they were constantly under indictment for reading their own peculiar views into Scripture. Many a lordly scholar dismissed them summarily as "eisegetes." Therefore, the sermons were a kind of test. Here were twenty-five passages of Scripture and the sermons in which Barth and Thurneysen opened up these passages for their hearers. Were the texts allowed to speak or did one hear only a pair of opinionated theologians who silenced the text in order to make themselves heard? The text was the judge. No one could deny that these sermons constituted expository preaching of a new order that brought the message of the Scriptures and the life of man into a confrontation that at one and the same time shook man to the depths of his being and opened to him the promise of a new future. There was both judgment and mercy in them in the same fruitful interrelation that they have in Scripture. To many there had seemed to be an exaggerated and overpowering emphasis on judgment in the 1922 "Romans," giving a negative cast to Barth's theology, but here were sermons from the same period and in them the gospel was preached as the best news man could ever hear, news, however, that was irrelevant to his life until, acknowledging his imprisonment in a world of sin and death, he became willing to hear it as the word of liberation. These sermons, for many far beyond Germany, became their introduction to Barth's theology.

4. Bultmann in Closer Agreement with Barth

Bultmann was silent in 1923, but in 1924 published a significant article on "The liberal theology and the most recent theological movement," [10] not however in the new journal but in the *Theologische Blätter*. The article is basically a confession of solidarity with Barth and Gogarten and an indication of specific points at which a break with liberal theology had become necessary. Bultmann in 1924 was much closer to Barth than he had been in his review of Barth's "Romans" in 1922. But perhaps his points of difference were deliberately concealed by his confining the scope of his article to the concepts of God and man, leaving the subjects of Christology, Scripture, and canon for another time. It was on Christology that he had differed with Barth most radically earlier and it was on the canon of Scripture that he was later to be most opposed to him. From liberalism Bultmann had learned the necessity of absolute integrity in historical research, even though it should endanger men's souls and lead them into shattering doubts. But the primary error of liberalism was in thinking that history could provide a basis for faith, and in particular in basing itself on its picture of the historical Jesus. Its second error was in failing to see that *everything* historical, without exception, is relative. Liberalism was intent upon finding the revelation of God in history, the power of God working through forces present in history, with persons as the bearers of those forces. But in identifying history with revelation the theologians were deifying man, and in doing it with Jesus as a historical person they made of him not God but an idol. " God is the absolutely other-worldly reality " and neither he nor his Kingdom can be identified directly with any human phenomenon or construction. It is interesting that in an autobiographical note, written in 1956, Bultmann claimed that before all else he had learned from the new theological movement that the Christian faith " is not . . . a phenomenon of religious or cultural history " but, rather, " is the answer to the word of the transcendent God that encounters man." [11] We have already seen that long before 1922, under the influence of Herrmann, he had decided that religion was beyond the reach of any historian and understood it as the total response of man to the reality of a transcendent God. Apparently what he learned from Barth and Gogarten was that the reality which alone could evoke such a total response was the word of God in the Christian gospel. The uncertainty that had plagued his thinking as to the " how " of revelation was at least in some measure resolved. From now on he bound it decisively to the kerygma of the early church which must be constantly reinterpreted if God's redeeming word is to be heard by man, though occasionally he may seem to waver still.

The remainder of the article echoes Barth's " Romans " of 1922 at almost every point. God is never a given quantity to be known by reason or experience. The Beyond ever remains the Beyond. This is not skepticism or irrationalism: on the contrary, if reason is followed relentlessly, it leads man to the point of crisis, i.e., to the great question of meaning that opens up at the limits of human thinking. God's judgment sets the whole of man's life radically in question but judgment is never separate from grace. Faith is man's response to the word of judgment and grace by which he is wakened from death to life. This is the scandal of the gospel that was evaded by liberal theology: that the natural man cannot inherit the Kingdom of God, that we become sons of God only when God raises us from death to life. Bultmann contrasted this with the standpoint of his former teacher, Johannes Weiss, who held that we perceive our sonship to God as we do the sunshine, which was closer to Stoic teaching than to the New Testament. Far from this, the gospel decrees that man must die to live. And the new man in Christ, the man who is justified by faith, is known only to faith, just as Christ is known only to faith. The new man belongs to the Beyond, and his identification with the man whom we know in this world cannot be seen but can only be believed. (This represents a major change from 1922.) The man of this world remains a sinner under judgment in his past, present, and future, and only as such can he be justified before God. To escape the judgment would be to escape God's grace. The final comment is the most interesting of all: "God is the object of theology and theology speaks of God in speaking of man as he is set before God, i.e., from the standpoint of faith." Insofar as that statement meant only that one can never speak of God without speaking also of man, it said no more than Calvin did in the opening pages of the *Institutes:* God cannot be known apart from man or man apart from God. But, knowing what was to follow in later years, and how inaccessible the Beyond was to the mind of man for Bultmann, one wonders whether already in 1924 it meant that theology speaks of God *only* in speaking of man as he is set before God.

5. First Signs of Bultmann's Anthropological Emphasis

This last theme becomes primary in Bultmann's next essay, published in 1925, "What meaning has it to speak of God?"[12] Existentialism now presses into the foreground. To speak of God as though one were a spectator, from outside the existential relation in which man stands before God, is not just meaningless but is sinful and godless. A science that attempts to make general statements about God occupies this godless spectator position and so must be repudiated. The reality out of which one must speak is the reality of a human existence that is determined by its relation with God. Therefore, to speak of God one must speak of himself in the same moment. But how does one speak of himself and at the same time of the God who determines his existence when God is the Wholly Other, transcending his existence? He finds himself merely speaking of himself and of his own human experiences, which may be illusions with no reference to God. But his existence is determined by God and to seek a God somewhere beyond his own existence, some metaphysical being, a complex of mysterious powers, a creative source, is to seek a phantom. Escape from one's own concrete existence is escape from God. But the God who meets man in his concrete existence is hidden from him by his sin: he is the Wholly Other in antithesis to a sinful world.

A spectator view of the world is actually an escape from the dilemmas of our concrete existence. We build up an objective picture of the world with ourselves in it, but it is abstracted from our real existence and God and man are merely objects in it. Seen from outside in this way, our whole world is godless. Only from inside our concrete existence when we have been addressed by the God who determines our life can we speak of God. And we can speak only when his speaking to us compels us to speak of him. We obey freely a necessity that makes itself felt from beyond us but we can only believe in this necessity; we cannot know it in any more definite way. And the faith which is our response to this compelling word, and which constitutes our very existence, is equally beyond our objective knowing. Only in this free act of faith do we become certain of our own existence. The word we hear and to which we respond is God's word of grace and forgiveness. God himself, like our own reality, remains beyond our knowing, but we have God and our real existence as we respond in faith to his grace which forgives us our sins and heals our alienation from God. " Faith therefore would be the Archimedean point from which the world would be lifted out of its place and transformed from a world of sin into the world of God."

This existential focus upon an inner response of faith which is evoked by confrontation with the reality of God himself and which is inaccessible to all objective description is in direct continuity with the confessional statements that we have been hearing from Bultmann since 1912 concerning the mysterious center of true religion, where a man's self is fulfilled in total response to the reality of God. Where man meets this reality was at first left vague, the cross of Christ being only a symbol for something that could be experienced quite apart from the cross. But now, since 1924, the reality is seen as manifesting itself in a word that is heard by man within an existence that has been determined by its relation with God. It is significant that in this article nothing is said concerning what relation this word which brings forgiveness bears to the New Testament gospel or to the church's preaching. Perhaps one is expected to assume that relation. But it seems as though Bultmann's mind was so concentrated upon the existential definition of faith that the word which alone evokes faith is left floating in uncertainty, undefined, as a word that, somehow, sometime, emerges out of the unknown Wholly Other as the medium of the divine grace which gives man his true existence. The assumption seems to be that, while both the reality of God and the reality of man are unknown quantities for human knowledge, so that objective statements about them are at all times impossible, faith lifts the cloud of unknowingness to some degree at man's end of the existential relation, so that firm statements may be made concerning his faith, but the other end of the relation remains completely hidden, so that nothing can be said of God or God's word except insofar as they manifest themselves in man's faith. The question is whether any such conclusion would have been reached had the starting point been the Biblical witness to the word of God rather than the faith by which man in his inmost being responds to the word of God as a present reality in his own existence. At the very time when Barth was turning to the exploration of the source of God's living word in Scripture and church, Bultmann, under the influence of Heidegger, was becoming convinced that we know nothing and can know nothing of God except what is reflected in the existence of man as he responds in faith to the word of judgment and grace which meet him in his existential confrontation with the unknown God. The foundation is here laid for the whole future project of existential interpretation in which every human statement concerning God, since it cannot be really a statement concerning God but is only an expression of man's existential relation with the Unknown God, has to be reinterpreted as a statement of man about his own existence. Already in 1925, Bultmann was on the way to reduce theology to anthropology.

6. A New Approach to Exegesis

Even more significant was a 1925 essay in *Zwischen den Zeiten* on "The Problem of a Theological Exegesis of the New Testament."[13] It was first of all a protest against the assumption of New Testament scholars that by a purely objective historical exegesis they could establish factually what was said. This "spectator" scholarship began when Lutheran orthodoxy regarded the Bible as a book of doctrinal truths that are immediately comprehensible and determine one's life directly. Rationalism merely distinguished between the rational and irrational among these truths, explaining the latter as divine accommodation to man's capacities or as limitations in the thought of the time. Out of this grew the modern historical explanation in which the antithesis between eternal truths of reason and historically conditioned elements disappeared and all of the phenomena were understood as the products of a general law that gave unity to history. New Testament science was long ruled by a Hegelian conception of this law according to which the absolute spirit shapes history through the power of ideas. This was succeeded by a naturalistic conception of it which sees all things as causally determined and man as a product of circumstances. The ideas, ideals, and institutions of an epoch are then the results of a natural development. The psychological approach, however, sees historical events as the product of psychological forces in men and groups and makes piety the theme of the history with the main attention upon the cultus and mystic experience. All these approaches view the text from a distance and thereby surrender the original claim of the text to be not an object of contemplation but an active subject determining the existence of the reader. As long as the interpreter remains in his spectator position he can find in the text nothing new, but only what he already has potentially in himself. He can never get beyond the surface of history to the reality that makes history what it is.

Bultmann now turns to theological exegesis, or, as he prefers to calls it, *Sachexegese,* exegesis that concerns itself not just with what is said but with the " matter " of which the author speaks. For this approach, " the surface of history is transparent and it focusses on the light which shines through from beyond the surface, believing that this alone makes clear what is meant. This deeper level is not psychological, for that would not take us beyond the man. We ask concerning the ' matter ' that is meant by the statements " (52). The word of an author points to a reality beyond the author, and its intention is to disclose that reality to others so that it will be an *event* for them. At this point Bultmann breaks off his development of what was to be the very foundation of theological exegesis, the recognition of a reality beyond the text to which the text witnesses and thereby makes possible a relation of the interpreter to that reality in his own situation and time. He breaks off in order to show that *Sachexegese* must be followed by *Sachkritik*. Having pressed beyond the words to the " matter " that illuminates their meaning, he has to measure the words by the criterion of what is meant. This is made necessary by the fact that the author as a man of his own time introduces elements into his statements that are either irrelevant or contradictory to what is really meant. The interpreter, having grasped what his author really means to say, must separate this from everything else in his words. This was what Bultmann had already accused Barth of having failed to do in his interpretation of Paul in " Romans."

When Bultmann picks up his theme of *Sachexegese* again, he begins at a different point from where he left off. Instead of focusing on the reality beyond the text that discloses itself to author and interpreter alike, he shifts to an analysis of the interpreter's self-understanding that conditions his approach to the text. Having asserted the realm of meaning beyond the text to be as wide as the possibilities of humanity, he finds that the interpreter's understanding of the text is conditioned by his understanding of his own existential possibility as a man. The exegesis of any historical text goes hand in hand with the interpreter's self-exposition. " There is actually no *neutral* exegesis " (55). Idealist, romanticist, aestheticist, and psychologist — all alike have their peculiar self-understanding which con-

ditions what they find in the text, so that their exegesis produces not just
what is said but rather what they understand to have been said. They
bring a fixed schema of human existence to the text and fit the text into
that schema. But for *Sachexegese* man's life is not fixed but uncertain and
problematic, so that he is ready to hear from the text a word that with authority calls him to decision and poses for him a new possibility of life.
Man's temporality (*Zeitlichkeit*) is recognized, that is, that he is constantly on the way in time toward the discovery of his true existence.
Here Heidegger's definition of man as moving from inauthentic to authentic existence makes itself felt, but the insight is in keeping with the
New Testament conception of man's movement in faith out of an imprisonment in a world of sin and death into a new existence that is never fully
realized this side of death. But we must remind ourselves that thus far
Bultmann is dealing with the interpretation of historical texts in general
and not specifically with New Testament exegesis. The hermeneutic he is
developing is intended to be generally valid. The problem is how *any* historian gets beyond the surface of history to the reality that alone gives the
events their true meaning. He has to approach the text with an openness
to hear from it something that may produce a change in his existence.
"The only guarantee for the 'objectivity' of the exegesis, i.e., that in it
the reality of the history comes to expression, is just this, that the text
works on the exegete himself as reality" (58). The word he hears from
the text is for him an event that leads to decisions and a new future, if he
is existentially alive. "Therefore" (and this conclusion points very definitely toward future developments) "exegesis must be guided expressly
by the question of self-exposition if it is not to fall into subjectivism" (58).
Barth would have agreed heartily to the impossibility of neutral exegesis
and the involvement of the exegete's self-understanding in his understanding of the text, but he would have gone to the opposite end of the relation
for the primary guidance in exegesis, not to the self-exposition of the
exegete but to the self-exposition of the reality beyond the text with which
the text is concerned.

Bultmann carefully guards against *Sachexegese* being considered a new
"method" of exegesis. He criticizes Barth for speaking of historical *and*
theological exegesis as though they took place in different spheres. There
is no method that can grasp the reality of history. Rather, the interpreter
must approach the text conscious of the problematic character of his own
existence and open to be grasped by the reality of history that expresses
itself with authority in the text. A third party, for whom the interpretation is made, also enters the picture, and his understanding of the interpretation is conditioned in turn by his own self-understanding. In this

complex of relations the possibilities are as inexhaustible as those which emerge from any meeting of an " I " and a " Thou," but definite and final results are not possible at all. The process of interpretation must by its very nature be endless. To show that these principles are generally applicable Bultmann refers to their development in the field of secular history and culture by Dilthey and their application to the interpretation of literature by Unger. Both recognized a philosophy of history as a necessary element in historical science, since " he only is an historian who understands the present." But when the philosopher assumes in his exegesis " that man can pose the existence-question himself and is capable of the free deed [of decision] in which he wins his existence " (66), the New Testament exegete has to part company from him. According to the New Testament, man does not have his own existence at his disposal, cannot of himself pose the existence question, nor is he capable of the free deed of existential decision. All of this is possible only for faith.

At last we have come to the specific problem of New Testament exegesis. That the existential approach to the text is possible only for faith seems to pose an insuperable obstacle, since the New Testament also says that no man of himself can know what faith is, since it is the fruit of a believing exegesis. How can a man approach the text with faith if faith is possible only in response to the reality that meets him in the text? At this point one would expect a Pauline scholar to say something of the Holy Spirit which, for both Paul and John, speaks with the Word to the sinner and unbeliever to create the response of faith. The omission is significant and was to remain a significant omission in all the later development of Bultmann's hermeneutic. Here in 1925 he found a way through this seeming impasse by pointing out that New Testament exegesis is the task of one who stands in the tradition of the church of the Word. Only when this is the existential situation of the exegete can he ask his questions in faith. Later Bultmann was to abandon this solution and in its place to look to philosophy to provide the exegete with an adequate self-understanding with which to approach the text. He was much closer to Barth when he defined the existential presupposition of theological exegesis as a faith that the exegete shares with all who have their life within the church of the Word. But again it is to be noted that all the attention is given to the *faith* that is necessary in understanding the text and none to the reality behind the text whose self-disclosure alone enables the interpreter to speak of what the text really means. The word of God is left in its hiddenness while faith which responds to it is brought out into the light.

After only two pages on New Testament interpretation Bultmann turns to the redefinition of theology in the light of the principles that he has been developing. " Theology means the conceptual representation of the existence of man as an existence which has been determined by God." That is, while it speaks directly of man, it can speak only indirectly of God as he is reflected in the existence of man. It is always mindful that it has to do with the speech of *sinful* man and can be justified only as such. Only as God in his revelation forgives the sinner does the sinner have his true existence, so that truth is real for him only in that event. But now, since the self-exposition of man and his exposition of the Biblical text are inseparable, " basically theology and exegesis, i.e., systematic theology and historical theology, become one " (68). The two have separate tasks. The theme of systematic theology is directly " the conceptual explication of the existence of man as determined by God," whereas the task of historical theology is to translate the exposition of man given in the texts out of the conceptuality of the past into the conceptuality of the present. Theology maintains its scientific character by concerning itself with conceptual thought. It cannot ever claim to be direct proclamation of the word, since its statements have only relative validity. The word alone has definitive validity but only for the concrete situation in which it is heard, never as a general timeless truth that theology has at its disposal. It is concealed in the text of the New Testament and is real only in the act in which the revelation of it is event. There is never direct and unmediated revelation. Exegetical theology is needed to translate the text into the conceptuality of the present and *Sachkritik* to discriminate between what is essential and what is irrelevant to the revelation hidden in the text.

Of course, the revelation is accessible to the exegete only if he understands the words in which it is hidden, and the human words themselves have a history with which the exegete must be familiar, although this history does not fully determine the meaning of the words in the specific instance. Thus the whole historical-philological work of the New Testament scholar which finds its climax in the production of a lexicon has its validity. His theological responsibility does not diminish or in any way interfere with his philological, historical, and literary methods of investigation and interpretation. The exposition does not become theological by methodological change. Historical and theological exegesis " stand in a connection which defies analysis because the genuine historical exegesis rests on the existential confrontation with the history and so comes together with the theological since the validity of the latter rests on the same fact " (72). Here Bultmann was resisting an unhealthy tendency to assign historical and theological interpretation to separate compartments, which although it had shown itself slightly in Barth, was later to become much more blatant in Windisch in New Testament and Eissfeldt in Old Testament exegesis.

7. BARTH'S GREATEST CLOSENESS TO BULTMANN

In 1924, Barth had published a study of I Corinthians entitled "The Resurrection of the Dead," [14] in which he found the unity of the letter in the fifteenth chapter on the resurrection and interpreted the whole book in the light of that chapter. In 1926, Bultmann reviewed the book.[15] There is perhaps a larger measure of unity in these two writings than appeared either before or since, and not just in an approximation of Bultmann's views to Barth's but in an inclination of Barth at least in some measure to follow Bultmann in the reduction of theology to anthropology. The two are agreed that Paul's slashing attack on the complacent religion of the Corinthian church proceeds from his eschatological standpoint. All things in human life, including the religious achievements of Christians, have been relativized for Paul by the light that shines from the Beyond in Jesus' resurrection from the dead. The Christians at Corinth have lost this perspective and have begun to think that corruption can inherit incorruption, that they and others can reach the goal of Christian knowledge and achievement within the bounds of this mortal life. Thus they are led astray into absolutizing what can be no more than temporary and giving to their beliefs and practices and to their leaders a finality that can never belong to them. But "with the rising of the sun all lights are extinguished." [16] Paul even relativizes himself and his standpoint for their instruction. "An inflexible Pauline dogma does not exist so far as he, its author, is concerned" (47). Also, in ch. 7, Paul confesses his own ascetic ideal but does not ask conformity to it. Even the gifts of the Spirit are of relative authority and must be exercised within the limits imposed by being within the body of Christ. The Christian dare not ever lose sight of the radical distinction between his human world in its brokenness and mortality and the world on which his hopes are set, revealed to him in the resurrection of Christ.

Little is said in enforcing the distinction between the two worlds that is not a repetition of the "Romans" of 1922. The world beyond, which because it bounds this world, marking it as finite and limiting time, can be spoken of as eternity, as the end of time, or as *Urgeschichte,* but when we speak of it we have to recognize that we are using the language of time to speak of eternity which is not time, the language of the dead to speak of a life in which there is no death. Therefore, it is an attempt to utter the

unutterable. Man in his finiteness cannot know the infinite. Chapter 15 of
I Corinthians consists of "the most vital things which Paul intended to
say and yet nowhere can say" (118). The resurrection is "the deed of
God, whom no eye has seen nor ear heard . . . a historical divine fact,
which as such is only to be grasped in the category of revelation and in
none other" (146). "Truth is dead, or at least mortally ill, as soon as it
receives a human name" (153). Love, which alone never ceases, is the
breakthrough of the divine world into our human world in which the last
things become reality in the life of the Christian. Love is the miracle per-
formed on man by God, the revelation of a life that is ruled by God which
discloses the alienation of our world from God and at the same time is the
promise of what our life will be in an eternity where God is all in all.
But to man in his finitude and sin, even to the man whose eyes have been
opened to the promise of the resurrection life, God remains hidden. Man
has only "indirect knowledge, a knowledge in a strange medium, *for it
reflects itself in man and as human knowledge,* and human knowledge
means broken, i.e., indirect, knowledge" (82). The italicized words (my
italics) show how far Barth had gone at this time in emphasizing the hiddenness of God even in his revelation and the brokenness of man's knowledge of him, the language of the dead being utterly inadequate to express
the reality of divine life. He even went as far as to say that "theology
really signifies an enterprise which is impossible to man" (116), i.e.,
possible only in the severely limited fashion that it speaks of God only as
the knowledge of him is reflected brokenly in man's existence.

It is not surprising that Bultmann found himself much less critical of
this work than of the "Romans." As before, he regrets the general lack of
Sachkritik, which would distinguish temporary world views from the
kerygmatic content of the letter. Barth is not sufficiently aware of the
Gnostic elements in the Corinthian community and in Paul's language.
But with some delight Bultmann discovers Barth himself exercising *Sachkritik* when he says that for Paul the resurrection of the dead is simply
another way of saying "God" and that it relativizes all things in time,
including the Christian religion. Since for Paul the resurrection of Christ
and the Parousia are *also* events in time, Barth could reach his conclusion
only by separating this latter element from the former more essential element in Paul's eschatology. But in doing this he "understands Paul better
than he [Paul] understands himself." [17] This is the function of *Sachkritik,*
to understand the author better than he understands himself and to distinguish what is essential from merely contemporary elements that contradict
or conceal the essential. What Bultmann likes best of all in the book is the
denial of the possibility of Christian gnosis, "For first of all God is no ob-

ject that exists in the same way as worldly things and so can be thought of like them; and second, for that very reason Christian knowledge is present only as a determination of man's life (as his obedience in response to the claim that is made upon him by God) which expresses itself as agape."

How close Bultmann felt he was to Barth at this time is evident in a second 1926 article on " The Question of the Dialectic Theology "[18] in which he undertook to explain and defend the use of dialectic. He uses the pronoun " we " to denote himself, Barth, Gogarten, and others. He first distinguishes the original Socratic dialectic from theirs. For Socrates, truth is hidden in the dialogue and appears as the conversation moves between question and answer. No simple statement can ever be the truth itself. The dialogue is ever on the way to truth. But for the dialectical theology the starting point is an event in time in which the truth of God has been revealed in Jesus Christ as the justification of sinful humanity. This is the center round which the question and answer of the dialectic are in continual movement and from which they cannot move away. Dialectic is the appropriate form of thinking in relation to the revelation because man in his finiteness does not have direct access to the revelation. Only God can speak God's word. When man attempts to speak it, all his utterances become a mixture of truth and error. The necessity of dialectic is rooted in man's very existence. Confronted with God, his entire existence becomes the question, God's judgment setting his whole life in question. But when he lets himself be open to God's question, God justifies him and the justification is the answer. But in being justified he knows himself as still a sinner before God, so that the question comes alive again. The question and answer of dialectic are thus not logical entities but the realities of our existence on the journey between birth and death. Only in movement between question and answer do we have knowledge of God's revelation. It is an eternal event that is constantly new through the action of the Holy Spirit (a reflection of Barth or a new element in Bultmann? It was absent in 1925), but man cannot grasp the event in his human words without falsifying it. It is refracted by the human medium through which it reaches him. Therefore, his words can never be more than witness to the truth which is a divine event beyond both his questions and his answers.

The revelation itself, however, has in it no dialectic. Dialectic is necessary to the thinking of the theologian, but, as the early church knew, the revelation as the event of God's judgment and grace calls for proclamation in a message. The church speaks not only in theology but also in preaching, and in its preaching, the Spirit of God takes the human words and performs the miracle of letting God's word be heard ever afresh in them. But the human words cannot as a consequence of the miracle be identified directly with God's word. They remain human words with their mixture of truth and error which conceals the revelation. This is true also of the dogmas in which from time to time the church seeks to bear definitive witness to the truth. They are only witness, not the truth itself, and have to be set in question afresh by the eternal event of revelation. To identify dogmas directly with the revelation by making them an extension of the event of revelation in time is to ignore not only the brokenness of all human knowledge but also the necessity that God in his Spirit should make his word truth for us. To claim possession of the truth of God directly in our preaching or our theology would be to engage in a *theologia gloriae* and to rob God of his freedom to judge all our human words. God alone decides whether the obedience of faith is present in our theology. We participate in the logos of God only through the free activity of the Spirit. In speaking of revelation, Bultmann, in his agreement with Barth, goes farther in his Christological statements here than one would have expected from both past and future developments. He is willing to say that Jesus Christ not only spoke God's word but *was* the word, where in future he would insist that the incarnation, demythologized, means only that Jesus was the bearer of the word. Also, the ascension of Christ is described as the miracle that broke the continuity of the revelation, so that there can be no direct extension of it in history, Christ being hidden in heaven and revealed only to faith through the work of the Holy Spirit. Neither is there as yet any inclination to demythologize the Holy Spirit. Our theology has authority only when the Spirit brings God's word to life in it. We undertake theology in response to God's command and to his promise that he will make our word a living word. We have access to his revelation only through the witness of the Scriptures and even there only indirectly. Thus far the essay is a faithful reproduction of Barth's thought in every detail.

The final paragraph, however, emphasizes this indirectness and its consequences for the character of theology. "In form theology is always exegesis of Scripture. In content it is speech concerning the revelation. But because this is the eternal event which the real man knows as judgment or forgiveness, the object of theology is nothing other than the conceptual representation of the existence of man as it is determined by God, i.e., as he must see it in the light of Scripture."

8. BARTH EXPLORES HIS THEOLOGICAL ROOTS

We must go back now and see where Barth was moving between 1924 and 1926. Much of his work at this time was a struggle to find a right relation with the past. He spent the winter term of 1923–1924 lecturing on Schleiermacher, recognizing alternately the immensity of his achievement and the perverseness of the direction in which he had sent theology for more than a century. Out of this research came two long essays eventually.[19] The second, delivered as lectures in 1926, forms a companion piece to the 1926 essays of Bultmann. For Schleiermacher, too, theological thinking was a dialectic that has its hidden center, not in a historical event of revelation that has to be mediated, but in the inmost consciousness of man where he is at one with God. Heaven and earth are joined and peace with God is attained at a level that is beyond all thought or action. It can be called a " feeling of the universe " that is like a union of lovers. " I lie on the bosom of the infinite world." The divine and the human spirit are joined in a union that obliterates all distinctions. But this ultimate center of reality cannot be known by man in any conceptual form; it can only be felt, a feeling of absolute dependence. Poetry and music are the most adequate forms of expression for it. The preacher has to speak of it in order to awaken the consciousness of it in others, but it is not so much the words as the impression made by them on the spirit that counts. The words attempt to express in systematic form the religious consciousness of the day. Schleiermacher's " consciousness determined by God directly " corresponds roughly to Barth and Bultmann's " human existence determined by God through confrontation with the word of God." The similarity within the difference is in the basing of theology entirely upon the reflection of God in man's existence. Schleiermacher divided dogmatic statements into three categories — concerning man's consciousness, concerning the world, and concerning God, but the latter two were derived from the first and he at one time considered discarding them as superfluous. He envisaged a time when the religious consciousness would maintain itself in all men without any words needing to be spoken, but he recognized that such a time was not yet present and mediators were necessary in the service of the God-consciousness. Historically, Jesus Christ was the bearer of the great peace, the originator and bringer of life, the awakener of men to their true life in God. A stream of life begins in history with him and flows through the centuries, making men participators in the redemption of human life achieved in the perfect God-consciousness of Jesus. (We can see reflections of this in the *Heilsgeschichte* of the 1919 " Romans.") But it was difficult for Schleiermacher on this basis to maintain any essential difference between Christ and the rest of humanity or between Christianity and other religions. His oneness of man with the universe could be mediated by culture as effectively as by Christ or the preaching of the Christian gospel.

Both Barth and Bultmann had transferred the locale of the primary reality in which God and man are one from time to eternity, from the inner being of man to the Beyond of God. Man in himself knows only the contradiction, but in Jesus Christ he has the promise of the restoration of the unity and lives a new life in the strength of the promise. Schleiermacher assumed the existence in every man of a relation with God that needed only to be awakened, but for Barth and Bultmann this relation was brokenly reconstituted in man only when in faith he responded to God's word. Allowing for this radical disjunction, many lines of continuity could still be found between Schleiermacher and both men. Their No to the past was both emphatic and conditioned.

This continuity Barth was to confess frankly in discussing Schleiermacher twenty years later in his " Protestant Theology in the Nineteenth Century." " No one today can say whether we have really overcome his influence or whether we are still at heart children of his age, for all the protest against him. . . . Anyone who has never loved here and is not in a position to love again and again may not hate here either." [20] But this made Barth's problem all the more complex. He had to get free of Schleiermacher without freeing himself from anything in Schleiermacher's witness that was essential to the truth.

He had also to deal with Herrmann [21] to whom he owed his beginnings in theology, and here again he had to distinguish between where he could merely reinterpret what he had learned and where he had to say something quite different. In spite of all changes, he was not conscious of any radical discontinuity with his most respected teacher. He found reason to suspect that before the close of his career Hermann had become more open to the mystery of God that comes to expression in the doctrine of the Trinity, more aware that the self-questioning of the ethically earnest man which for him was the starting point of theology depends upon a confrontation of the self with God, and more inclined to find in the Bible and the church's tradition definite norms for his theology. His strength had always been in his negations, his violent repudiation of orthodoxy, rationalism, mysticism, intellectualism, and both conservative and liberal dogmatics, i.e., in showing what was *not* the basis of religion. But his positive statements had been indefensible, what he presented as self-evident experience or historical fact being highly vulnerable. He was seeking a visible basis for that which could have no basis except in God, placing in the human consciousness what belonged in another consciousness which meets ours from beyond. He wanted to guard theology against the contemporary historicizing and psychologizing of it, but he let down the barrier when he ascribed to the real experience of man what can belong only to the Holy Spirit. He wanted to bind dogmatics to the person of Jesus by finding in him the reality in which God is revealed, but he defined that reality in human and historical terms alone rather than as the divine word made flesh. What he really meant by " the inner life of Jesus " was God's self-revelation in him. His emphasis upon sincerity and freedom was not that of a vulgar liberalism, because he recognized an authority in Jesus, Scripture, and church that set a limit to the scholar's freedom, so that one might ask whether his concern were not really for the freedom of God's sovereign word to be heard by each man for himself.

During these first years of his professorship Barth felt the necessity of developing historical breadth. By this he meant exploring in the past the roots of the theology which he was teaching. Man lives in time. What he is, what he thinks, believes, and does, is determined far more than he ever realizes by the past from which he comes. Witness to the truth by which alone he can live comes to him out of the past, first in the form of a sacred Scripture and then in the witness of the church through the centuries. In neither does he have the truth directly. It is hidden in the human witness of Scripture and revealed only to faith, and hidden also even more brokenly in the witness of the church in its confessions, teaching, preaching, and varied activities, so that one has to wrestle with the problem of truth and error in regard to everything that comes to him out of the past. Hence the earnest critical discussions of Schleiermacher and Herrmann, of Luther, Calvin, and Zwingli, and the exploration of the Reformed heritage, which found even in some of the most rigidly orthodox theologians insights that had to be retrieved. Then in 1924 the roots were traced farther back into the early church fathers. In preparation for his lectures on dogmatics Barth read Justin, Aristides, Minucius Felix, Celsus, Tertullian, Athenagoras, Gregory of Nyssa and Augustine, also Thomas Aquinas. He was on his way to achieving the catholic breadth for his theology that was to give it such profound ecumenical significance in the future and to make some Roman Catholic theologians confess that he was more truly catholic than they.

9. A New Emphasis Upon the Church

It was inevitable, then, that the church should press more and more into the forefront of Barth's theology, although in 1927 he was still to call his dogmatics " *Christian* Dogmatics " and only in 1932 adopt the significant title " *Church* Dogmatics." Thurneysen, in a lecture in 1926, spoke of the awakening of men to the question of the church as characteristic of the historical moment and one of the most hopeful signs for the future.

Cultural Christianity, finding the focal point of life in the midst of the cultural forces of the time, tended to bypass the church.[22] So also did religious socialism, which pinned its hopes on the massed forces of an oppressed proletariat to bring a new order to the world. But now Barth turned decisively to the church as the instrument of God's saving purpose in the world. On its human side it would always be an aggregation of sinful human beings, with all the afflictions to which flesh is heir, but by the grace of God it would be hiddenly the channel by which the word of God, to which prophets and apostles bore witness, would reach the world in each new generation.

This turning to the church brought with it no softening of Barth's criticism of the contemporary church. In replying [23] to a criticism of his theology by Erik Peterson (to which Bultmann's essay "The Question of the Dialectical Theology" was also an answer), he first attacked critics of Peterson who dismissed him as holding an essentially Catholic viewpoint. Barth found in contemporary Protestantism no secure standpoint from which such a firm negation could proceed, but rather an evolutionistic historicism, moralism, and idealism that was closer to the Erasmians and Anabaptists of the sixteenth century than to Luther or Calvin. Thomas Aquinas was no farther from Luther than the disciples of Schleiermacher. Peterson held that the knowledge of God communicated in the logos-revelation in Jesus Christ was continued directly in the church in the form of authoritative dogma, and that theology consists in concrete obedience to the concrete authority which is manifest in this revelation of which the church is the channel. He objected to Barth's twin doctrines of the hiddenness of the revelation and the necessity of dialectic rooted in man's inability to speak God's word for him, on the ground that they denied the church any certain knowledge of God. Barth agreed with Peterson that theology has no basis for existence except in obedience to the revelation of God in Jesus Christ which becomes immediate and contemporary revelation through the church's witness in preaching, teaching, and dogma. Without the church and its dogma as witness to revelation there could be no theology. But he pointed out that all authority in the church is secondary to and derivative from the authority of Jesus Christ himself. The Head remains Lord over the body and his presence is known through the Word and Spirit. He does not abdicate his authority but only lends it to his church as it is willing and able in faith to receive it. Dogma, therefore, has only *relative* authority and has to be subordinated to the primary authority of God's word which makes itself heard in the exegesis and preaching of Scripture. Peterson desired a continuity of revelation in the church that would make the truth directly accessible to the theologian, but he was forgetting that church and theology are carried by sinful men who of themselves are unable to speak God's word for him. All theology is only prolegomena to God's speaking. We have to leave the way open for God to speak. The church must await its Lord, not act as though it were itself the Lord. And in this waiting, the speech of the theologian is ever broken, a mixture of truth and error, and therefore must take the form of a dialectic as it seeks to escape from the error of each of its statements into a fuller knowledge of the truth. In assigning the church this radically humble role, Barth was nevertheless claiming for it a uniquely divine destiny as the chosen instrument of God for the reconciliation of the world and its restoration to its true order.

A second essay in 1926 dealt with the relation between the church and culture.[24] This is of great interest when it is compared with the earlier essay of Bultmann on " Religion and Culture." For Bultmann the two belonged to sharply separated areas of man's existence. Both religion and culture were essential to man's life. With only culture he was doomed never to find self-fulfillment, since this could come to him only from the Beyond. But with only religion his life would remain empty of content. In the realm of culture, in which ethics was included, reason would be his guide, but in the realm of religion the decisions in which he grasped his existence and laid hold on his future would be possible only in confrontation with God's word. For Barth no such separation of life into realms was possible. Both church and culture were defined theologically in relation to the word of God. His description of the church was very similar to Bultmann's description of religion. The church is constituted in a faith and obedience that are man's response in decision to the word of the unknown, unsearchable God. But even in the act of faith men remain sinners as long as they live so that the visible church is always a human, sinful church. The divine institution called into being and sustained by the ever-renewed hearing of the word, the instrument of God's dealing with humanity, remains invisible, i.e., visible only to faith.

The definition of culture then begins by drawing out the implications of the fact that the Christian's obedience to the word is *human* obedience *in the world*. It is the obedience not of animals but of men and in it humanity comes to realization. The perfect obedience of Jesus Christ to God was the perfection of humanity. It is in faith, therefore, that man becomes conscious of the problem of being a man. By setting him before God, it sets him before the problem of his existence. He can no longer endure a contradiction between soul and body and seeks a unity of self. " Found by God's word, man knows that the Spirit must shape nature and nature must fulfil and realize the Spirit. . . . The inner must appear in the outer and the outer find its being in the inner." [25] In culture, therefore, man is continually searching but never finding the unity of which he has heard the promise. Were he really to think he could find it in his culture, his culture would be a Tower of Babel by which he would expect to join earth with heaven and restore paradise. Because his world is sinful and human, he must be content to seek and never find. This is the urgency and fearfulness of the problem of culture, that man in the obedience of faith must continually seek the fulfillment of his humanity and that the goal must ever remain beyond his reach.

Barth's doctrine of creation is highly significant here. " From the standpoint of the creation [realm of nature], culture is the promise originally given to man of what he is to become." The man who is lost in sin remains God's creature. No sin, however much it hides God from man, can hide man from God or dissolve God's relation with him as his creator. God's word, which in the fullness of time was incarnate in Jesus, fills heaven and earth and rules in the realm of nature.[26] It can be known only through the revealed word, but nevertheless, hidden in the creation, it is the promise of what is to be, the promise of humanity, the promise of culture. It is a relation of God with man, undisturbed by sin, that makes it possible for God's word to be heard in a world of sinful men. This was Barth's answer to those who, like Brunner, posed the question how blind, sinful, faithless humanity could respond to a revelation that could be known only to faith and who therefore posited in man a connecting point, a remnant of the divine image, a fragmentary capacity for God, untouched by sin. For Barth this was a reconstruction of the bridge from man to God which had been man's most fatal illusion. The bridging of the rift in man's existence was wholly from God's side and was possible because no sin of mankind could ever deliver the world out of the hand of God or make it other than God's good creation. The sinful man remains homo by God's hidden grace. He has the promise in his created being of humanity, i.e., fulfillment, unity, wholeness, in his sphere as creature. His cultural work in which he struggles to overcome the split in his existence can thus be an analogy, a pointer to that which man as God's creation and likeness should become. The light of the eternal word can be reflected in culture. Therefore, the division between church and culture can be only a practical one, never a division in principle. The church does not see the Kingdom of God in any cultural achievement but holds itself open for signs in many areas of culture that the Kingdom is near at hand.

To the sinner who has died and risen with Christ and so has found reconciliation with God, what formerly was only the promise hidden in creation becomes the law of God in which God demands of him humanity. " Always the content of the law is quite simply culture. Always the content of sanctification, of being set apart for God, of doing the will of God, is humanization." The goal is beyond the limits of our world. Only in Christ has humanity appeared in its full reality. Nevertheless one obeys the law if he has been reconciled. In reconciliation he has his fulfillment only in faith, a faith in which there is always unbelief, uncertainty, and brokenness, but there is a final redemption in which all is fulfilled. Because of this eschatological perspective, the man of faith is not tempted to build a Tower of Babel with his culture. " Christians are men who know better than anyone else what kind of judgment hangs over the heads of men and how incurable — not the others but they themselves — are." The sinfulness of all things human, including the church, does not lead them to despair or to inactivity. They know that on its humanly visible, sociological side the church is swept along in the stream of human culture, but this does not negate its hidden reality as the church of God, and as the church of God it must ever call men both to the shouldering of cultural tasks and to the recognition that no cultural achievement constitutes the fulfillment of man's destiny.

The point of difference from Bultmann stands out sharply here. There is no separation of man's existence into separate compartments, one ruled by reason and the other by the word of God. God's word is sovereign over the whole creation, over the outer as well as the inner life of man, over culture and over history. Just as Bultmann separated the human existence of Jesus sharply from his significance as the Christ, the bearer of the eternal word which alone redeems, so also he separated the flesh of the world, the outer events of history, from the inner world of primary reality which he called the Beyond. This was why in 1922 he declared what Barth in " Romans " wrote concerning the incarnation to be simply incomprehensible. For him the word could not *become* flesh, the inner could not *appear* in the outer, the Spirit could not be *fulfilled* and *realized* in nature. The separation of heaven from earth and of God from man for him was final and absolute and not just a rupture created by sin which was overcome and healed in Jesus Christ. On this point there was never any agreement between Barth and Bultmann and it was so crucial for their theologies that it was certain to divide them more and more as each of them drew out more explicitly the implications of his thought.

CHAPTER VIII

THE WIDENING GULF,
1926–1927

In 1927 Barth published an essay on Feuerbach [1] which had been part of a series of lectures on the history of modern theology at Münster in the preceding year. Why he chose this particular lecture for publication at just this time is a nice question. Feuerbach he interprets as doing in a completely open and thoroughgoing fashion what nineteenth-century theology was doing in a surreptitious and partial fashion: substituting anthropology for theology. The essay was thus a polemic against all the representatives of the old theology who in the 1920's were trying to hold their well-established line against the assault of the new theology. In *Zwischen den Zeiten*, Barth added a postscript to the essay in which he answered a critic, Wilhelm Bruhn, who had accused him of a complete pessimism that could no longer see God in the world since he had lost his faith in a " God-filled humanity." [2] But when one sees the direction in which Bultmann and Barth, together with Gogarten, were moving in 1926, one begins to wonder whether this sharp attack on the anthropologizing tendency of nineteenth-century theology was intended also as a kind of warning to himself and his friends not to slip back into this well-worn groove of the past.

1. FEUERBACH AS A WARNING AGAINST SUBJECTIVISM

Feuerbach was distinguished as a philosopher by the intensity of his interest in theology. He was what Barth called an " antitheologian " who sacrificed his academic career to his passion to destroy once and for all the supernatural orientation of theology and establish the inner reality of man as its proper focus and concern. His aim was " to make friends of man out of friends of God, thinkers out of believers, workers out of prayers, students of this world out of candidates for the beyond, men, whole men, out of Christians who in consistency with their own confession are half animal and half angel," to turn men " from God to the world and man, from faith to love, from heaven to earth, from Christ to ourselves, from the empty ghosts of supernaturalism to real life." Feuerbach was in radical reaction not only against the theology of his time but also against the idealistic philosophy of Kant and Hegel with which it was saturated. " I hate idealism which tears man out of nature," he said. He found the whole of reality in the life of man with his fellowmen. " Truth is only the total-ity of human life and being." " Man with man — the unity of I and Thou — is God," and the true dialectic in which truth comes to light is the dia-logue between I and Thou. In this dialogue man comes to consciousness of himself and his world. In short, Feuerbach was not abandoning God but merely transferring his locale from the heights of an abstract and otherworldly transcendence to the depths (*pace* Bishop Robinson) of man's being, where he can be more concretely known. He then proceeded to reinterpret the attributes of God and of Christ in terms of the divine being of man. The infinity of God is the infinity of universal man in con-trast to the finiteness of the individual. The resurrection of Christ is the satisfied desire of man for direct certainty of his personal survival after death.

For Barth all of this was actually an unmasking of the intention of nineteenth-century theology from Schleiermacher on. The intention was concealed even from the theologians themselves by their constant efforts to maintain an element of transcendence, but however hard they tried, man and not God remained central for them. Barth was particularly in-terested in the support that Feuerbach thought he found in Luther for his program. Luther seemed to him at times to speak of faith as though it were a kind of independent and active divine hypostasis. Faith not only justifies, comforts, and produces love and good works, but overcomes sin and death and makes man blessed. It can even on occasion be called a creator of divinity in us. Also, Luther's assertion that God became man in order that man might become God and his emphasis that God is to be sought on earth in the man Jesus left a door open not only for Feuerbach but for others who would come after him. For Barth, Feuerbach struck a healthy note in his realistic concern with the whole existence of man in contrast to those who were concerned only with the spirit, heart, con-science, or inner being, of man, but in his identification of man with God he showed himself a child of his century, ignorant seemingly that man must die and that all men are involved irretrievably in evil. Little did Barth realize the renascence that Feuerbach was soon to have.

There could be no fear at this time that Bultmann and Gogarten were sacrificing the divine transcendence. On the contrary, like Barth they were under constant attack for having left no vestige of a divine immanence in the world or in man. A church that had become accustomed to thinking of God as generally available in nature, history, culture, and the inner life of man felt harshly stripped naked of its spiritual clothing. The infinite qualitative difference between God and man was so central and decisive for all these new theologians, and the revelation of God to man in Jesus Christ so firmly the basis of all theology, that the break with a theological tradition which even in the slightest confused man with God or God with man would seem to have been complete. And yet in the writings of Gogarten and Bultmann there was a persistent tendency, having defined faith as man's response to the word of God which comes to him from completely beyond himself, to focus the interest of theology upon the human end of the relation, upon the faith of man rather than upon the God who meets him in his word. This tendency was the result of a conviction which Barth shared, that man's finiteness and sin make it impossible for him to speak with assurance concerning God, since God is always for him the Unknown who is revealed only in the act of forgiving man his sin and never becomes an object of observation. But neither does the forgiven and justified man, the new man of faith, become an object of observation. Why, then, should one assume that a knowledge is available for theology at the human end of the relation but unavailable concerning the God with whom man comes into relation? Therefore, through these years Barth focused his attention not on the faith-response of man but on the word to which faith responds: how Scripture is witness to this word, how the church in all its life but particularly in its preaching and its confessional dogmas witnesses to it, and what it means for the shape of the church's ministry that it has the task of proclaiming this word.

2. Developments in Gogarten's Thought

Gogarten came to theology from an angle different from that of Barth. He was deeply immersed in the study of Luther at a time when Barth was almost totally engrossed in Scripture, and he found in Luther something of what Barth found in Scripture. This was what brought them together. Gogarten, nourished on Luther, wanted to establish faith and justification by faith as possible only when God makes it possible. He went from Luther to Kierkegaard who sharpened for him the antithesis between eternity and time, between God and man, and made him see the world and the existence of man as the place where time and eternity meet and stand in contradiction to each other. The battle for decision between the two is our being, our substance. " We have no being which is not this battle, this antithesis." [3] Both idealism and materialism try too quickly to resolve the antithesis and reduce all to unity. The antithesis that creates such unrest, anxiety, hunger, and dissatisfaction in man has to be understood as the setting in question of all human existence by God, the bending of man under the wrath and judgment of God. Yet the contradiction presupposes a unity with God that has been broken. To exist in time is to know only this brokenness, to be " sick from God," but to be able neither to die of the sickness nor to become whole through the strength of one's own organism. Both the sickness and the healing can come only from God. The solution of this dilemma is for God to become man, for eternity to become time, but the moment of fulfillment in time remains hidden for us, since we stand continually under the mastery of the human contradiction. For us where we stand, the incarnation seems contrary to reason, the " impossible " for conscientious critical thought. Yet this which can only be believed in defiance of reason is the one possibility of our contradiction being healed — that " we men in our body of death [should] be born again in the eternal body of the original man, the Son of God."

It is not hard to understand why Barth and Gogarten felt that, traveling different routes, they had both come out at much the same theological destination. But, as we have already seen, there were differences between them that disturbed them both. Gogarten saw the enemy who was to be destroyed as idealistic philosophy with all its theological progeny, so that the echoes of Plato and Kant in Barth must have made him shake his head. But Gogarten's reluctance to go behind Luther to the Scriptures and his practice of weaving a fine network of logic in which he caught all his opponents and then brought in Jesus suddenly at the end "like a club " [4] left Barth critical. Also, Barth found in the polemical zeal of both Gogarten and Brunner an overconfidence in the present state of their own theological constructions and a danger of shifting their theological base in order to meet their opponents on their own ground. Was Gogarten in his attack on idealistic philosophy tending to develop a new philosophical basis for the gospel and so merely to continue the old error in a new form? His attempt to develop an ethic that would provide a basis for family, nation, and other institutions in orders of creation seemed to be withdrawing such institutions to some degree from under the judgment of the gospel, and so also from its promise. At the same time he was taking over from Buber and Ebner an " I-Thou " philosophy that located man's confrontation with God in the "I-Thou" relation with his neighbor. The appeal of this latter was that it enabled him to contrast the "I am I" individualism of modern thought, in which man made himself as God and disrupted society, with the community created between "I" and "Thou" when one or the other speaks the word of God with authority to his brother. But it was left undefined how the word of man is to become this binding word of God.

An article on "Belief in God the Creator" in 1926 [5] shows the direction in which Gogarten's thought was taking him. For any man to profess to understand the creation would be to claim to be as God. God's being is hidden and revealed only in his works. To believe in God the Creator is not to believe in an act of creation at the beginning but in something which now happens: it means to know that we live not in eternity but in time, and we know what time is only in confrontation with the Creator. Time is the place of decision where reality has its beginning and its end. In a creation-faith this world has the decisive reality and to seek another timeless, spaceless world behind it is to evade our decisions and to make the world a mere appearance with secondary reality. Our only knowledge of the Creator is our knowledge of ourselves as creatures in time. There is no invisible eternal world that stands in antithesis to our world. The primary reality is here where we are. Faith is the recognition of the particular situation in which I find myself as belonging to the creation, as provided for me just so by God and therefore to be acknowledged by me. Faith is not knowledge but acknowledgment by the creature of his bond with the Creator. We know the bond, we know our creatureliness, but that is all. We cannot generalize about the creation. God meets us only in the specific situation where the "Thou" of the neighbor stands over against us and the decision of the moment is for self or for the other. If one puts "I" before "Thou," there is no faith. The reality is in the personal relation, that is, in human history, so that in the doctrine of creation on this basis nature disappears and only history remains. This conclusion was to be increasingly important in the future for both Gogarten and Bultmann. It is significant that in evolving this concept of creation no attention whatever is given to any Biblical witness concerning creation, and Jesus Christ does not enter the picture in any way. History rather than some ideal order is made the primary reality. It is a triumphant move to demolish idealistic thinking, but its implications for a Biblically-based theology are ominous. While the transcendence of God is maintained, man's knowledge of him is so completely in the indirect form of a knowledge of his own existence as confronted by God that it is difficult for theology not to be transformed into an existentialist anthropology.

3. BULTMANN'S " JESUS "

In 1926, Bultmann published his book *Jesus*[6] — in English entitled *Jesus and the Word* in recognition that it is centered more on the words of Jesus than on Jesus himself — and in 1927 Barth produced the first volume of his Dogmatics, " Christian Dogmatics in Outline." [7] The two books provide an excellent opportunity to trace the orbits of our two theologians.

One of Bultmann's severest criticisms of Barth had been, as we have seen, his failure to exercise *Sachkritik* in his interpretation of Paul's letters, i.e., to separate the essence of his gospel from elements in his thought which are the temporary conceptual expressions of it or borrowings from the contemporary milieu which actually are alien to it. Barth disagreed with this approach to Paul, holding that the essence thus extracted was an abstraction and not the real historical Paul and that to hear Paul's witness one had to let him speak as the Christian who absorbed Jewish, Greek, and all manner of contemporary elements into his speech, giving them his own meaning as he did so. But for Bultmann this seemed to be an attempt to transplant a first-century theology into the twentieth century and to force the mind of today's Christian into the thought patterns of a vanished age. The gospel, in order to become actually and decisively contemporary, had to be liberated from its first-century Jewish and Hellenistic clothing and reclothed by the theologian in language and forms of expression meaningful to our day. It is evident that what he called *Sachkritik* in 1922 and 1926 is what he later was to term " demythologizing " and " existential " interpretation.

The book *Jesus* is a demonstration of the operation of *Sachkritik* upon the traditions concerning the teachings of Jesus. In his first chapter Bultmann makes it very clear that the *person* of Jesus is of no concern to him. " We can now know almost nothing concerning the life and personality of Jesus " (8). Whether or not he considered himself the Messiah is of no importance. Our interest is wholly in his work, his purpose, his message, as they meet us as historical reality in his teachings. " We know enough of his *message* to make for ourselves a consistent picture " (12). We cannot be certain, however, whether even the earliest layer of tradition disclosed by form criticism comes directly from Jesus or whether the oldest community preserved a true picture of him and his message in its tradition. But actually this need make no difference to us. Our encounter is with a message that was heard in history. Whether it originated with Jesus or with his church is a secondary consideration. The " historical phenomenon " of the message itself is primary, not the person of Jesus. The desired encounter is with *reality in history*. As spectators we are incapable of such an encounter. Man "must admit himself to be a part of history" (3) and must enter into living dialogue with it. The meaning of history is not revealed unless we listen to the demand that it makes upon us with authority and are prepared to give up our presuppositions. "The essential in history is in reality nothing *super*-historical, but is event in time." (Note the antithesis to Barth's *Urgeschichte*.) Objective historical method is successful only with external facts and can see nothing new in history. Psychological explanation merely interprets the past by fitting it into what we already know. But in confrontation with reality in history one comes into a place of decision where he is freed from the past and is given a new future. In regard to Jesus this reality meets us in his teachings, but it is hidden in them and concealed from us by his extensive involvement in a Jewish conceptuality in speaking to the men of his time.

Bultmann then employs his *Sachkritik* in three analyses of the teachings, first of the eschatology, then of the ethics, and finally of the understanding of God. In each he begins at the periphery with the contemporary Jewish concepts, showing where Jesus merely adopted them, then points to what is distinctive in Jesus' teaching, though still involved in a time-bound conceptuality, and finally penetrates to what he considers the essence of the teaching, which is not a truth that can be expressed in statements of any kind but is an existential encounter of man with God in which man has to choose between obedience and disobedience and by his decision has his very existence determined.

The whole perspective of Jewish faith was eschatological, focused on the Beyond. The purpose of law was "to release man from the world, to separate him from any interest in an independent cultural development and to humble him in obedience to the transcendent power of God" (17). By its chosenness, Israel "is lifted out of the world, out of the world's interests and ideals, and has its centre of gravity in the Beyond" (18). The nature of what lies beyond is not spelled out with any definiteness. Jesus shared this basic orientation, the events of the last week of his life showing how he and his disciples expected the Kingdom to dawn at any moment. "In this last hour, the hour of decision, Jesus is sent with the final decisive word" (30). Men must surrender all for the sake of the Kingdom. The intense eschatological expectation thus has as its present significance the bringing of men into the place of decision, setting them before an absolute "Either/Or." Jesus as a Jew might conceive the Kingdom as a tremendous eschatological drama, a future event with no significance for Gentiles, entirely for the benefit of the Jewish people (43). But the essence of its meaning was a call to decision, a present deliverance from the past, a separation from the present world to have one's life in the Beyond. The individual could find this deliverance only because he belonged to the eschatological community and he was called not to a mystical or pietistic culture of the inner life but to decision and obedience in his concrete situation in the world. Jesus encouraged no pessimism about the world, no asceticism. The Kingdom thus is not to be conceived as a future event in time but as the reality that determines man's life now by setting him in the crisis of decision. The vital center is the conception of human existence as being realized only in decision, in short, the existentialist concept of man which is to be contrasted with the prevalent idealist one for which man is a personality in pursuit of an ideal realization.

Alongside Jesus, the eschatological prophet, one must set Jesus the rabbi. " Jesus actually lived as a Jewish rabbi " (58), conforming in many respects to the rabbinic pattern, especially in his recognition of the authority of Scripture and his basing of man's conduct on unconditional obedience. For Jesus as for the rabbis, man has no claim on God but has only to obey, which contrasts with the Greek and modern rationalistic idea of man in his autonomy perfecting his nature by his own achievement. In general the rabbis conceived of the relation with God as a legal contract, but some broke through this to teach a service of God that was not for reward. Where all commands in Scripture were binding for the rabbis, for Jesus only the ethical commands were binding and he distinguished between the essential and the nonessential in Scripture, setting one passage against another. " The external authority of Scripture is given up . . . and man is trusted and expected to see for himself what God commands " (76, 77). Again we come to the essence of the matter which is described in terms of man's existential situation. Man in the place of decision is absolutely insecure with no ethical system for support (85). The " intrinsic significance of the demands of God [is] not mediated to man through Scripture as a formal authority . . . but they arise quite simply from the crisis of decision in which man stands before God. . . . With every choice he decides and limits his own possibility " (87). Only in the crisis of decision does man know good and evil. General ideas about the highest good are a spectator ethic. Jesus' ethical precepts do not constitute an ethical system. There is little or nothing that is original in them. Most of them have parallels in the rabbinic sayings. They dare not be made into a new law, for their intention is to express God's claim for complete obedience from man. Jesus " always refers the questioner back to his own judgment " (89). When he demands poverty of a man, he is not setting up an ideal of poverty but in a particular instance he is asking for a man's surrender to God. " God demands the whole man, not merely specific acts from the man "

(92). "God speaks to him in every concrete situation, for every concrete situation is a crisis of decision" (102). "God is for Jesus the Power who constrains man to decision, who confronts him in the demand for good, who determines his future. . . . Only in the actual comprehension of his own existence can man find God" (103). Jesus is "not interested in character building, personality values, and the like" (105). His "only purpose is to make known the position of man before God" (107). What to do must be the decision of the man himself, but, since a decision for God is the renunciation of any claim for himself, it turns him outward to his neighbor, so that obedience to God issues in love toward the neighbor. Again, it will be noted that the focus is on the human decision rather than on the divine initiative in the relation. The significance for ethics of a personal covenant relation in which the nature of God makes specific claims upon man's life, so important in the Old Testament, but also in the New, receives no mention. The whole emphasis in Bultmann's description of man's encounter with God is upon constraint to decision, claim for surrender, and demand for good rather than upon grace and mercy. Perhaps this is a consequence of the encounter's being with a reality of history which meets one in a teaching rather than with a living person who identifies himself with man the sinner and in speaking to him the word of pardon opens to him a new life in fellowship with himself.

Again, in regard to Jesus' understanding of God we move from the periphery of Judaism to the center of existentialism. For the Jews, in contrast to the Greeks, God "does not in any sense belong to the world of objects about which man orients himself through thought. . . . [He] is primarily Will, and moreover, sovereign, uncaused Will" (133, 135). Because he is Creator of the world and the world belongs to him, there can be no ultimate dualism. Satan is an intrusion in the picture. Only man's will is evil, corrupting a world and a humanity that are not evil by nature. The Creator is known to man through his law. These are the assumptions of Judaism and also of Jesus' preaching. It must also be said that God is both remote and near but that the remoteness of God receives more emphasis than his nearness. His nearness as Creator expresses "the dependence of man on God throughout his whole existence . . . the consciousness of being a *creature* before God" (140). Also, God directs history, and man stands in a divine plan that moves toward its goal. But God's sovereignty in the future is so emphasized in Judaism, the present age as a time of Godforsakenness being distinguished from a future age of fulfillment, that it becomes a problem how he can be the God of the present. He is accessible now in prayer and he is to judge what man is now, but because the judgment is future, man thinks of himself as standing before

God in the place of decision not *now* but then (145). This prevents both sin and grace from being conceived radically.

Jesus' understanding of God was very much that of Judaism. He was restrained in speaking of him and used circumlocutions. He also conceived God as communicating through angels. There is no access to him through cult or sacrament and there is no talk of his attributes. " Jesus speaks of God not in terms of general truths or dogmas, but only in terms of what God is for man, how he deals with man " (151). " He speaks of God in speaking of man and showing man that he stands in the last hour of decision, that his will is claimed by God " (152). There was " a childlike belief in providence and a naïve optimism in his view of nature and the world " (160), similar to what one finds in the psalms and the literature of Judaism. But this was combined with a realistic resignation to the inevitable as in Ecclesiastes. He does not offer any explanation of human suffering, but even in suffering the meaning of the moment is decision for or against God. Happenings such as his own healing of the sick and the expelling of demons were for him the direct action of God, not proofs of God but experiences of God's action for those concerned, visible only to their faith. Prayer for him was with simplicity a talking with God in which there was a union of trustful petition with the will to surrender. Faith is an awareness of the nearness of the living God which is possible only if one is obedient (190, 191). Both Jews and Greeks called God " Father " and men " children of God," but, while for the Greeks sonship to God belonged to man by nature, the Jews were sons of God by God's free choice and by their obedience. For Jesus, however, " sonship to God is a miracle." We are sons only by the Father's forgiveness (194).

The schema into which Bultmann has built the teaching of Jesus breaks down completely in this last stage. He had found its essence in each instance in the existential moment where man, in confrontation with God, hears his claim upon him and by his decision has his future determined for him, whether he is to be a sinner in a world without God or righteous and in fellowship with God. He had said earlier that " the essence of his [man's] own life consists in the full freedom of his decision. . . . Through the decision of his will, through obedience, he can win fellowship with God " (154). Therefore, the long section at the end on sin and forgiveness does not seem quite to fit into the established pattern. The question is whether God's grace and forgiveness will ever fit where they are not primary but secondary, in this instance to an existential concept of how human existence comes to its realization. We are told that " only when the requirement of obedience is wholly grasped can the thought of grace and forgiveness be wholly understood " (201). One would expect the order to

be the other way around: God's grace and forgiveness in Jesus Christ determining the total character of man's obedience in faith. But the grace
and forgiveness are not the grace *of the Lord Jesus Christ* and *his* forgiveness of man, but are specifically detached from his person. The church was
wrong in placing the decisive act of forgiveness and deliverance in the
death or the death and resurrection of Jesus as though it were an objective
event in history, or perhaps a cosmic event (213). Forgiveness was and is
through his words or the words of his church. Jesus was not, as Greek
Christianity was soon to represent him, the Son of God with a divine nature, but was a prophet-rabbi who was " sent by God as bearer of the
word." Since words do not go in search of sinners or bear the weight of
human guilt but have to wait to be liberated from their time-bound trap-
pings by the scholar, the grace and mercy of God expressed in words is
not quite the same as the grace and mercy of God incarnate in a person
who on his cross gives himself to man and through the cross reaches out
to bind men to his person so that through all time they are the channels
through which his grace together with his judgment, or his judgment together with his grace, flow out to heal the world of its brokenness.

The word, which is the "reality of history" in which man is decisively
confronted with God, and which may be either the word of Jesus or of the
church, is here specifically separated from the person of Jesus by Bultmann.
Later in his *Theology of the New Testament* he was to make this separation even more emphatic when he defined the word as the kerygma of the
church for which Jesus' ministry and teaching were only preparatory. The
most that he is willing to say of Jesus is that he was the *bearer* of the word,
and Bultmann takes that to be the full meaning of the incarnation. That
the word should become flesh and should be identified with the person
of Jesus is for him an impossibility. It is here that he and Barth stood far
apart already in 1922. For Barth the central miracle of the gospel was the
incarnation, God's word and in it the whole new world of God breaking
in upon our humanity in the person of Jesus Christ. In him was revealed
a humanity restored to its original nature as the reflection of the very nature of God and therefore the foundation of man's hope and confidence
concerning himself and his world. Why did Bultmann find this impossible
and incomprehensible? For him the infinite qualitative difference between
time and eternity had become a fixed principle. Just as he divided the Beyond sharply from this world and separated religion as man's concern with
the Beyond from culture as his concern with this world, so he divided the
word in which the reality of the Beyond comes to expression from the person of Jesus which was a phenomenon of first-century Jewish history. The
core of revelation was not and could not be in Jesus' person but only in

the " word event " that became reality when the message of Jesus, divested of its merely temporary features, sounded in the ears of men as the divine word that could liberate them from their past into a new future.

A later essay on Christology,[8] read in the light of this 1926 exercise of *Sachkritik,* makes clear just how radical these conclusions are for Christology. *All* Christological statements about the person of Jesus are mythological and must be understood not as statements about Jesus' person but as " the theological explication of the new self-understanding of the believer " (264), " the explication of the believer's understanding of the new being " (267). Every time and culture must express the decisive kerygma, or word, in its own conceptions. But it is little wonder that the picture has become somewhat blurred when we note in this later essay that Bultmann uses the Pauline and Johannine terminology — that the word is Christ, that God has reconciled the world with himself in Jesus Christ, that whoever sees him sees the Father — and asserts that the early church in calling him Messiah showed that it had understood him, i.e., had understood the event character of his mission. He even says that Jesus' person, not his personality, is the decisive thing. But the use of this Biblical language has to be understood in the light of the prior statement of principle, that all such statements are meant not as assertions about the *nature* of Jesus Christ but as explications of the believer's new self-understanding. A certain amount of confusion is bound to result if the reader fails to note that the Biblical language has already been reinterpreted existentially in Bultmann's own mind. That Christ is the word means only that he is the bearer of the word, and that God reconciled the world with himself in Christ means only that he reconciles man with himself through the word of which Christ and the church are the bearers.

4. The " Christian Dogmatics " of 1927

It is a long step from Bultmann's *Jesus* to Barth's " Christian Dogmatics." Barth had begun to develop his dogmatics in lectures in 1924 at Thurneysen's urging in order to draw out in an orderly fashion the implications of the kind of theology at which he was working.[9] Commenting in the preface on the fact that theologians usually write their dogmatics at the end of their career whereas he was writing his early, he justified what might seem presumption as having been made necessary by misrepresentations of his thought, not just by opponents but also by colleagues closely associated with him. What makes misunderstanding inevitable is the sharpness of the rupture between this new theology and the whole central tradition of theological thought since Schleiermacher. Even Herrmann he sees now as " the last stage of a development with which with the greatest goodwill I could only break " (VI). His dogmatics is thus a pioneering venture that at present can be no more than an outline, a prolegomena to dogmatics, protesting against a two-hundred-year tradition and opening up the problems that must be discussed if a new dogmatics is ever to take shape (VIII).

In an earlier essay [10] Barth had stated the dilemma of theology in the paradox that the church in order to be truly the church must speak of God, but, because it is a human, sinful church, cannot in any moment speak the truth concerning God. The solution of the dilemma lay in God's hands alone, in his freedom to speak the truth concerning himself through the broken and ever questionable witness of the church to him. This paradoxical situation was now to form the starting point of theology for Barth. The last thing in the world that he would claim (though he has often been accused of claiming it) was that he had direct access to the word of God, both in Scripture and as a present reality, and could now make it the basis of a theological system. He had to begin with the acknowledgment that the word of God, divine revelation, was not and could never be at his disposal. The fundamental error of earlier theologies was the assumption that they had direct access in some way to such truth: orthodoxy that it had it in propositional form in the confessions and in historical form in the Scriptures, pietism and mysticism that they had it in an experience of God, Schleiermacher that every man had it hidden in him in his relation with the universe, Herrmann that it was available through the historical reality of the inner life of Jesus. The question may be asked whether Bultmann did more than modify Herrmann's view when he made the revelation available in the historical reality of the message of which Jesus and his church were bearers. Bultmann was at pains to insist that " the essential in history," i.e., the word event that has in it the possibility of revelation, " is in reality nothing *super*-historical but is event in time " (*Jesus,* p. 8), just as for Herrmann the inner life of Jesus was a historical event in time. The passion of modern theology had been consistently to find some solid basis in history or human experience, something in man, on which to build. Barth's basic recognition was that to build on *anything* in man was to build on sand. The truth of God could have its source only in God. As it passed into the human medium, a fatal refraction always took place and what man saw was a mixture of truth and error. Nowhere in history or experience, not even in Biblical history, or in the experience of prophets and apostles, or in the historical life of Jesus, or in a historical kerygma of Jesus and his church, had the theologian direct access to truth. Where, then, could he find a starting point for his theology?

The answer was quite simple, yet epoch-making: that theology must begin at the point of the church's most serious embarrassment, where, having claimed to speak and act for God, it has in all humility to confess its failure. Theology exists as a human discipline to deal with a human problem. Its subject matter is Christian speech concerning God and man, a describable reality, which by its very nature demands a criterion to determine what is valid in such speech. Christian speech exists not by permission of the theologian but because the church hears an imperative in the witness of prophets and apostles in Scripture which compels it to preach. The message that they proclaimed demands that it be proclaimed ever afresh, and the church responds to this demand, daring to believe that God himself will speak his word to man in such proclamation. Christian speech is the responsibility of the whole church and not just of the preacher. It reaches its peak in preaching and the Sacraments but includes the mother's word to a child, the conversation of a Christian with his neighbor, and all that Christians say and do. Speaking God's word can be a very dangerous thing, as past experience demonstrates, for truth creates serious disturbances in life, and theology can be an equally dangerous occupation as it seeks to distinguish between truth and error in Christian speech. It is noteworthy that Barth refused to deny the possibility that God's word may be heard elsewhere than in the message of the church and pointed only to the fact that the church alone makes the positive claim that it proclaims the word of God and alone accepts the responsibility in its theology of testing the validity of its claim continually (27).

Thus far the approach has been what Barth calls phenomenological, though it is difficult to see why that term was necessary. He has simply described a human situation. Theology has been defined as a human science, a search for knowledge, which takes as its subject matter human material, what the church has to say concerning God and man, and examines it in order to distinguish, according to a criterion intrinsic to it, what is valid in it and what is not. The criterion, however, the word of God which God alone can make reality in the church's speech, is not directly accessible to theological science. Preaching and Scripture, which witness to the word, are historical and thus accessible, but the word of God is hidden in them. This creates a problem of definition. It is *in* history when God chooses for it to be in history, but it is on the boundary of history and hidden, so that it is never directly accessible to the theologian (45). The concept of *Urgeschichte* (primal history) is necessary, therefore, to denote a reality in history that is not directly accessible. At this point Barth made a transition which was to create wide misunderstanding. Having begun phenomenologically " as though we were spectators " with no word of man's involvement (but was he really not involved?), he felt that he had to shift gears to an existential methodology in which spectator thinking would be aban-

doned and it would be taken into account that every word had to do with
the totality of man's life. His real concern is evident in the fact that he
considered " ethical " as satisfactory a term for this as " existential," but
since existential philosophy was just coming into vogue, it was generally
assumed by readers of the " Dogmatics " that he was making existential
philosophy the basis of his theology from this point on. But the full extent of his concern was that every statement concerning God should be
recognized as having the existence of man involved in it.

Barth was confronted with a serious problem as he attempted to define
how theology actually finds its criterion in the word of God when that
word is hidden. Modern theology had identified revelation with an element in the human consciousness. Barth quoted nine theologians to show
the varied forms of this, a modified Cartesianism, which merely changed
Descartes' " idea," to " experience " or " faith " and held that " since the
experience of God or faith in God has existence in us, God has existence."
But everything in human experience is world, participating in the relativity and sinfulness of the world, and is *not* God. The hearing of God's word
makes man conscious of the contradiction in his existence between being
and not being, between angel and beast. He sees in himself a world that
is alienated from God, a life that is radically set in question. It is God's
answer, God's word to him that has set him in question, but the answer is
hidden from him in the question, or, to use his earlier formulation, God's
Yes is hidden in his No. But when man responds in faith, accepting God's
judgment upon his life in the No, the Yes of God's grace is revealed to
him in the No and is his justification. It would seem, then, that an honest
consideration of the nature of faith should point one beyond faith to the
word of God to which it is response (90). Not Christian faith but the
hidden word of God to which faith responds is the object of theology. The
Christian faith is grounded in God's word, not God's word in Christian
faith. The axiom that knowable reality is present only as a reality in our
consciousness makes God an element in man's consciousness. But the
word of God, defined as God speaking in person, cannot be an element in
our consciousness. (Here Barth was refusing to follow the anthropological
trend of Bultmann and Gogarten.) How, then, can it be known? The
severity of the dilemma for Barth in 1927 is evident in the fact that he
speaks of " the almost insuperable difficulty of this quesiton " (92), and of
how it makes one appreciate why Schleiermacher took faith as the starting point of theology rather than this elusive word of God to which faith
responds.

Anselm was eventually in 1930 to be of great help in breaking a way
through this impasse, but already here in 1927 he was pointing the way. In

his *Proslogion,* Anselm hopes and prays for revelation while confessing himself God's creature with God hidden from him. He wishes to understand God's truth which his heart believes and loves. Faith is a reality of his consciousness, but not God. God he can only pray to know (97–100). Man's consciousness can be filled with the Spirit of God, but this does not mean that the Spirit in man's consciousness can be the object of theological research and description. There is no way of access from man to God, only from God to man. Direct knowledge of God, face-to-face, belongs only in the *eschaton.* In time we know God only indirectly, in being known by him, in being the objects of his judgment and grace (103). The dilemma of the theologian is that as a Christian he lives only by the word of God which judges and redeems him and yet nowhere in human history or experience can he point to a phenomenon and say "*That* is the word of God." Even in the moment of reconciliation God withholds himself and his word from human observation. One thing, however, is certain, that the concept of the word of God comprehends the man who hears it as well as the God who speaks. (Here Barth gave real comfort to his existentialist friends.) It is heard only as it takes human form as human word and spirit, i.e., in historical clothing and through the medium of human witness, but the human word is never of itself God's word. It *becomes* God's word only when God himself speaks in it (111).

Wrestling with this strange reality of revelation which comes to man only in human form and yet is hidden completely in the human form until it is revealed to faith, Barth draws into the forefront of dogmatics the mystery of the Trinity which for him is the mystery of God's self-revelation. None of the human forms of revelation can be identified with the revelation itself, neither the witness of prophets and apostles in Scripture, nor the human life of Jesus himself. To worship the historical Jesus is to engage in idolatry. God's revelation is God himself in his whole being. This is the test and the downfall of what men call natural revelation: God is wholly revealed or not at all. God's word is God, and what happens in us in response to God is wholly human, a faith that has no direct continuity with God's action, yet on the human level displays analogies to God's action (139). God is reflected in man's response, but the reflection, the analogy, provides no bridge from man to God, since it is evident only to God. Man sees only the brokenness of his knowledge and the sinfulness of his life. We have to confess then, that God is the Revealer, that he is also the revelation, since in the act of revealing he makes the human word his own, and that he is himself what is revealed in the life of man. The Trinity designates these three moments in revelation, the three ways in which God is Lord. The incarnation, thus, is the possibility of revelation.

God, to be known to us, must become man and meet us in human form
and yet remain Lord by remaining hidden in his revelation. Therefore,
he remains hidden in the Scriptures and in the human life of Jesus and
hidden in the immediacy of his presence with man in the Holy Spirit. God
remains ever the active subject in his relation to us and never becomes an
object for our knowledge.

Barth asks the question why God should reveal himself in man, and
here the old tendency to seek answers in the nature of man shows itself.
We encounter in man the reality of the " I " and therein a valid cloak for
the Trinity of God. The " I " does not become the " Thou " in order to
know the " Thou." The " Thou " remains subject even as object to my
" I " and therefore remains hidden from me. Alongside this is the simple
fact that only man can speak to man. But, having said this, Barth seems to
apologize for introducing such an argument, claiming that his intention
was only to demonstrate the rationality of what is believed so that even
the outsider may see that what is said is meaningful in its own context (227).

It now becomes clearer than ever how necessary the concept of *Urgeschichte* is to Barth's definition of revelation. There is no revelation for
man except through a human historical medium, whether it be the person
of Jesus Christ, the history of Israel, the witness of the prophets and apostles, the text of Scripture, or the preaching of the church. But none of
these is revelation of itself. Only the action of God speaking in them and
by his Spirit opening the heart and mind of man to hear his word makes
them the media of revelation. The revelation event is thus *in* history and
yet *beyond* history and beyond the observation of the historian. The revelation event is therefore placed in the sphere of *Urgeschichte*. The acts of
God in creation, reconciliation, and redemption are all events in *Urgeschichte* and it is what God does in *Urgeschichte* that ultimately determines
what happens in history. The meaning of the events of man's history is
hidden from even the most acute historian because the source of the visible events is in the invisible (230–232). The error of the conservative theologians is that they regard the incarnation as a historical event like any
other, as though God's act of revelation were directly accessible to the historian. But Bultmann, while he differs from the conservatives by his radical recognition of the relative character of all historical phenomena, oper-
ates with the same concept of history as they do (whatever is an event in
history must be accessible to the historian), so that for him the historical
character of Jesus' life excludes the possibility of incarnation (236). But
Barth sees it differently. " In history of itself there is nothing, so far as the
eye sees, on which faith can be grounded. The historical event as such is

and remains ambiguous. As such it can be a banality or a myth " (237). It can be no more than witness to or prophecy of revelation. Revelation or *Urgeschichte* is the prototype or hidden meaning of all history because in it the contradiction in man is overcome. The content of *Urgeschichte* is the logos through which all things were created. Finally, the denial of any identity between history and revelation has to be slightly but significantly conditioned, not to relax the denial but to take account of the effect upon the outward history when it becomes the medium of God's revelation. Insofar as history in Israel and in the church is witness to revelation it becomes " qualified history of second grade " (239).

The prime example of this qualified history is the canon of the Scriptures. The Old Testament and the New Testament find their unity not primarily in any human characteristics they possess but in being both of them witness to the same revelation, in part very incomplete witness, yet uniquely witness. The Old Testament has this unity with the New not through prediction of the when, where, and how of Christ but by its witness to the word which was to be incarnate in him. A purely historical, untheological scholarship cannot grasp this because it focuses exclusively on the historical phenomena and ignores the *Urgeschichte* to which they point beyond themselves. The possibility of extra-Biblical witnesses cannot be excluded. After all, the Bible itself includes the non-Israelites Melchizedek, Ruth, Naaman, Cyrus, the Wise Men from the East, and the centurions of Capernaum and Caesarea. The church may be greater than it knows. It is not the visible church or Christianity as a historical phenomenon that is absolute but the revelation to which they point. But when one speaks of revelation beyond the Scriptures and the church, he dare not forget that such revelation must be the self-revealing of the Triune God, God become flesh, the hidden God revealed (250).

Against this background Barth comes to the decisive heart of the matter in Christology. The foundation has already been laid in the exposition of the Trinity as the unfolding of the truth that Jesus is the Lord of life (140). The revelation of God requires his flesh in order to communicate itself to man and yet is hidden in his flesh. The word of God in Jesus and the human existence of Jesus are therefore two and yet one, distinct and unmixed, and yet by God's act a mysterious unity, mysterious because it defies human explanation. The God-manhood of Jesus, therefore, has always to be understood as deed, God's deed in his word, and not as " thing " (*Sache*); otherwise, it becomes an absurdity. Here Barth and Bultmann stand far apart. For Bultmann, there is no unity in the *Person* of Jesus between the divine word and his human historical existence. The humanity of Jesus is essentially irrelevant to the word of which he is the bearer, and no statements are admissible concerning his nature. When he has been described as prophet and rabbi, the whole truth concerning his human existence has been spoken. But for Barth the divine revelation in Jesus and the human flesh in which that revelation confronted men were inseparable, just as *Urgeschichte* and history are always inseparable. The being and reality of Christ's humanity is that of the Lord who acts as Person or Word. Christ even in his human nature can be no other than the Son of God, and there is truth even in speaking of Mary as the mother of God (265). His flesh is our flesh, our God-resisting, sinful manhood. He bears it with us and for us, but he is not guilty of its resistance to God. In him the contradiction between humanity and inhumanity is overcome.

Barth pointed out an important difference between Lutheran and Reformed Christology. For Lutherans who follow Luther's emphasis on the flesh of Jesus, the word of God does not exist apart from his humanity and they attribute all the marks of divine majesty to the humanity. But this makes the finite to be *capax infiniti* and so is Docetic. Contrary to this, the *extra Calvinisticum* maintains the identity of the word in creation with the incarnate word so that the word has an existence beyond the human earthly life of Jesus. The *Urgeschichte* in the history of Jesus, hidden in it to be revealed, makes the incarnation a miracle that in its unhistorical character " belongs under the concept of myth " (273) and as an event is analogous to the mythical. But theological recognition of the true character of the event removes it from the realm of myth and this recognition becomes possible through the continuity between the event of revelation in Jesus Christ and the event of revelation in the church. Only in this way is the incarnation known as reality and not fantasy. " By its own participation in this event the church confesses: conceived by the Holy Spirit, born of the Virgin Mary." The Virgin Birth at the beginning of Jesus' history and the resurrection at its end mark this piece of history from A.D. 1 to 30 as different from all other history, absolutely unique, through the unity of God and man, of *Urgeschichte* and history (275). At this point an element of speculation enters in again as Barth tries to rationalize the absence of a father in Jesus' conception: a man gets his name, position, rights, place in history, and character as an individual from his father. Therefore, the old Adam has no part in the coming of the new Adam. " As *his* son Christ would be a sinner like all other men " (279). God had to take the place of man in Jesus' conception to make him the firstborn of a new creation and to make our redemption possible through him.

A section on religion adds little to Barth's earlier polemic against a religion-centered theology and against Schleiermacher as its typical representative. The man who no longer dares to speak of God speaks of religion.

He replaces Scriptural exegesis with history of Biblical religion, which enables him to bypass revelation, and he substitutes philosophy of religion for dogmatics. The reality of religion is found in a relation with God which is a natural possession of every man but in which some men have virtuosity and so become mediators of it to others. Each man is regarded as already possessing God in his own innermost being and having no need to receive him in his Word and Spirit. The God of this religion cannot be equated with the Trinitarian God. The reality for which it is searching within man is none other than the Holy Spirit, but in confusing God's Spirit with man's spirit it brings into being a man-centered religion. However, just as sinful man can be redeemed, so also can his perverted and sinful religion, by recovering its true center of worship in God's self-revelation (317).

True religion is faith and obedience which are possible only through God's coming to man. "In faith and obedience man himself enters into the continuity of *Urgeschichte*" (320). This is a highly significant statement because it signals the reappearance of *Heilsgeschichte* (sacred history) in a new form. In the 1919 *Romans* there was a stream of *Heilsgeschichte* in the midst of history. In 1922 with good reason this disappeared as the full dimensions of historical relativity were recognized and God's acts were placed in *Urgeschichte* or the *eschaton* on the boundary of history. *Urgeschichte* represented for Barth the revelational depth of significant events in history. But now there is a "continuity of *Urgeschichte*" into which men enter in each new generation as they respond in faith and obedience to the word of God. Faith and obedience are inseparable because gospel and law are inseparable. God is known only in both grace and judgment. No man can receive God in his grace without being exposed to the will of God which contradicts his human will and commands his obedience.

The continuity of *Urgeschichte* provides the basis for the interpretation of Scripture, for *Urgeschichte* is nothing other than the continuity of revelation, the continued activity of God in history revealing himself to men, and the continuing presence in history of men who respond to that revelation with faith and obedience. But that is the church. Only a faith that presupposes the Christian church can understand *Urgeschichte* or revelation. The historian can call the Bible "Holy Scripture" only if at the peak of his thinking he becomes a theologian. "As a historian he sees and recognizes here as everywhere only the words of men" (334). Therefore, historical science can neither help nor hinder the church in its hearing of God's word (336).

Bultmann was right in his accusation that Barth made too sharp a distinction between historical and theological interpretation,[11] between the text as it hides the revelation and the text as it becomes the medium of revelation. The text is a historical and at the same time a theological reality but in such a way that the two can never be held completely apart. Barth has always recognized the necessity and importance of historical interpretation as well as theological, but he has insisted that it is only preparatory to the theological and can neither help nor hinder the theological. He seems never to have recognized that the facing of the historical questions is theologically necessary and has important theological consequences. It is at this point — the understanding of the interrelation of revelation and history — that much greater clarification is needed. Bultmann saw the deficiency in Barth's position, but he himself confused the problem still further with his absolute separation between this world and the Beyond and his dualistic conception of historical knowledge.[12]

Barth's doctrine of Scripture is analogous to his Christology. The word of God is both hidden and revealed in the human words of Scripture. "The Word of God became history. But it has no history" (341). Therefore no human endeavor can extract revelation directly from the Biblical text. Orthodox literalism, whether Roman or Protestant, and pure historicism are alike in error in thinking that the content of Scripture is directly accessible to them. What they find on the surface of the words is not the living word of God for man now but the ancient, time-bound witness in which the word found its expression in history then. The Roman Church attempts to bridge the gap between then and now and to provide the means whereby the revelation may become contemporary through the vicariate of the church with its interpretative tradition, but the tradition as the expression of present revelation inevitably takes precedence over the Scriptures as witness to a past revelation. Against this it must be asserted that it is not the church but God in his Spirit who makes the word contemporary. But it has to be recognized also that not just the Roman Church but everyone reads the Scriptures in the context of a tradition. Nineteen centuries of interpretation speak together with the Scriptures. The context in which we read them has been created for us by Augustine and Luther, and by a host of other influences. "No one reads the Bible directly: we all read it through some one, and indeed more than one, medium, whether we want to or not" (366). The meaning that words have in our present existence condition our hearing. The church with its cumulative understanding of Scripture, embodied in its tradition, must be recognized as having a certain authority in interpretation, but that authority dare not become primary; it must always be secondary to the authority of the original revelation in the Scriptures. Thus a translation such as the

Vulgate or the Luther Bible may receive from the church an authority that is withheld from private translations, but the way must be held open for new translations embodying new understanding.

The three stages in interpretation are summarized in the three words: *nachdenken, mitdenken,* and *selberdenken,* which are hard to translate. *Nachdenken* is the whole historical process by which we imaginatively enter into the original situation of the text and *think* the author's thoughts *after* him. *Mitdenken* signifies a second stage in which, beyond observation, there takes place a *mingling of our own thoughts* with those of the text. The text speaks but the hearer also speaks. He cannot help bringing to it a certain theory of knowledge, a certain logic and ethics, a certain idea of the relation of God, man, and world, certain ideals, " in short a certain philosophy." Luther was a Neoplatonist, Calvin an old Platonist, Augustine a Platonist, Thomas an Aristotelian. Without some such organization of thought we cannot think at all. But no philosophy is either a guarantee of a good theology or an obstacle to it. Philosophy becomes dangerous to theology only when it inhibits its freedom in hearing and responding to the word of God (406). At the third stage, *selberdenken,* the identification of the interpreter with the author becomes so intense that he forgets that he is not the author and yet states the substance in his own terminology. This has been misunderstood as though the identification with the author meant taking over — very much like a literalist — every detail of the author's point of view and attitude. But far from this, it means *finding oneself together with the author,* in unity with him, in openness and obedience to the same revelation of God and thinking it all through for oneself. Hearing the word of God together with him constitutes the communion of saints (389), in which each saint has to speak in his own situation with absolute integrity. The two participate together in *Urgeschichte* and by this continuity in *Urgeschichte* the true succession in the life of the church is maintained.

In this unity with the Biblical author, not on the level of time-bound attitudes and practices but on the level of revelation, the church, or the individual in the church, must take the responsibility of bearing witness to the revelation in the language and thought forms that are pertinent to the problems of his present situation. " They must themselves think and express the thoughts of Scripture on their own responsibility and in obedience to their own commission, and not just reproducing them but making them their own " (439). This is what the Biblicism of Bengel, Hofmann, Beck, and others in the past had failed to do. Such Biblicism fails to take account of the involvement of the word of God in the broken words of men. A *true* Biblicism is not content to cite Scripture but gives its faith and obedience to the revelation which is *hidden* in the words and lets that revelation come to fresh and contemporary expression. This third and last stage in hermeneutics, the *selberdenken,* is ignored by those who accuse Barth of reverting to a Biblicistic literalism. The *selberdenken* represents his alternative to Bultmann's demythologizing and existential interpretation. First, the communion of the interpreter with the author must be established so that they stand together under the light of the same revelation, and then the interpreter must take the responsibility of witnessing to that revelation in his own day and in the thought forms of his day. The interpreter cannot parrot the Bible any more than Paul could parrot Jesus, or Jeremiah could parrot Isaiah. What Barth distrusts in Bultmann is not the endeavor to let the gospel find a contemporary form of expression but the assumption that historical and philosophical scholarship can detach the essence of the gospel from its first-century conceptuality and prepare for it a conceptuality more meaningful to the modern mind.

The volume ends with some final guidelines for dogmatic thinking. In a divided church, dogmatic thinking takes place in the context of a tradition — Catholic, Lutheran, Reformed — but, since all traditions are relativized by the revelation, there can be no absolutizing or repristinating of a Luther or a Calvin or a Thomas. Dogmatics has its focus upon the problem of how the church is to speak the word of God *for today* with *authority*. It cannot become a system, once the relativity of all human statements and the hiddenness of the revelation are acknowledged. Lutherans have a tendency to make a system of dogmatics, seizing upon some one basic statement and building a system upon it. Again, God is never the object of the thinking in dogmatics but always the subject, so that it is a thinking that in faith and obedience follows God's thoughts concerning us. Because the truth of God in its fullness remains ever hidden from us and appears only brokenly, our thinking has to be dialectic, making every answer a new question and never coming to a final word. Only God speaks the undialectic word which simply *is* truth. We speak brokenly as sinners, the contradictions in our existence being reflected in the contradictions of our thought.

5. GOGARTEN'S RESPONSE

Two years after the appearance of the *Christian Dogmatics,* Gogarten reviewed it [13] and in his review drew attention to the way in which Barth was diverging from the course followed by himself and Bultmann. He had difficulty in seeing why Barth started from the second Person of the Trinity to develop the full doctrine of the Trinity. He found no adequate explanation why Barth took the church's preaching as the starting point for the development of a dogmatics. Also, the doctrine of God the Creator seemed to him to have received insufficient attention. But what impressed him as the most serious weakness was the lack of an anthropology. He was willing to agree that the widely prevalent attempts at theological anthropology must be rejected, but that seemed to make it all the more necessary to develop a true one as a defense against the false. He was hurt at the failure of Barth to appreciate what he and Bultmann were doing to provide a right anthropology with which to approach the Bible. It was at that point that philosophy had a contribution to make to theology, but Barth was closing his eyes to this interrelation. For Gogarten, the only way one could be saved from speaking speculatively of God was to start not from the word of God or the preaching of the church but from the reality of the life of the man who is accepted of God and in whose existence revelation is actual. Only in this way will one be starting from the incarnate word, the word *incarnate in man now*. It was also a disappointment to Gogarten that Barth ignored the work which he and others were doing on " a new and improved doctrine of history." This was the concept of history as the primary and only reality which was being developed in dependence upon Heidegger's existentialism and was to issue in the varied forms of existentialist theology. Barth was not ignoring it. He had considered it and was rejecting it as a blind alley down which one must not go. The review shows clearly that by 1929 Gogarten and Bultmann were fully conscious of the basic divergence between themselves and Barth.

6. Other 1927 Publications of Barth's

During the winter of 1926–1927, Barth delivered a series of lectures on Paul's letter to the Philippians to the university students at Münster and published them as a commentary in 1927.[14] The contrast in form to the " Romans " of 1922 is striking. The twisting and turning of dialectic and the Kierkegaardian terminology are gone. With simplicity the mind of Paul is allowed to express itself and bear its distinctive witness to the gospel. Barth had been accused of practicing " pneumatic exegesis," of bringing forth under the inspiration of the Spirit all manner of revelations for the present day which had only a slender connection with the Pauline text, and he wished to show that in his theological interpretation he was as faithful to the text as any purely historical exegete. In the preface he writes: " That I myself — though my intention remains the same — do not bind myself to the procedure earlier employed in the case of the Epistle to the Romans, but am still seeking, is a thing the present work will perhaps make clear at least to some." How historical and theological exegesis were best to be combined was still an open question (and remains one of the most urgent and intriguing problems of present-day Biblical scholarship, though many English and American scholars ignore it). In concentrating so heavily in the "Romans" of 1922 upon what the text means in the present day and upon the reexpression of its content in the thought forms of the modern theological situation, Barth had left himself open to the misunderstanding that he was attributing to Paul theological and philosophical ideas which were nonexistent in the first century. Therefore, in the exegesis of Philippians he leaned in the opposite direction, leaving no one in doubt that his one concern was to let Paul speak with his own distinctive accents into the modern situation.

The year 1927 also saw the beginning of a contact with Roman Catholicism that was to be increasingly significant in the future. Barth was asked to address a group in Münster that belonged to the Roman Catholic " Centre " political party and chose to speak on " The Concept of the Church."[15] He recalled with nostalgia the sixteenth and seventeenth centuries when Protestant and Catholic had looked each other in the eye and disagreed, which was so much more preferable than the modern tolerance and politeness with which they merely looked past each other. To take each other in earnest must mean to take in earnest the antithesis in their understandings of the church. First, he established that, in spite of all differences, Catholic and Protestant see the same reality when they speak of the church. He took the creedal statement " I believe in one holy catholic apostolic church " and showed that each can repeat it and must repeat each word of it with complete sincerity. Then, when he examined the confessional statements of the churches, in a number of instances he found that the Roman Catholic statement supported what was generally assumed to be the Protestant position, while the Protestant statement sometimes gave comfort to the Roman Catholic. The church is a people called of God, ever one, the body of Christ on earth, the mother of the faithful. As to the instrument of his purpose, God lends to it his holiness and as his spokesman it witnesses to an infallible word. It is catholic, not because of its numbers or its geographical distribution, but in the same way that Christ himself is catholic and universal. It stands in succession to the apostles and under apostolic authority, being a true church only insofar as the apostolic faith finds continuance in it. The secret of its existence lies not in itself but in God's grace and man's faith.

Against this background Barth asked why the two churches in the sixteenth century pronounced their anathemas against each other. The answer was that in spite of what seems to be a formal agreement in doctrine, each church has understood every point of its doctrine in a different way. His own task is to state the Protestant understanding and thereby provoke his Roman Catholic friends to formulate their own position. Fundamental to his statement was the definition of faith as man's receiving and grasping of the grace of God in such a way that grace remains God's grace and is never at man's disposal, being the reality of the word and Spirit of God. They receive power over man so that in Word and Sacrament he perceives them, has rational knowledge of them, and experiences them in his heart, but without having them in his power as other things he knows are in his power. The church, as the place where God's grace exercises this power, has authority over us, but only as the means of grace. The church cannot control the grace. " The God-relation is an irreversible relation in distinction from all other relations." The bridge from God to us cannot be made into a bridge from us to God. God enters into time, " into the twilight, into the relativity and questionableness of history and of human life, but in that hiddenness in which he is never known directly, never as self-evident, but always only through a present act of will, a present act of his love." We can have the church only as we have God, with the same hiddenness and in the same lowliness of the human means of grace. Barth then goes back over the creedal statement to sharpen each point of it in the light of this basic distinction. The church is one only as God makes it one by freeing it from all that is false. It is holy only insofar as it is obedient to God's holy will. It is infallible only insofar as it witnesses to the infallible word of God, the infallibility being in what it hears and not in what it speaks, its dogmas as witness having only a limited secondary authority. It is catholic not by being ancient but by sharing in the catholicity of Christ himself. And it is apostolic only as it continues to serve the same word and Spirit to which the apostles bore their faithful witness.

This encounter with Roman Catholics was the beginning of Barth's own private ecumenical movement. From this point on he began to engage the interest of Roman Catholic theologians. In his reformulation of dogmatics he had been forced back beyond the Reformers to take account of the witness of the church in earlier centuries, so that in a real sense, without the slightest betrayal of his Protestant principles, he spoke as a Catholic to Catholics. Hans Urs von Balthazar, a Jesuit university chaplain in Basel, who was to have long conversations with him in the thirties and forties and who published an able volume on his theology in 1951 [16] (much more competent and understanding than any previous Protestant treatment of it), declared that he was more catholic than any Roman Catholic theologian. A remarkable number of theological works by Roman Catholic authors have appeared in the last twenty years which either deal directly with Barth's theology or show in their thought the effects of his influence.[17]

CHAPTER IX

THEOLOGY VERSUS
ANTHROPOLOGY

LATE in 1933 the partnership which for ten years had produced the journal *Zwischen den Zeiten* was dissolved at the insistence of Barth and Thurneysen. In the preceding year Barth had remarked rather pointedly in the foreword to the new edition of his *Dogmatics* that the only colleague with whom he could make common cause in theology was Thurneysen, and in the body of the work he had criticized sharply not only Bultmann and Gogarten but also Brunner. He saw all three developing their theologies in such a way — Bultmann and Gogarten their anthropological interest and Brunner his eristic or apologetic interest — that they must eventually divert theology back into its old channel in line with Schleiermacher, Ritschl, and Herrmann. More serious, he saw in them a surreptitious reintroduction of natural theology, contrary to their own professed intentions, and with dangerous implications for the now precarious church situation in Germany. The former colleagues refused to take their differences with Barth with the same seriousness that he did and regretted his decision to end the partnership. Brunner in particular insisted publicly that there was no essential theological divergence between Barth and himself. Therefore, in 1934, Barth published a pamphlet with the title " No! Answer to Emil Brunner," [1] which was intended to make clear to everyone that Brunner's standpoint was not at all to be taken as an indication of where he, Barth, thought theology should be going. The vigor of the repudiation owed something to the fact that for ten years Barth had been impatient that Brunner was frequently in various countries taken to be an authoritative interpreter of his theology. So widespread was this impression in America that Barth's attack on Brunner in 1934 was interpreted by many American theologians as a sudden brutal and bad-tempered outburst against a theological companion for daring to differ from him. But when the history of the six years, 1927 to

1933, unfolds before us, we see that there was nothing sudden about any of these ruptures of relationships. The differences had long been there, but they had been pushed into the background and their seriousness had not been recognized. The colleagues had been united in their revolt against the theologies of the past. But when they turned to the task of theological construction, it began to be evident gradually that they were not at all of one mind.

As early as 1928, H. M. Müller, in reviewing Barth's 1927 " Dogmatics," commented that the " dialectical " theologians were as disunited as the political generals in China [2] and drew forth from Gogarten the retort that his own criticisms of Barth's present development of dogmatics in no way set in question the essential theological solidarity between the two of them. Barth's assesssment of the situation was a less optimistic one. If we had the post-1925 correspondence between him and Thurneysen to supplement the already available pre-1925 letters, we would be able to determine how early he knew that the relation was basically untenable. Certainly when in 1930 in an article on " Theology and the Present-Day Man" [3] he classified the anthropological and eristic approaches to theology (without naming Gogarten, Bultmann, and Brunner) under the heading of Protestant parallels to a Thomistic compromise with natural theology, he had already decided that their alliance was at an end. In the light of that fact it is surprising that the public break did not come until 1933 and 1934.

1. The Anthropological Project

To understand the developments of this period from 1927 to 1933 we need to bring clearly into view what Bultmann and Gogarten were talking about when they insisted that a valid anthropology was essential to the future of Protestant theology. The question was not whether a doctrine of man can or must be worked out. Every dogmatics must include anthropology and on that score there was no argument between them and Barth.[4] The question was whether theology must by the nature and conditions of its knowledge have not just its beginning but its primary form as an anthropology. We shall use the writings of both Bultmann and Gogarten to show what they meant by anthropology, since Bultmann himself made very clear in 1930 that he shared this project with Gogarten and stood very close to him in his thinking.[5] He acknowledged his indebtedness to both Gogarten and Heidegger.

Under the influence of Heidegger, Bultmann had come to the important

conclusion that the theologian must look to the philosopher for the basic
analysis of human existence (93 ff.). He was impressed by Heidegger's
critique of the self-understanding of man in all the earlier ages of human
thought and particularly in nineteenth-century German idealism and romanticism and by the revolution implicit in Heidegger's formulation of
the self-understanding of modern man. The error in all earlier self-understandings was that in them man assumed a fixed knowledge of himself
and his world. The essence of Heidegger's reformulation was the indeterminateness of man's existence in any given moment of history. Man
is a historical being, which means that his existence is not and cannot
be fixed but is constantly being determined by the decisions that he makes
in each moment of history. Therefore, he cannot proceed as though he
possesses a fixed knowledge of himself and his world. What he is and the
nature of his world are disclosed to him only in the moment of decision
in which he puts behind him his inauthentic being and lays hold upon his
authentic being. To Bultmann this was the philosopher's secularized description of the Christian experience of salvation. Inauthentic being was
the Pauline natural man's life in a world of darkness, sin, and death, and
authentic being the life of the new man set free from sin and reconciled
with both God and man through Christ. The indeterminateness of man's
existence corresponded to the Pauline conception of man as all his life
long being on his way out of the life of bondage into the life of the new
age, with the goal always beyond the bounds of time. Where Bultmann
refused to follow Heidegger was in attributing to man the ability by his
own decisions to put inauthentic being behind him and to realize his own
authenticity in a new future. For Bultmann, man remained imprisoned
in the inauthenticity of his past until there sounded in upon him the
word of God's forgiveness which freed him from his past and opened to
him a new future. Philosophy could describe the realities of the human
situation but it could not speak the liberating word: that remained the
task of the church's proclamation. Only in the church's gospel could man
hear the word of forgiveness which was at one and the same time God's
judgment upon his past and the grace of God offering him a new life.
He could not have the grace without the judgment. Under God's judgment he died to the past and by God's grace he came alive to a new future.

What others called Heidegger's atheism, his leaving God totally out of
account in his philosophizing, did not trouble Bultmann at all because he
saw in that the necessary limitation of the philosopher's knowledge. To
speak of God the philosopher would have to become a theologian. He
should as a philosopher speak neither of God nor of the word of God nor
of the action of the word of God in man's existence. But what the phi-

losopher *can* describe with a conceptual accuracy that is helpful and essential to the theologian is the existence of man, both in its inauthentic and in its authentic state, *as well as on its way from the one to the other.* What seemed to make this service of the philosopher to the theologian particularly necessary was that the theologian carried with him out of the past a confused and confusing mixture of self-understandings which vitiated his thinking and obstructed his comprehension of Scripture. As we have seen earlier, one of the most revolutionary insights of Bultmann and Barth had been the recognition that pure objectivity in the approach to historical records is an impossibility for any human being, however skilled he may be in historical method. What the historian finds in the record is strongly influenced by the presuppositions with which he approaches it. Bultmann saw in the work of his predecessors in nineteenth-century New Testament scholarship that their idealistic or romantic conceptions of themselves and their world had a profound effect upon their interpretation of the content of the New Testament. Gogarten found the whole thinking of the age, both in theology and in culture in general, perverted by being saturated unconsciously with idealistic assumptions. Therefore, for both men the immediate and most urgent task of theology was the clarification of concepts, the cleaning out from one's thinking of the old inadequate self-understandings and the formulation of a new self-understanding adequate to man's knowledge of his own existence in the mid-twentieth century. At this point theology should welcome all the help that philosophy with its sharp conceptual tools can furnish. Barth seemed to Bultmann and Gogarten to overlook the seriousness of this problem and to be blind to the proper function of philosophy in relation to theology. One of their repeated criticisms of his 1927 " Dogmatics " was that in it he was too uncritical in the employment of his concepts.

The problem was further complicated by the fact that the Biblical authors had their own self-understanding which was only in part determined by the revelation of God to which they witnessed and which had made them what they were, and inevitably in part determined also by the self-understanding of the age in which they lived. There was thus in the words of Jesus a conceptuality that belonged to the self-understanding of Judaism and that would involve one simply in absurdities if the attempt were made to transfer it bodily to the modern age. So also Paul, as an inhabitant of a Hellenistic age, united in himself a self-understanding that belonged to his age with a self-understanding that was the fruit of his hearing of the gospel, the latter alone having power in it to break out of that age into a new one. The interpretation of Scripture, therefore, requires a critical approach by the scholar both to the conceptuality of the

Biblical author and to his own conceptuality with which he is approaching the Biblical text. But such critical activity is impossible without a dependable criterion. The ultimate criterion is, of course, the revelation itself which alone can bring man to the true realization of his existence, but that ultimate criterion is not available to man in his *approach* to Scripture. In this dilemma philosophy comes to his aid by providing him with a dependable working criterion, a preliminary description of human existence, freeing him from false conceptions, but needing to be deepened and corrected in dialogue with the revelation of the Scriptures. The task of philosophy is to provide the theologian with the conceptual tools with which to distinguish between valid and invalid self-understandings both in the Biblical text and in his own approach to the Biblical text. The acceptance of Heidegger's definition of self-understanding as a working criterion was based on the conviction that it penetrated beneath the confusion of religious language and stated in secular terms the essentials of a Christian understanding of man's existence. The accusation that Bultmann took over Heidegger's existentialism uncritically is unfair. For him it was a point of departure from which as a Christian theologian he could begin the interrogation of Scripture, in dialogue with which his understanding of man would constantly be under correction from the revelation of God which was inseparable from the revelation of man.

The dimensions that Bultmann attributed to the philosopher's knowledge of man's existence must not be underestimated. All phenomena of man's life are open to the philosopher, including the phenomena of faith. He can describe accurately not only the natural man but also the man who has come to the fulfillment of his humanity. There are no possibilities of man that are hidden from him. He can also bring under his scrutiny the human process in which man moves toward fulfillment. But the important distinction must be made that the philosopher knows all these things only as possibilities of man, structures of human existence. Actual existence in faith is hidden from him just as God is hidden. Existence in faith is the domain of theology. Philosophy clarifies conceptually the meaning of such things as proclamation, word, address, hearing, which are central for theology, but " it does not teach one to understand some concrete proclamation in particular " (93). Philosophy explores existentiality but not concrete existence. It can demonstrate the ontological possibility of sin and forgiveness, but the meaning of sin and forgiveness is accessible only to the man who sins and is forgiven. " All the basic Christian concepts have a content that can be determined ontologically prior to faith and in a purely rational way " (96). While the Christian *meaning* of love is known only to faith, it is knowledge of the care-structure in man's nature that enables one to give a clear conceptual statement concerning it. More than once Bultmann uses the illustration that the friendless man knows what friendship is but passes to a different kind of knowledge of it when he possesses a friend. Similarly, the natural man knows what revelation, life, grace, and forgiveness are. Faith only adds a knowledge of what they are *for him,* knowledge of the actuality from within. But the man of faith, in order to express in words this " knowledge of the actuality from within," has to use the language of the natural man, and for that reason is dependent upon the philosopher for the clarification of concepts in his language. Only a theology which recognizes this dependence upon philosophy can attain the character of a science. Theology without this conceptual clarification remains indistinguishable from preaching (97).

The article then proceeds with a comparison of Heidegger's and Gogarten's interpretations of historicity. For Heidegger it was the encounter with death, but for Gogarten the encounter with the " Thou " of the neighbor, that made man aware of his historicity, i.e., the indeterminateness of his existence, and so constrained him to the decision in which he " freely chooses his possibility of existing authentically " (107). The encounter with the " Thou " contains two possibilities, hate and love. The " Thou " becomes visible only in love. " Love alone is the possibility of authentic existence " and " only in love is man historical " (105). But love is possible for the " I " only when the " I " is loved. Therefore, the Christian gospel and Christ come into the picture as the proclamation of God's love for man which makes man's love not just a possibility but a reality. But theology, when it speaks of this *reality* of love which is known only to faith, does so in the same human conceptual realm in which philosophy belongs. Theology and philosophy are conceptualizing activities, the latter focused on existence and the former on existence in faith, but both are attempts to capture in concepts realities that must ever in some measure elude the human mind, a truth forcefully evident in the fact that the conceptuality of one age in history is valid only for that age and not for any other. Philosophy and theology therefore represent for Bultmann two levels in man's knowledge of his own existence, the philosophical being the indispensable preliminary to the theological, since implicit in the language and concepts of every human statement there is an understanding of existence without which no statement concerning any reality can be made.

It may be helpful to note the implications of this existentialist approach for the interpretation of all historical records and not just the New Testament. At a conference in October, 1927, Bultmann spoke on " The Mean-

ing of the 'Dialectical Theology' for New Testament Science,"[6] attempting to answer the criticism that dialectical theology approached the Bible
with a set of fixed dogmas and read them into the text. He denied the
charge categorically, defining dialectical theology as no more than a deepening of historical methodology by the recognition of the historicity, i.e.,
the indeterminateness, of man's being. Every historical text expresses not
just facts about the past but a possibility of human existence. If we would
understand it, we must bring to it an understanding of such possibilities
through the knowledge of our own existence. There must be a dialogue
between the understanding in the text and my own understanding of myself, and in this dialogue one never reaches finality. The understanding of
history is therefore an endless dialogue with history. Thus, if the text
speaks of revelation, I have no possibility of understanding it unless there
is already in my self-understanding some preliminary knowledge of what
revelation is. This preliminary knowledge, however, is always a "not-
knowing knowledge" (128) because the reality that is present only in the
act of revelation is hidden. I know the *possibility* of death, but death itself
I cannot really know until I die. Only this preliminary "not-knowing
knowledge" makes it possible for me to ask questions of the text and so
to enter into dialogue with it. But if my self-understanding has been determined largely by rationalism, romanticism, and idealism, and is dominated by Greek conceptions of being and existence, I will, in the reading
of a Pauline text, arrive at a radical misunderstanding of such terms as
"world" and "flesh." The historian needs the philosopher to make him
critical of the conceptuality with which he is approaching the text and
to help him to a conceptuality that is tenable for a twentieth-century man.
Thus, dialectical theology, far from reading dogmas into the text in
such a way as to silence its intrinsic meaning, lays both the historian and
the text open to each other so that the past can really speak to the present.
It will be noted that here Bultmann identified "dialectical theology"
specifically as an existentialist deepening of historical methodology in general which attained its theological significance when it was applied to
theological texts such as those of the New Testament. One can hardly fail
to see that not only the interpretation of New Testament texts but the
whole structure of Christian theology has been made dependent upon the
validity of the existentialist preunderstanding, or "not-knowing knowledge," of human existence. The whole of theology is like an inverted pyramid of knowledge that rests ultimately upon what is assumed to be the
philosopher's solid rational objective analysis of the structures or possibilities of human existence.

An essay on "The Concept of Revelation in the New Testament" in

1929 [7] furnishes an excellent illustration of the operation of the new methodology. First, there has to be a clarification of the question through an examination of the guiding preunderstanding of revelation. Revelation is usually conceived as the disclosure of what is veiled or hidden, but this may be either the communication of knowledge or information, or an occurrence that puts me in a new situation as a self and may at the same time bring me knowledge of myself in my new situation. The discussion from this point forward is confined to these two possibilities. (A third possibility, which would combine the two in some degree, holding revelation to be an occurrence that puts me in a new situation as a self and in doing so brings me knowledge not only of myself but also of God, is not allowed to appear, although the reading of the New Testament would certainly suggest it as a possibility. Thus, one must say that in the formulation of the preunderstanding the dice are loaded in the direction of existentialism.) We know about revelation in a not-knowing way because we know about our own authenticity in the midst of our inauthentic life, just as we know about our death long before it comes.

A historical survey then demonstrates how dominant the concept has been that revelation is a communication of knowledge. In Roman Catholicism the knowledge is given partly by reason and partly by revelation but in both it is rational knowledge. Once revealed, it is " known " and becomes man's possession. In Protestant orthodoxy the Roman pattern was retained, revelation being " a supernatural arrangement for communicating doctrine," although faith was defined as trust in the word of forgiveness in such a way as to break through the pattern. In Rationalism, revelation was natural through reason, not supernatural, and comprehended all knowledge. In Idealism and Romanticism, revelation became " the emergence into consciousness of the omnipresent and eternal basis of all phenomena," an awareness that comes as man reflects on himself as spirit and finds the source of his life in a supertemporal essence. Revelation was defined as the irrational, but the awareness was not of God but of man himself and the whole concept led to a confusing of the devil with God. In Liberalism the concept of revelation was trivialized, being equated with " what one can perceive in moral achievements and the phenomena of culture." " Everything is revelation." Yet all were agreed that revelation is the means whereby man comes to his authenticity.

Turning to the New Testament, Bultmann found no basis in any part of it for a concept of revelation as the communication of knowledge or doctrine. Revelation there means life for a man who is limited by death. " Revelation can only be the gift of life through which death is overcome." It is nothing other than the fact of Jesus Christ, his life, and the

promise of life to us, a life " yet to be revealed, for our life is still hidden
with Christ in God." The revelation takes place in the word of preaching, a word that for Paul spread death as well as life, " not illumination,
or the communication of knowledge, but rather an occurrence . . .
which takes place in us ourselves " (78). One cannot go behind this event
of revelation in the word of preaching to a historical Jesus or to a cosmic
process belonging to the past. The content of the revelation is designated
precisely as love (85), the love of God in Christ which frees us to love him
in return. " Just as little as the preaching communicates something that
happened in a certain place and at a certain time, but rather speaks of
what has occurred to the person being addressed, so little is faith the
knowledge of some fact within the world or the willingness to hold some
remarkable dogma to be true " (87). Faith is obedience to God in the
now. In faith, man is freed from his past by the grace that encounters
him in the word, sees the other person as his neighbor, and in understanding the neighbor understands himself. Revelation thus in invoking
love communicates life, not supernatural knowledge. The only knowledge
that is given in the revelation is of myself (88). The content of the word
of God cannot be " exhibited, but rather can only be heard in the immediate moment." Looking back, one realizes that a central assumption on
which the whole discussion is based but which is never allowed to appear in the discussion is that God himself remains entirely hidden in his
word of revelation. God remains so completely Subject in his word of
judgment and mercy, love and forgiveness, that he never becomes an object of knowledge even for the man who responds to his word in faith
and receives the gift of life. Theology, therefore, as knowledge is confined to what man knows in himself as a hearer of the redeeming word.

It was perhaps in the consciousness that his doctrine of the philosophical
preunderstanding would lay him open to the charge of reconstructing
natural theology (the charge that Barth actually made at this time) that
Bultmann wrote an essay on " The Problem of Natural Theology "[8]
which remained unpublished until it appeared in his first volume of essays and addresses. He begins with a flat rejection of natural theology as
being impossible in Protestantism, since God can be known only to faith.
But he then proceeds to outline three factors that make natural theology
still a problem. First, there is the understanding of existence, including
faith as one possibility of existence, which even the unbelieving man possesses and must possess if he is ever to understand the gospel. His rejection of the gospel implies an understanding of it as the negation of his
own self-understanding. Second, there is the non-Christian use of the
word " God." Missionaries do not have to invent a new word. A knowl-

edge of God is hidden in the idolatrous use of the word just as a knowledge of God's demand is hidden in the stirrings of man's conscience in confrontation with his neighbor. Unbelief as well as faith knows the moment of decision and the historicity of human existence which it implies, and to that extent knows God. But what is "intended" at all these points is visible only to faith, which is born of the word and so cannot become the basis for a natural theology. Third, there is the ontological knowledge of existence which the philosopher attains by existential analysis. There is no phenomenon of existence visible to theology that is not also visible to philosophy. But philosophy sees faith only as a possibility of existence, not as reality. As transformation of existence faith is not perceptible. Neither God nor God's justification of the sinner are demonstrable in existence, since man even in his justification remains a sinner and is justified only in the sight of God. Thus, the ontological knowledge of existence remains on a plane where it can never be a foundation for dogmatics or for a natural theology. One wonders why this essay remained unpublished when it was so pertinent to the debate with Barth. It would have invited Barth to show where an incipient natural theology lay concealed in Bultmann's development of anthropology.

Gogarten dealt directly with "The Problem of a Theological Anthropology"[9] in an address in Copenhagen in May, 1929, and, while his thinking parallels that of Bultmann fairly closely, some elements of their joint concern come out more clearly in his presentation. As in his review of Barth's "Dogmatics" of 1927, Gogarten lays great weight upon the inseparableness of God and man in the event of revelation. His concern in the review is to hold together the word of the gospel and the man addressed by it as one reality in the phenomenon of revelation. The word is not only *from God* but also *to man,* and the revelation is not an actual event in history unless the man is included in it. He scolded Barth for conceiving God and man in isolation from each other and for distinguishing between the incarnation as the objective possibility of the revelation and the Holy Spirit as the subjective possibility. For existential thinking, "such distinctions as objective-subjective are simply impossible." This was to be an increasingly important theme for Gogarten — the overcoming of the objective-subjective antithesis. Therefore theological thinking must begin "from the God who is not isolated from man, and does that not mean that one must begin his thinking with the man?" The second half of this statement is not as obvious as Gogarten assumed. In fact, it becomes obvious only when one assumes with Gogarten and Bultmann that God remains totally hidden in his revelation while man is revealed to himself in the event.

In the Copenhagen address Gogarten is mainly concerned to vindicate the placing of anthropology at the center of theology. He denies any intention of substituting anthropology for theology and agrees with Barth that God and his word must be the primary theme of theology. But God cannot be separated from man in a Christian theology, nor man from God. An understanding of man cannot be imported into Christian theology from outside but must be derived from the gospel. Reinhold Seeberg with his comprehensive science of man, employing the resources of psychology, epistemology, philosophy, ethics, philosophy of history, and sociology, conceives man as existing apart from the revelation of God, with a natural religious capacity to know God and to set himself in a relation to him. But for a Christian this is to misconceive man. The problem of anthropology is not new but has commanded the center of interest ever since the Renaissance. At that time man and his world lost their place at the center of the universe and man had to find in himself the significance which earlier the world had lent him. He made the discovery that history was not something that happened to him but rather was the objectification of his human spiritual existence in time and space. He was himself the *maker* of history. He was a historical being who in history was unfolding his own reality. This impelled him in theology to start from himself in approaching theological problems, and the epoch-making significance of Schleiermacher was his frank recognition of this anthropological orientation of theology. Thus the modern age began with man's discovery of his own historicity, something in himself that previous ages did not know, even though it always was there: " the consciousness of his own inmost, most personal aliveness, the knowledge of the historicity of man." This made it the age of humanism and in such an age Christian theology is forced by the focus of interest upon man and by the proliferation of false doctrines of man to concentrate its interest upon the development of a right anthropology with which to resist the false ones. Not one step would Gogarten go with Schleiermacher, but because of the tradition stemming from Schleiermacher, he called for anthropology to be given the center of interest. The question of man is central whether we like it or not and should be treated under every theme of theology.

The first task, then, is the critical one of bringing to light the self-understanding that is implicit unconsciously in theological statements. No man arrives at his self-understanding by deliberate and conscious decisions; he absorbs it unconsciously from his epoch, so that today it will be that of post-Renaissance man. The second task is more difficult: to find a criterion of truth and falsity with which to measure the self-understanding. The obvious suggestion is that the Biblical self-understanding of man provides the necessary criterion for Christians. But one cannot have the Biblical self-understanding without understanding himself as the Biblical authors did, that is, as persons addressed by God. We can share their self-understanding only by hearing the same word of God that they heard. There is no ideal concept, however, which we can extract directly from Scripture and apply ideologically as a criterion. The obstacle is that our own unconscious self-understanding makes us misunderstand the text of Scripture. Our actual situation is that in our hearing of Scripture the self-understanding of the author enters into bitter conflict with the self-understanding on which our lives are based. At this point Gogarten differed from Bultmann in an unwillingness to take over from Heidegger a modern formulation of self-understanding as a working criterion with which to approach Scripture. He insisted that no direct and conscious formulation of a modern self-understanding is possible. It comes to sight only in the conflict that is generated by the hearing of Scripture, in the conflict between the word of God and the human conscience. Man constantly tries to understand himself apart from God. This is his fall from grace from which he is saved only by the word of God. The function of anthropology, therefore, is to take away man's self-security and leave him broken in spirit to hear the word of God.

2. THE POSSIBILITY OF KNOWLEDGE OF GOD

For Barth as for Bultmann, theology was a thoroughly human science dealing with thoroughly human subject matter. For both, the error of the nineteenth- and early twentieth-century theologies that lay behind them was in their assumption that theology must have direct access to divine reality, that God had somehow to be made the object of human thought. Each theologian had his own way of doing this. A Schleiermacher laid bare a union of man with God, or with the universe, at the hidden center of man's consciousness. A Herrmann found God revealed in the historical reality of the inner life of Jesus. Others found God directly revealed in the human conscience. Orthodox theologians posited a directly accessible revelation of God in the text of Scripture. All found God present somehow in human experience, or ideas, or history, or historical records, in such a way that their thinking could grasp God directly. The revolutionary insight which came to Barth and Bultmann and set them thinking in a new direction was that God is Subject and never object for man. God is never at the disposal of man, so that man may possess him either in his experience or in his thought or in human documents or doctrines. God

is God and man is man, and there must be an end to the modern confusing of man with God and God with man. God is never captured by
a church or by a theology or by an individual, so that they can proudly
claim: "We have him." God remains free in all his dealings with men
to give or to withhold himself, to reveal or to hide himself.

But God has revealed himself, does reveal himself, and will reveal himself. Again Barth and Bultmann were agreed that theology comes into
being in the church as a consequence of the testimony of the church and
of Scripture to the reality of revelation. The whole New Testament points
to a word of preaching, a proclaiming of Christ crucified and risen,
through which God somehow judges and redeems humanity. The central significance of Scripture is not in religion but in revelation, and the
function of the church is not the promotion of religion but the service of
the unique divine revelation to which the Scriptures testify. But the revelation itself is not a quantum of supernatural information about God, man,
and the world, but is God himself in his word. The human witness to
God's word in Scripture is therefore never to be confused with the word
itself. It is *human* witness and, as such, conceals the revelation until God
reveals himself in it to faith. Where there is no faith, only the human
words, ideas, and experiences are visible. For this reason, a purely objective historical science could find only religious phenomena in Scripture
and could regard revelation only as a human concept with which to interpret the phenomena. So also in the church's preaching of the gospel,
although the hope that sustains it is that God may speak his word to man
by means of it, even in its most successful form it cannot be identified
directly with revelation but remains a fallible human witness. The same
is true of the dogmas and doctrines that come to formal and impressive
expression in the church's creeds and confessions. They are testimony to
revelation, but *human* testimony and always open to correction in the
light of better understanding of the revelation. Therefore, although theology exists only because of this witness to revelation, it does not and cannot ever have direct access to the revelation, that is, to God himself in his
act of revealing himself in his word.[10] It cannot base itself directly on the
word of God. This is the acute dilemma in which theology finds itself
when once it takes seriously that God in his freedom never lets himself
become the prisoner of man's thought but constantly in his self-revelation
breaks through all the religious and theological constructions that men
erect in his honor as dwelling places for him in time.

How, then, is theology to begin if it does not have the revelation of God
available to it as the basis and starting point of its thought, if, in fact, it
is blasphemous presumption for it to think that it can grasp and retain

the living God in the categories of its thought? As a human science it must begin with human subject matter. Barth met this requirement by defining theology as the critical examination of the church's very *human* speech concerning God to discern where in its *human* witness it is faithful and where unfaithful. But how was this discernment possible when the criterion was hidden in the revelation itself and theology could have no direct access to the revelation? To this question, and in fact to this whole problem, Barth and Bultmann gave quite different answers. Crucial for Barth was the incarnation, that God became man in Jesus Christ, that the word of God was manifest in human flesh, concealed indeed in the humanity of Jesus but also revealed in it, and revealed in it in such a way that witness to that revelation *remains* the medium of revelation through all time. For Bultmann this was an absurdity. The humanity of Jesus was irrelevant to the revelation of which he was the bearer except in the bare fact (the *dass*) of its existence. The revelation was in his words and in the words that the church preached in dependence upon him, but concealed in them by the conceptual forms of the age in which it was expressed. A personal relation with Jesus Christ was possible only in his lifetime and is impossible now. Our relation is with the word of the gospel, the kerygma of the church, which had its origin in him. We know Christ only in that word and must not try to go behind it to a person who once lived in history. Barth agreed that it was futile to attempt to reconstruct a Jesus of history behind the kerygma of the church, but he was unwilling to shift the focal point of revelation from the *person* of Jesus Christ to a word event of which he and his church were the bearers. There were not only words of Jesus in which God spoke his word, but there was the man Jesus, a human being in history whose human historical existence in his life, death, and resurrection, became the decisive event of God's revelation of himself to man.

What, then, was the significance of this difference for the structure of theology? One would expect it to be very great, and it is. The church's faith is centered for Barth not just on a kerygma but on a person to whom that kerygma constantly points, and not on a person who is dead but on a person who is alive and active in the life of the world through his word and Spirit. Christian faith is faith in Jesus Christ and in God through him. To have faith is not just to be known by him but to know him in being known. To abide in him and to have him and his words abide in us is to be his church. Therefore, theology has its existence in a church which, while its unfaithfulness ruptures its relation with Christ and conceals the revelation of God, nevertheless has been sustained through the centuries by the faithfulness of God. In spite of human sin and blindness, he preserves in his church ever a witness to Christ through which faith in him is constantly renewed. The only criterion of a true faith is its object, Christ the incarnate word. Theology does not have him at its disposal in an ideological fashion to use as a measuring stick of truth, but it does have him present in the witness of the Scriptures and in the witness of the church, both through the centuries and in the present moment, if it is willing to open its eyes to him in faith. It dare not recognize any other criterion of truth, for the importation of any secondary criterion will be the recognition of some other authority over the church than the personal Lordship of Jesus Christ.

Bultmann agreed that the ultimate and absolute criterion of truth for Christian theology is in God's self-revelation in his word, but since this word is located not in a living person but in a kerygma, and is concealed in the kerygma both in Scripture and in the church's preaching by conceptual forms alien to the mind of our day, the word of revelation has first to be liberated from its inadequate conceptuality before it can be available to theology as a criterion of truth. Therefore, as we have seen, a preliminary working criterion has to be found elsewhere. Bultmann found it in Heidegger's existentialist analysis of man's existence. Here was a solid, rational human basis from which to start. In a brief note on Heidegger in RGG[2], Vol. II,[11] Bultmann described him as taking up the problems of ancient ontology to radicalize them and to outline a universal ontology that comprehends also the region of history, a work that can be fruitful in providing " an ontological basis for theology as a science." The criterion would be valid only for the anthropological element in theology and even there only conditional upon its ongoing correction in dialogue with the Biblical self-understanding. But since theology had been limited to a knowledge of man's existence in faith, and this knowledge was to be expressed in the conceptuality of the existentialist self-understanding, severe limitations would necessarily be imposed upon theology by the philosophical ontology so that what was supposed to be a subsidiary working criterion was already seizing the primary authority and, by its definition of human possibilities, restricting the freedom of God in his revelation. Philosophy was being allowed to define the conditions in man's existence within which revelation was possible.

We need to remember also that Barth refused to recognize in the faulty and unchristian presuppositions with which men approached the Scriptures an insuperable obstacle to the revelation. No matter how sinful they were and no matter how idealistic, pantheistic, or materialistic their self-understanding, it was possible for God's word of judgment and grace to reach them and to create for itself an understanding. Beneath all perversions of men's natures and no matter what their self-understanding might be, they remained God's creatures. Nothing they did could deliver them out of God's hand. No disruption of *their* relation with God could disrupt *his* relation with them. There is no human defense against the Spirit of God. Therefore, there did not need to be any formal image of God, any elementary bridgehead of the divine, in man as a connecting point for God in him, as Brunner was teaching. God himself was there, hiddenly present with every man, to provide his own connecting point. So also in the hearing of God's word in Scripture and in the preaching of the church, the possibility of a genuine hearing lay not in some readiness of man but in the presence and power of the Holy Spirit bearing witness within to the word which was heard from without. The words of Jesus were better understood by sinners than by the scribes who were schooled in "Biblical concepts." The other side of this truth was that no clarification of concepts, no adjustment of one's self-understanding, could prepare the way for God's revelation. He would reveal himself where and when he chose, and perhaps, as with Paul, to a man whose religious presuppositions were most in contradiction to the truth of the revelation. Every man will have a philosophy of some kind as he approaches Scripture, some idealistic and some realistic, some consciously and some unconsciously. Among the great theologians there have been Platonists, Aristotelians, and Neoplatonists. All have made use of philosophical principles in the organization of their thoughts. But their philosophy should be neither a help nor a hindrance to their hearing of the word of God. They must let it, like all else in their lives, come under the judgment and critique of the revelation so that anything in it that stands in contradiction will be overcome. The revelation itself must be allowed to create the mind and heart to receive and understand it. Here again the incarnation was significant for Barth. The word makes a temple for itself in the flesh of man. The revelation conquers the resistance of the flesh. It enters the flesh and conforms it to itself so that the human history becomes, not itself the revelation, but a permanent witness in time to the revelation. *The history is conditioned by the revelation.* And the revelation is at one and the same time the revelation of God and the revelation of man, never the one without the other. This was the principle on which Gogarten had been so insistent, that God and man are inseparable in the actual event of revelation. But in his and Bultmann's anthropological development of theology, man was revealed in dialogue with the revelation but God remained hidden, to be known only indirectly as he was reflected in the changes in man's self-understanding. To Barth this was nothing less than the denial of the possibility of theology and a substitution of anthropology in its place, actually an existentialist reversion to the anthropocentric tradition of Neo-Protestantism.

In 1926 and 1927 Barth did not as yet see the full seriousness of this problem and he made certain concessions which were promptly interpreted as signifying that he was basing his theology to some degree on an existentialist philosophy. Torrance in his book on the " early Barth " [12] has exaggerated the extent of the concessions, seeing somehow in the Barth of 1927 some "remnants of an *analogia entis* in its existentialist form " which was only finally overcome in the " Dogmatics " of 1932. On the contrary, as we have seen, Barth and Bultmann were moving in divergent directions from the very beginning and more swiftly after 1926, though they themselves were slow to realize it. There is no trace of Barth's being seriously tempted by any form of *analogia entis* and, though Bultmann's anthropological venture captured his interest slightly between 1924 and 1927, even in his " Dogmatics " of 1927 he was determinedly, though with difficulty, pursuing the route from God to man in revelation and not from man to God.

3. THE CONTRIBUTION OF ANSELM OF CANTERBURY

It was at this point, in establishing the possibility and reality of knowledge of God in revelation, that Barth found Anselm of Canterbury a great help during these years. He was reading him as early as December, 1920.[13] Already in the 1927 " Dogmatics " Anselm had made an important contribution to his thinking, but a seminar on Anselm's *Cur Deus Homo* in the summer of 1930 at Bonn, followed by the publication of the volume *Anselm: fides quaerens intellectum* in 1931, greatly enlarged the contribution. Barth, in reviewing the years 1928 to 1938,[14] claimed that his book on Anselm was written with greater love than any other of his books, though it was the least read. One can understand this considered judgment when one sees how it set him free to work at theology with confidence and joy. It is not to be imagined that he agreed with Anselm in all his conclusions, but he found in Anselm's theologizing " a vital key, if not the key, to an understanding of that whole process of thought that has impressed me more and more in my ' Church Dogmatics ' as the only one proper to theology." [15] Anselm has been consistently misunderstood as though he belonged in a direct line with Descartes, offering proof of the existence of God in much the same way as Descartes formulated his proof of the existence of man. Anselm's primary aim was not proof but understanding, although the achievement of understanding then operated as proof. His purpose in theology was "to give the faithful joy in believing by a demonstration of the *ratio* of their faith" (15). The *ratio* of faith was the inner coherence and reasonableness of its content, that is, in the understanding of all things to a knowledge of which it brought the believer. Such inquiry is "the spontaneous desire of faith." The believer wants to understand because he believes. Faith itself is for him "a creaturely participation in God's mode of being" (17), and the character of his faith is wholly determined by what God is to him. He believes in response to the gospel. "Therefore, the aim of theology cannot be to lead men to faith, nor to confirm them in the faith, nor even to deliver their faith from doubt "(17). "It is the presupposition of all theological inquiry that faith as such remains undisturbed by the vagaries of the theological 'yes' and 'no'" (18). Faith is to be sought not in theological inquiry but in hearing and responding to the gospel.

It belongs to the very nature of faith, then, that it summons us to knowledge. Because God is truth, faith in him is faith in the truth which God is and, therefore, knowledge of the truth in him. Because there is no faith in God without a movement of the human will which is the will of a rational creature, faith means choosing between justice and injustice, between true and false, between good and evil. The word of God to which faith responds encounters in man a potestas which is a trinity of capabilities— a recollection, knowledge, and love of an *optimum et maximum omnium* — the image or reflection of the holy three-in-oneness of God. It is this vestige of the Trinity in us that makes us human in distinction from the animals, and in faith this potentiality is actualized so that man remembers, recognizes, and loves God. Thus faith, in restoring man to his true nature in the image of God, cannot complete this aspect of its task without bringing with it a knowledge of God. How could man reflect God's nature, his love, his justice, his purity, and not reflect also his truth? There is also an eschatological dimension in the knowledge that is given in faith. It is not the final vision in which man sees God face-to-face, but a broken seeing. It belongs not in the realm of glory but in the realm of grace. The knowledge is somewhere between faith and vision. Faith participates in God in such a way that it attains within the realm of grace a certainty that theology can never possess. Theology "comes up against the inexorable limitations of humanity in a way that faith, as such, does not." But "just because we possess the certainty of faith, we must hunger after the *ratio* of faith" (21).

The possibility of theology is thus inherent in the nature of faith. Faith arises in response to the word of Christ, but always to that word as it is heard from the Scriptures and interpreted by the church. Dogma, tradi-

tion, the church fathers, and the pope, all had their place in interpreting
the word of Christ to the believer. The credo (with a small *c*) of the
individual believer was always in the context of the Credo (with a
large *C*) of the church. The word to which faith responds has a content
that is explicated in the Credo of the church, and, even for the simplest
and most unreflective credo of the individual, that content is present in
the word of Christ to which his faith responds. Faith, therefore, has in it
in nucleus an understanding that differs only in degree and not in kind
from the understanding that it seeks in theological reflection and discourse. The Credo of the church as a larger and clearer unfolding of the
credo of the believer thus makes the science of theology possible and gives
it a basis.

Barth then outlines eight "conditions of theology" according to Anselm. First, the knowledge that theology seeks is "an extension and explication of that acceptance of the Credo of the church which faith itself already implied" (26). It reflects on the Credo that has been already
spoken and affirmed. This does not mean that it simply adopts some dogmatic formulation on the authority of the church, but that it recognizes
in the dogmas of the church the necessary endeavor to say with authority
what the church knows in consequence of its faith. Theology begins not
by challenging the validity of this knowledge but by attempting to understand it. Second, there is a limit beyond which the theologian cannot press
his questions without ceasing to be a theologian. He asks, "To what extent is reality as the Christian believes it to be?" Insofar as he asks for
a certainty other than that which is given within faith itself, he abandons
the very basis of theology. Third, "Every theological statement is an inadequate expression of its object. . . . God shatters every syllogism" (29).
We cannot get beyond conceptions of objects, none of which is identical
with God. Yet, because nothing exists apart from God and what is not
God is something only because of God, the language of our human world
can be used to say what is true when it is applied to God. Fourth, theological statements have a scientific certainty that is not to be confused
with the certainty of faith. Scientific certainty is always less than ultimate,
since further investigation may modify it. Fifth, the achievement of theology, like that of the church fathers, is always incomplete. New grace is
given to new ages. Some elements in understanding remain hidden and
have yet to be revealed. Therefore progress in theology is possible. Sixth,
the validity of any theological statement rests with God, but the criterion of its present admissibility is the text of Scripture. Scripture as
witness to the word to which faith responds is both the decisive source
and the determining norm of theological understanding. Seventh, a right

faith is necessary to a right understanding. A theologian without faith will be without understanding. His dedication is essential. A pure heart, open eyes, a childlike obedience, life in the Spirit, rich nourishment from Scripture, all condition the theologian's capability for his task. Barth set in line with this Melanchthon's demand for fiducial faith, pietism's insistence that the theologian must experience rebirth, and the insistence of present-day theologians on existential thinking. (Elsewhere he has spoken of Kierkegaard as ultimately the originator of a superpietism.[16]) He pointed out that for Anselm this seventh condition was provisional in nature and was not the final question. Eighth, Anselm set the whole of theology in the context of prayer and gave his *Proslogion* the form of an explicit address to God. This final condition, the intimate relation between theology and prayer, conditions all the others and makes them relative. God alone guides man into truth. The capacity for understanding has to be bestowed upon the reason in prayer. Anselm prays for God to " let him see his face, let him see his very self." [17] He knows that God must stand in encounter with him if his *intellegere* is not to be delusion and if he himself is not to be a mere *insipiens* (39).

4. THE CRUCIAL ISSUE FOR THEOLOGY

Here, then, is laid bare the decisive issue between Barth and Bultmann (together with Gogarten) which was to become, and is, the decisive issue in modern theology, dividing it into two streams according to the decision which is made. The revelation event in which faith is born is agreed by both to be an encounter between man and the living word of God himself in which God comes to man, a word that is to be heard through the Scriptures and the preaching of the church. There is no question but that theology belongs in the service of this revelation event upon which man is dependent for his life's fulfillment and has as its task the explication and clarification of the knowledge that is given in revelation. The crucial issue is whether theology is to be focused upon the word to which faith responds or upon the faith that responds to the word. Neither can be known without the other, for God's word is hidden until it is revealed to faith and faith is wholly determined by the word to which it responds. Bultmann seems to have made the decision very early that no knowledge is available to theology except from the faith side of the relation, that God, even in his speaking of the word in which he judges and redeems man, withholds from man any knowledge of himself. God never offers himself to man in such a way as to become the object of his thought. Yet God is known, indirectly, as he is reflected in his determining of human existence in the revelation event. Man can know God only by what God does to him by his word of forgiveness which is both judgment and grace, or in existential terms, by the change that God's revelation makes in his self-understanding as he is released from inauthenticity into authentic existence.

Long before 1927, Barth took the other fork in the road at this parting of the ways. As we have seen, even in 1922 the Unknown God was for him a known Unknown. He offended Bultmann in his " Romans " by his insistence that God became man and the word of God was revealed in the flesh of Jesus Christ so that the years of his life became the years of the central decisive revelation *in history*. Between 1922 and 1927 he was wrestling on this rocky uphill path of clarifying what to him was the objective side of revelation, the word of God in Christ, in Scripture, and in the witness of the church, but without forgetting that it had also its subjective side in faith and that the two sides were inseparable. He was open to the emphasis of Kierkegaard that truth has no reality except in the existence of men, which Gogarten and Bultmann were pressing as the antidote to idealistic and romantic speculation in theology, but he resisted firmly their increasing tendency to make the faith of man rather than the word of God the basis of theological knowledge. The " Dogmatics " of 1927 was written to bring clearly into the open for himself and his colleagues, as well as for his opponents, where he stood on this issue, but it created so much misunderstanding through its failure to break clear of existentialist terminology that even men as close to him as Gogarten and Brunner failed to grasp the full implications of the direction in which he was going. Even as late as 1933 they were still insisting that in spite of all differences, they were essentially on the same theological road as Barth. Just as in 1914, so now it took an ethical issue, the political situation in which Germany found itself in 1933, to bring out the implications of the theological issue. For himself, Barth's work on Anselm brought the final resolution of the problem of where theology was to find its basis. It did not mean any radical change in the structure of theology for him but rather a confirmation of the structure to which he had already committed himself. It brought a clarification and a joyful confidence that has never since left him. But one has to look very closely to find changes between the " Dogmatics " of 1927 and the " Dogmatics " of 1932 which are more than an enlargement of the historical background and a debating of the issues with other theologians of the past and present. The basic pattern was already there in 1927, but in 1932 there was much less likelihood of anyone's misunderstanding either where he stood or in what direction he was going.

5. THE RELATION BETWEEN THEOLOGY AND PHILOSOPHY

Bultmann, as we have seen, postulated a very positive relation between theology and philosophy. He argued from the inescapableness of some philosophy in the theologian's thinking and in his mental equipment as he approaches the Bible to the necessity that he should accept the help of the best existing philosophy in clarifying and purging his self-understanding and his language in preparation for theological discourse. Gogarten was not prepared to take over an analysis of the structures of human existence ready-made from Heidegger, but he agreed with Bultmann that the theologian needed the help of philosophy if he was to clean out of his thought and language every trace of the romantic and idealistic understanding of man which for a century and a half or more had been leading theology astray. The polemical task of freeing men of the philosophical presuppositions that vitiated their understanding of the gospel and prevented them from moving into the new era in their thinking impressed both Gogarten and Brunner as the most urgent task of the moment. All three were critical of Barth's refusal to join them in this task or to welcome the co-operation of philosophy at this point. They accused him of a blindness to the interrelation between philosophy and theology and of a carelessness about the purging of inadequate philosophical elements from his language and conceptions. Out of this dispute have come various misconceptions of Barth's attitude to philosophy, at the one extreme that he simply ignored the existence of philosophical problems and turned his back on all philosophy, and at the other extreme that while condemning Bultmann for his dependence upon Heidegger, he himself is naïvely dependent upon Plato but less honest about his dependence.

Barth cannot be justly accused of neglecting philosophy. His introduction to it was not likely to be neglected in such liberal schools as Berlin and Marburg, and in Marburg he became acquainted with the neo-Kantians Cohen and Natorp. In June, 1916, when already he envisaged the coming time when he would have " to strike the great blow against the theologians," he reported to Thurneysen that he was beginning more extensive theological *and* philosophical studies and was working on Kant as though he were preparing for an examination.[18] One of the factors in his rethinking of basic questions after 1919 which made him rewrite his " Romans " was the better understanding of Kant and Plato that he attained under the guidance of his philosopher brother, Heinrich. The greatness of his respect for Plato is unconcealed in all his earlier writings. At one point he even spoke of him as a noncanonical witness to the resurrection, an exuberance that was soon to disappear. Heinrich Barth was a Christian existentialist in his philosophy and the points of agreement and disagreement between him and his brother would form an interesting subject for investigation. Then there was the impact of Kierkegaard's philosophy during the years 1919 to 1922 and the struggle to free himself, not wholly but largely, from its influence for some years after 1922. Barth certainly gave considerable attention to philosophy, and anyone who has read the introductory chapters in his "Protestant Theology in the Nineteenth Century " [19] will be unlikely to accuse him of being philosophically naïve or incompetent. He does not disparage the importance of philosophy or its value for man in his attempts to understand himself and his world. He would insist that no man, and certainly no theologian, can escape from involvement in a philosophy of some kind. That Thomas Aquinas was an Aristotelian and Calvin a Platonist does not of itself set in question the validity of their theological thinking. Every man who thinks must use some kind of thought structure to organize his thoughts. The vital question is whether or not it becomes a secondary source of revelation and so a secondary authority alongside the word of God in his theology. This was what Barth criticized in the anthropological projects of Bultmann, Gogarten, and Brunner and to some extent in his own earlier thinking. In using philosophy to clear the ground for a new theological structure, they were, consciously or unconsciously, permitting philosophy to function as in some measure a criterion of truth and reality in the realm of theology and were thereby cutting a channel that would eventually divert the new theology back into the old Neo-Protestant stream. The camel of philosophy needed only to get the tip of its nose inside the tent of theology to begin a process that would one day negate the authority of revelation by reestablishing some form of natural theology. Barth's concern was the construction of a theology that once more, as in Luther and Calvin, would recognize the sole authority of God in his word, and by its negation of any secondary criterion of truth in which man would be seeking to protect some coveted concern of his own would preserve for the word of God its full revolutionary force in its impact upon the total life of man. He saw in even the slightest concession to a natural theology a possible bridgehead for man's defense of *his* understanding of himself and his world against God.

The basic document in this discussion from Barth's side is a forty-page essay which appeared in *Zwischen den Zeiten* late in 1929, having been delivered in lectures in Dortmund early in the year. It was entitled " Destiny and Idea in Theology," [20] but in order to give a broader conception of his concern he indicated that he could have called it " Reality and Truth " or

"Nature and Spirit" or "The Special and the General" or "The Objective and the Nonobjective" or "The Conditioned and the Unconditioned" or "Being and Thinking" or "Heteronomy and Autonomy" or "Experience and Reason" or "Realism and Nominalism" or "Romanticism and Idealism." The basic problem of philosophy is that when we examine our existence, we find our thought moving constantly between two poles. The advantage of the chosen title is that it indicates poles not just of thought but of life. Reality has a double aspect for every man whether he be philosopher or theologian. Theology as a science has its own area of investigation in the church just as medicine has physiology as its area. It investigates, not the truth of God directly, since God cannot be the object of knowledge, but the truth or falsity of the church's teaching concerning God. It is a human science with human thought and speech for its instrument. Theology exists, therefore, only when we have heard God's word proclaimed, only as God has found us, not in a vacuum above and beyond the church. But because it must employ human language and thought, it exists in the area of philosophy in much the same way as the church must exist in the area of the state. Although the source of its knowledge is in God, it has no special language or categories in which to express itself and thereby differentiate its statements from philosophical ones. "It can never say the special thing which as theology it has to say in such a way that the philosopher could not, in case of necessity and perhaps meaning it somewhat differently, say it too" (312). The theologian can only erect a sign by his witness to revelation. He or the philosopher become theologians when they speak God's word, but they do so only from grace, as God wills. The danger is that the philosopher will think he can use the witness of the theologian to enrich his human knowledge, and that the boundaries between philosophy and theology will become blurred, so that theology tends to become philosophy, either openly or surreptitiously, behind an orthodox front. What is inescapable, however, is that theology, while speaking of God, must take account of the double aspect of reality. The crucial question is whether through the word of God the duality can be overcome. Thinking that remains stuck in the duality capitulates to philosophy. But in the reality of God who is Lord of all reality, the relativity of the duality is exposed and transcended.

Man may begin his thinking from either pole, but destiny, reality, the given, the objective, being, experience, or however the one pole is described, is more likely to capture his interest than idea, truth, or spirit. He seeks God in the given, both in the world about him and in himself. God participates in being and is himself Being. Merely by being, we and our world stand in relation to God, and because we participate in being to-

gether with him, we think we can by *analogia entis* read God out of the
given. Being has a double aspect, an inner side in man and an outer side
in all that is beyond man, and God is found sometimes in the one and
sometimes in the other. Thus man searches in the depths of his own being by psychoanalysis, or in the stars by astrology, to discover his destiny.
Luther saw a similarity between the givenness of the Spirit in the enthusiasts and the givenness of the Spirit in the pope. Pietism found God in the
inner world and rationalism found him in the outer world. The one produces a theology of experience and the other a theology of history, but
both have the same starting point, God in the given. Realistic theology
begins with the assumption that the actuality we experience without and
within is God. For it, the incarnation means that the Word, and so the
God with whom we have to do, entered our way of being, the way of
being of nature and history. God is the reality within which our self and
our world have their reality. He is the reality hidden in all other reality,
and yet not quite hidden, and so available to be the object of our experience.

Realistic theology has in it a legitimate concern and cannot be completely negated. The vital question is whether one can really find God in
a subjective-objective givenness. Is that in accord with God's revelation?
Was Thomas Aquinas right that revelation confirms what is there by nature, and Wobbermin that man is capable of experience of God? The
word of God, however, always comes as God's *judging* and forgiving
grace and reveals what is *wholly new* to man. In relation to God's grace
man is ever sinner. "If he hears what he basically knows already, then
certainly he hears something other than the word of God" (324). There
is no reality of God apart from God himself. God cannot be possessed
apart from his act of grace in which he judges and forgives; in short he
cannot be found in nature and history as given. The likeness of God is
not given men as something they then possess of themselves but is given
them new in each moment in God's relation with them. An inner experience of God is possible, not however in such a way that God is captured
in man's experience but only as encounter with God's Spirit. Realism af-
firms a God who *is* rather than a God who *comes,* and in identifying him
with the given makes him a god who might better be called Nature. Instead of theology, we then have demonology.

Thinking may begin, however, from the opposite pole of idea, truth,
spirit, the not-given. "The question of truth is the question of an entity
superior to reality, validating reality as such, indeed ultimately giving reality its basis" (328). The Not-Given is the noetic and ontological presupposition of the Given. Idealism means self-contemplation of the spirit

over against nature, " discovery of the creative logos as the whence of the givenness of the correlation of subject and object " (328). No earnest theology has ever been able to escape this idealist problem. It need not imbibe idealist philosophy, but it must distinguish the Not-Given from the Given in order to distinguish God's revelation from all else that is revealed. Understanding necessarily involves abstraction from the Given and interpretation of it. In order to think of the reality of God one must transcend it in the direction of its not-given truth. But this absolute truth need not be allowed to swallow up the relative. The concentration on the " I " does not need to eliminate the " Thou," which means that the finding of God in the Not-Given, the non-Objective, and the denial that he is to be found in destiny, nature, the Given, the Objective, history, does not mean that the life of man in nature and history is negated or left without meaning. The revelation of God becomes the crisis of the Given, the divine judgment upon it that reveals its contradiction, but this breaking of it is actually a strengthening, for it sets in question its realistic self-understanding and restores it to its genuine relation. The idealist emphasizes " God is truth," over against the " God is reality " of the realists. God is not nature or history. Flesh is not the Word. Rather, reality or flesh or history is transparent that truth may shine through.

It sounds like a warning to Bultmann and Gogarten in their polemic against all idealism when Barth says that whoever opposes all idealism in theology at this point does not show himself a seriously Christian theologian but only a naïve realist. " Idealism is the necessary antidote to all demonology that pretends to be theology " (333). It guards against the confusion of God as the object of theology with other objects when it emphasizes his nongivenness and focuses theological thought and speech on the God who in his genuine otherworldiness is really God. Theology purged of all idealism would be a pagan monster. The danger of idealistic theology, however, is that it constantly tends toward the erection of an ideology. Seeking truth beyond reality, it begins to think of this as a way to God. But the Christian theologian sees revelation not as a possibility of man but a possibility of God alone in Christ and in the Biblical witness. Augustine and Calvin were idealistic theologians, but *under,* not above, the word of revelation. The divine word cannot be confused with any human word. No direct representation of the word of God is possible. Nor dare it be forgotten that the human spirit is *world. The Beyond of God is not to be identified with the Beyond in our own spirit.* God is known in his word only to faith, that is, only in the divine act in which man is known by him. Knowledge of God is only recognition.

The philosophical problem is thus inescapable for the theologian as he develops the theological problem, since "theology is active in the same area as philosophy " (338). He has to reckon with the two poles of human thought, truth and reality. Both idealism and realism have in them valid concerns. The theologian can turn his back on neither of them. In response to the word of God he has to resort to dialectic in order to bring together in his thought the truth that is found at both poles. His theology may be realistic or idealistic, depending upon the pole from which his thinking begins, but it must take account of the valid concern that comes to expression at the opposite pole, and in doing so his thinking runs parallel to a similar movement in philosophy. But the philosopher differs from the theologian in that he must attempt a synthesis. Idealist and realist alike make concessions in order to establish a third position that will overcome the dualism. The one makes being the reconciling principle and truth a predicate of reality, the other makes the logos the reconciling principle and reality a predicate of truth. But the theologian dare not follow either of them in their synthesis or his theology will be betrayed to philosophy, as Thomas was to the realism of Aristotle and as others have been to idealism. Philosophy *must* attempt the synthesis, but it should recognize that its synthesis lies *this* side of the boundary on which the question of God appears and refrain from confusing its synthesis with God. For theology, truth and reality are one in God and this synthesis which exists only in God is beyond the grasp of human thought. Theology is *human* thought and as such cannot lay hold upon the unity beyond the antitheses but must move dialectically from the truth in the one to the truth in the other. Its thinking has its source in the hidden unity that philosophy is trying to reach. Therefore, theology dare not confine itself to an anthropology that is focused upon the reality and truth of man's existence, because its true focus is upon " the reality and truth of the word of God which is spoken to man " (341).

There need be no conflict, then, between theology and a philosophy that knows its limits, but rather there should be a community of work. But let philosophy become theosophy, confusing its synthesis with God, and war is inevitable. Theology must brand as sheer illusion the man who " in his self-contemplation (no matter how existential, and even though it were the self-contemplation of the I addressed by Thou) thinks he can now really discover in it, within his own reach, the ultimate word, the reality of God " (341). The concept of sin must be validated against both realism and idealism. Man as sinner has no way of access in his thought from himself to God. Man's ultimate concept of the reality and the truth of his sinful life is an idol, a reflection of himself, a devil, judgment without grace, an endangering of life itself.

Neither philosophy nor theology can dispense with dialectic. Both have to go the same road. And this becomes the Trojan horse by which the enemy can enter the city. Luther had to use the Erasmian weapon of theological dialectic in order to contend with Erasmus. Every theologian is exposed to the danger of forming a concept of God that is not really God. The danger is of thinking we know what we do not know. The synthesis in God is always beyond our knowing, believed in but not known, the hidden center round which the dialectic of theological thought must ever move. The danger is that the penultimate will be confused with the ultimate, the concept of God with the living God. Because we ourselves are in the same danger as all other men, we can only question other theologians whether they leave this point open or capitulate to a synthesis and go over into theosophy. Theological dialectic remains open because of the freedom of the word of God. Only as God chooses do we hear his word and is theology of the word possible. God has to make my human concept of him a true witness to him. This leaves us no basis for the kind of self-confidence which triumphs over opponents. In conclusion, Barth pointed to Jesus Christ as the center of theological thought, in whom truth and reality are one, the truth of God's word and the reality of man's flesh, and in their oneness the justifying and healing word.

Barth's attitude to philosophy begins to be clear — not a blunt rejection, not a prejudiced neglect, but a frank recognition of an inescapable relation in which the theologian must think responsibly and not naïvely and in which he can undermine the obedience of theology to the word of God which is its source if he fails to define rightly the boundary between the two. Barth one time gave a group of students the advice: " Be a little with all the philosophers. You can learn something important from each of them. But let your theology become tied to any one of them and you are lost." [21]

CHAPTER X

A MATTER OF LIFE OR DEATH

In 1922, Karl Barth had been widely hailed as "prophet of a new Christianity." The thundering "No!" of his "Romans" to the whole complacent order, not just in theology but in every sphere of life, sounded into his time like the word of a Jeremiah who was sent "to pluck up and to break down, to destroy and to overthrow" in preparation for the building and planting of a new day. His destructive negatives caught the ears of men more than his heralding of the Kingdom and his proposals for a new way of theological thinking. But Barth was not pleased with the role of prophet and he had no intention of continuing in it. His vocation was theologian and the task to which he had set himself was the restoration to theology of its true nature as the critical discipline by which the church submits all things in its life to the criterion of the word of God which it is called to serve. Only by such self-criticism could it escape from its errors and unfaithfulness and lay hold more firmly upon its true gospel. The constructive task was much more awesome to him than the destructive one. When Brunner demolished Schleiermacher so completely in his "Mysticism and the Word" in 1924,[1] Barth wondered whether Brunner quite grasped the dimensions of the gaping hole that was left when once Schleiermacher was gone.[2] Both Brunner and Gogarten troubled him by what seemed to him an overconfidence in their own theological constructions and an underestimation of how radical a task in dogmatics lay before them all. Brunner's eristic and the Bultmann-Gogarten anthropological project were to him diversionary movements that obscured the urgency of the dogmatic task. But when Barth began soon after 1922 to draw upon the resources not only of the Protestant orthodoxy of the seventeenth and eighteenth centuries but also of the ancient fathers of the church in exploring the problems of dogmatics he was accused of turning from prophecy to Scholasticism. Bultmann in particular, a devoted student of the Herrmann who had waged a lifelong war against orthodoxy, was suspicious that Barth was swinging over to a repristination of the outworn dogmatic positions of the past.

Actually, Barth's backward look between 1922 and 1927 took in not only the early church fathers, the orthodox Reformed theologians of the post-Reformation period and conservative theologians of the nineteenth century, but also Luther, Calvin, and Zwingli, and a whole succession of unorthodox theologians from Schleiermacher to Herrmann. The latter are most in evidence in the essays of the period and in his lectures on the history of modern theology, while the former show their influence quite naturally in his "Dogmatics." Just because people expected from him a "new" theology, he was determined to strip away everything that was merely novel and to establish the continuity of his theology with an unbroken confessional tradition that spanned the centuries. His conviction of the relativity of all doctrinal constructions, including his own, permitted no repristination of any past era. However much he might learn from Luther or Calvin, his approach to them had always to be critical and not naïvely adulatory. They belong to their own time and cannot be transported into the twentieth century. Every era in the history of theology has its own task and there may even be more than one such era in one man's lifetime. Theology is the attempt to describe the bird in flight, the word of God which will never "stay put," since God has ever a new word to say to man in his new situation. The movement in theology must ever be forward. Yet a theology that fails to listen to the theologians of the past will be impoverished and will commit all the old heresies over again. The movement forward is impossible without a critical evaluation of the past and a willingness to let oneself be instructed by the past.

From the beginning, it was basic to Barth's thinking that theology is the concern and the task of the whole church. One of his sharpest criticisms of the " science of religion " which was replacing theology at the turn of the century was that it was a purely academic discipline, divorced from the life and problems of the actual church and increasingly irrelevant to the church's primary tasks. He wanted a theology that would focus its attention upon the dilemma of the preacher who had each Sunday to stand between the Scriptures and his congregation and dare to speak God's word to them, and upon the dilemma of a church that could not close its eyes to the contradiction between what it professed and what it was. A church in which there was no such theological discipline was a church with no defense against the unconscious permeation of its life and teaching by other gospels than the one true gospel and therefore was exposed to destruction from within. Barth's assessment of the church situa-

tion was that it had long been in a dangerous state of theological confusion and that nothing was more urgent than the awakening of ministers
and laymen alike to face the theological issues which were beginning to
stand out with clarity.

1. Barth's Conflict with the Church Administrators

Early in 1930 Barth was shocked to read in an official church yearbook
a triumphantly optimistic evaluation of the church situation by a Professor Schneider who spoke the mind of the church administration. The years
since 1918 had been very difficult. There was a time when atheists thought
the church was about ready to be buried. But according to Schneider, the
religious idea was more deeply rooted in the soul of the German people
than appeared to outsiders. The church leadership dealt with its problems
masterfully. The church as a result was now stronger and freer than ever,
the threat to its existence a thing of the past. It had come out of the narrow pass and could see an open field before it. Barth published a response
in *Zwischen den Zeiten* entitled " Quousque tandem . . . ? " [3] in which
he declared that it was a scandal that this should so often be the voice of
the church. He had no doubt that Schneider spoke for dozens of officials
and thousands of pastors. Fortunately this was not the only church, but
this was undoubtedly the official church whose voice was heard by the
workingmen, by the intellectuals, and by the other nations. This church
was paying no heed whatever to all that had been said theologically in
the past ten years. Therefore, Barth asserted, the hour has come when
one must declare rudely and publicly that the very substance of an evangelical church has been lost by such a church. The mentality expressed by
Schneider is more dangerous to the church than Russian atheism. But the
substance of the church, far from being destroyed, stands forth with a new
clarity in antithesis to the falsification that is evident in the church's concern for itself, its success and its power and in its complacency about its
present state of health. The year 1930 was to be the four hundredth anniversary of the Augsburg Confession, and Barth predicted that there would
be many anniversary addresses in the same key as Schneider's comments,
with none in angry protest. On such a road one who loves the church
must surely cry " Halt! "

Gogarten in an address in Bavaria in June, 1930, on " The Meaning of
the Confession," [4] spoke out in support of Barth's protest and against the
church administrators who so blithely took for granted that the gospel
was being preached adequately. But his polemic against the false self-

understanding of modern man which stemmed from the Renaissance and from Schleiermacher, and against Christian socialism, was much sharper and more sustained than any criticism of the church.

Barth struck again at the problem in an address which he delivered in Berlin, Bremen, and Hamburg in January and February, 1931, on " The Dilemma of the Evangelical Church." [5] Otto Dibelius replied for the church administration within nine days of the Berlin meeting in an address which was immediately printed and circulated.[6] It is important to note that Barth was engaged in a public debate with the church authorities concerning their imperilment of the church by their blindness to realities and their indifference to doctrinal issues a full two years before the controversy over the nazification of the church broke out.

First he pointed to the permanent dilemma of an evangelical church, from which it cannot ask to escape, which distinguishes it from the confident Roman Church, and which prevents it from making any confident claims for itself. It must always be the church under the cross. " The crucified Christ is the God who has humbled himself in the profoundest depths of human being, in the death of the criminal who was decisively expelled by the human community." He is Lord of the church only as the crucified, as the one who has ever to come to his sinful church from without and as to his enemies. Never can his presence be taken for granted by the church as its immanent principle. In each moment the sinful church becomes the true church only by God's free act of forgiveness. It has no possibility of serving man except by serving God and confronting man with the will of God that destroys all man's self-security. An evangelical church is not the Kingdom of God on earth, not a continuation of the revelation and reconciliation achieved in Christ, not the repeater of Christ's sacrifice, but only the *servant* of God's work. The church is visible only as God makes it visible. Even a great united world church would not necessarily have visible unity. Christ is not at our disposal. Therefore, the church can only seek its visible unity and can never count itself to have found it. There are signs of it in preaching, prayer, Sacraments, theological confessions, home and foreign missions, witness in life, but only signs. An evangelical church has only as promise what the Roman Church claims as reality. In philosophical terms, it lacks the synthesis that the Roman Church claims to possess. At the point of synthesis it stands with empty hands. This dilemma it must embrace as the necessary condition of its existence.

The second dilemma in which the church's very existence is threatened is not necessary but arises only when the first is not recognized. It belongs only to the church which has forgotten that it is under the cross. One as-

pect of it is a flight from the visibility of the church. Barth detected this
error in men such as Tillich and remembered it as a characteristic of his
own idealism in student days.[7] The painful contradiction between what
the church claims to be and what it is, between ideal substance and actual
form, impels men to flight. They long for " the invisible church! Free
church! Church of the Spirit! " Another aspect is the very opposite, a demand for visibility, and this was now the greater problem. The postwar
era was characterized by a realism that emphasized the visible and concrete. The current demand was for a religious organization that could
give moral and spiritual leadership. Realism was making itself felt in both
philosophy and theology, and in society in general it was producing a demand for ordinances, discipline, subordination of the individual to the
whole, an emphasis upon destiny and community, an emulation of Roman Catholic order, and an affirmation of the physical body.

It was the second error that was responsible for the most recent developments in the church. It had taken over uncritically the slogans of the
realists — destiny, social necessity, history, reality, community, givenness,
corporeality. The constant cry was for the church to have character and
will to action, but there was no facing of the theological question: what the
church must be to be true to its nature. Press releases by the administration, Sunday church papers, mass conferences, and published sermons, all
gave no indication that the church was in any dilemma but on the contrary radiated the most incredible self-assurance: " We have the gospel.
We are the Christians." The sinners were all outside and the church, unconscious of its own sin, was terribly preoccupied with the sin and unbelief of the outsiders. It took man's sin much more seriously than God's
grace. If it really had the gospel, it would know that man's sin and unbelief are forgiven in Jesus Christ and would set the forgiveness of sin
in the forefront of its message. Instead of this, it was preaching ideals,
that is, laws, and human ideals and laws at that. Even God's law should
be proclaimed only in the context of the gospel. It was only too obvious
that the primary concern of the church was for its own power and influence, its security against the state, its influence in the schools, its power
over society and particularly over the masses. How a church under the
cross could cherish such power was not even asked. But most preaching
in the church had no crucified Christ at its center but rather a mysticism
flavored with moralism or a moralism flavored with mysticism. Finally
came an accusation that was soon to make all the others pale into insig-
nificance, the accusation that in the church Christianity and German nationalism were being welded together into a unity which so pervaded the
oral and printed utterances of the church that their union was becoming

the real criterion of ecclesiastical orthodoxy. "All manner of heresies are permitted as long as one is orthodox on this point."

The answer of Dibelius to Barth was weak in the extreme. He dismissed Barth as a theologian moving in the realm of theory while he himself was a practical churchman. As a Swiss, Barth naturally lacked the national sentiment that would make one sympathetic to the union of Christianity with German nationalism. The repentance for sin and failure that Barth demanded of the church belonged in the inner chamber before God and not in the open before the world. Dibelius spent most of his time demonstrating the need for a concrete program in the church, which Barth had not challenged, and ignored completely the question of the church's indifference to the vital theological issue concerning its substance. He ended on the complacent note that in a world without hope or love we have a church in which with one another we can hope, love, and rejoice. Not yet had Dibelius come awake to the nationalist peril. This was the mind of the official church, and in a large degree of the actual church, just two years before the confrontation with national socialism was to put it to an ultimate test and ruthlessly expose its fatal weaknesses. If theology is Ezekiel's watchman on the wall of the city, charged with the task of warning the city of its danger before it is too late, then Barth must be credited with having been such a faithful watchman in 1931, and we must ask why so many of his colleagues were silent in that hour.

2. THE BASIS OF COMPROMISE

The political tragedy of Germany was that social democracy secured its first opportunity in the German scene when it replaced the monarchy in the postwar period and immediately had to grapple with the confusion of a nation broken by defeat in war, with an inflation that impoverished wide sections of the middle and upper classes, and at the same time with the intransigeance of Germany's enemies which prevented an economic recovery. Then in 1929 came the American stock-market collapse which triggered a worldwide depression, with serious consequences for Germany. Twelve years after the close of the war at least ten million of the population were living on the edge of starvation. Only a small percentage of university graduates could secure work. Social democracy was held responsible for the inability of the nation to meet and overcome its problems. The " good old days " of the monarchy were remembered with nostalgia. Nationalism, always strong both in the universities and among the clergy, had its opportunity. By 1932, under the leadership of Hitler, it was on its way to political dominance, promising a restoration of internal health and strength and a recovery by Germany of its proper place in the international sphere.

Barth had made the acquaintance of nationalism in its alliance with Christian theology long before. It was this that in 1914 disillusioned him concerning the theology of his former teachers and mentors, awakening him to the peril of a cultural Christianity that in an hour of crisis could sell its soul to a national culture and its political interests. He met the nationalist theologian again when in 1921 in Göttingen he was associated with the Kierkegaardian scholar, Emanuel Hirsch, who was a fanatical nationalist and was later to become a devoted Nazi. All through the years a primary concern for Barth had been the establishment of theology upon a basis and under an authority that would make impossible such a compromise with a national culture in any form. The compromise he found always to be based upon a natural revelation of some kind which was admitted alongside the revelation of God in Jesus Christ. For Hirsch, it was the revelation of God in the human conscience that became the validation of what the German conscience demanded of the German people. For others, it was the revelation of God in history or in nature or natural law that was essential to the health of the social order. But always these natural revelations which became the bases of a natural theology were the divine validations of an order in life that men considered essential but for which they could find no authority in the Christian revelation of God's will for man. The effect of natural theology, therefore, was to protect some area of human interest from the judgment of the word of God. But to be protected from God's judgment was to be deprived of the promise of his grace and abandoned to destruction. This was the concern which made Barth suspicious of all natural theology, even in its most reduced form. Man in all his life, and especially in his national and cultural life, can be open unconditionally to the grace of God only when he abandons all his human defenses, including the ultimate defense of his values in a natural theology, and lets himself and his whole world stand unconditionally under the judgment of God's word in Jesus Christ. Only then is he free of the infinitely subtle peril of subordinating his Christianity, his Christ, his God, to the interests of his national culture. (Here let the English and American theologians for whom the negation of natural theology is an irrational absurdity take note of what was at stake in the German scene.)

Against this background the developments in Gogarten's theology during these years become highly significant. Social democracy was for him one of the products of the idealistic and humanistic self-understanding of modern man that had been responsible for the perversion of theology, philosophy, culture, and life in general. It encouraged every man in an individualism that made him think himself a sovereign and so disrupted the bonds that held society together. The elimination of the idealistic self-understanding would carry with it the elimination of social democracy. What would take its place was not clearly defined. Man would renounce his individualism and submit himself to the community, subordinating all his interests to its welfare. He would recognize in the claim of his neighbor upon him the claim of God himself. This became a focal point in the thinking of Gogarten. On the basis of Matt., ch. 25, response to the neighbor was interpreted as the basic response to Jesus Christ and so to God. The decision for or against the neighbor was the decision for or against God. Bultmann published an article on this in French in 1930 and Gogarten one in *Zwischen den Zeiten* in the same year.[8] Gogarten defined history as something that happens between men as one responds to the other. Man divorced from his interrelation with others becomes a mythical being and thinks of himself as transcending history. Mutual involvement is man's original being, and recognition of Jesus as Being-for-the-other brings with it the recognition of ourselves as being-against-the-other. On the surface this sounds very Christian, but in the context of a repudiation of social democracy and a friendliness toward a reviving authoritarian nationalism, it could encourage Christians to identify the claim of the neighbor and thus the claim of God with the claim upon him of the new national community and its order.

Bultmann's essay has points of contact with Gogarten's, such as the definition of man's being as being-with-each-other and of ethical action as response to the claim of the " Thou " upon the " I," as well as the identification of socialist ethics with the individualistic tradition which, stemming from Greece, reaches the modern world through the Enlightenment. The concept of man as a master who shapes his own life and seeks to establish a cosmos is set over against the Hebrew and Christian recognition of man's inescapable involvement with his neighbor, a relation in which he ever hears an authoritative command and either obeys or rebels. Philosophical ethics can do no more than describe the formal structure of ethical action. It can show that the decision about what is to be done can only be made by me, but it cannot tell me what to do. That can be known only by the individual in his immediate relation with the " Thou." Love of the neighbor is not entirely new in Christianity. In Seneca it is regarded as necessary for the completion of human virtue, an element in the self-fulfillment toward which *erōs* ever strives. But Christian *agapē* which gives and does not desire demands a revolution in the life-direction of the natural man who seeks to free himself from the "Thou" and to assert himself against the "Thou." Christian love demands self-conquest. But no man can decide to love in this way. Only in knowing oneself loved does loving become a possibility. Only in relation to the love of God does mistrust and self-assertion become impossible. But "I can believe in the love of God only when it is real and meets me in the history in which I stand" (242). It alone can free me from my lovelessness and hatred by forgiving it. Therefore, the possibility of Christian love lies in the hearing of the word of God in which God in his love forgives my sins and frees me to love both him and my neighbor. Love of the neighbor is inseparable from love toward God. We know ourselves as bound together in the same situation as our neighbors, as sinners like them and as forgiven in Christ like them. We cannot upon the basis of love work out a Christian ethic that will tell us what to do or not to do on all occasions. But the love that lays us open to the claim of the neighbor upon us tells us what to do in the concrete situation, since in our self-love we know what we would want done to us.

The one point of weakness in this exposition of the ethical situation is the assumption that in the confrontation with the neighbor the Christian in whom love has been engendered by the forgiving love of God will know what to do for his neighbor by knowing what he wants for himself. Gogarten, operating on a formula similar to this, was convinced that loving his neighbor demanded of him that he cooperate with his neighbor in the creation of a sovereign state which would put an end to the anarchy of idealistic individualism and open a new future for Germany. The word of God has been too much narrowed in its significance here to be merely the word that brings forgiveness, with no mention of the commands that it contains for the man who has been forgiven. God's word does not leave him to deduce from his own self-love what he must do for his neighbor but spells out very specifically the nature of a true obedience to God in all the relationships of life.

Gogarten had also been interested for some time in evolving a doctrine of "ordinances of creation." This was the discovery of evidences of God's will in the nature of the created order. The physical and mental characteristics of man and woman in their distinctiveness were taken to indicate God's will for them, providing an ethical foundation for family life and the order of the home. In a similar fashion the existence of different nations and races was seen as divinely ordained. One can at once see the danger of such a doctrine in any situation where nations or races stand in conflict with one another.

Gogarten endeavored to take account of the phenomenon of nationalism

in two essays published in 1932. In the first, on " State and Church," [9] he
found promise in the fact that the nationalist movement was showing a
passionate concern about its relation to religion and the church. He deprecated any criticism which suggested that this concern was motivated by
a desire to use the church politically and he made the curious statement
that in some of its forms nationalism is itself religious — as though that
were a hopeful feature! The relation to religion is basic to it and whether
or not it leads to a new and genuine state will depend upon the healthi-
ness of the relation to religion, a healthful relation being defined as one
that will do justice to both partners. The new state is envisaged as having
power over the life and possessions of its subjects. Such power must have
a religious basis if it is not to become brutal. Gogarten in his opposition
to social democracy as an expression of the bourgeois state, a society of individuals ruled by the will of the majority, desired such power for the
state. He was critical, however, of those who sought a relation of church
and state based on the national existence, which could only lead to a
" German Christianity." The church stands or falls with its confession of
the crucified and risen Lord, but " German Christianity " with its faith
in German man and in racial uniqueness is only another version of the liberal faith in man as man.

The point of relation between church and state for Gogarten lay in the
fact that each manifests a sovereignty. The church is not a society for spiritual purposes but the place where God's sovereignty is revealed and man
has his *eternal* origin. The crucified and risen Lord deposes the powers of
sin and death which deceive man and which make him think himself sovereign, so that God may have his true sovereignty over man. Sin and death
have their power only by concealing their basic lie " in all the splendor
of ethical knowledge and the shining promise of a full life," but the cross
strips away the concealment. The state, similarly, is not a society of individuals but a sovereign power to which man owes his *earthly* existence.
Because it sustains its subjects and gives them their life, it has the right
to power over them. Gogarten was careful in his rejection of the modern
liberal democratic state, as a product of modern culture that makes the
individual autonomous and identifies his spirit with God, to exempt science and religion from the control of the power state. They must stay
free or the state will dig its own grave. The state must not touch the
place where man's soul stands directly before the eternal truth. Gogarten
thus established two separate sovereignties, one valid for man's *eternal* life
and the other for his *earthly* life. The sovereignty of the state is analogous
to the sovereignty of God, being the source of man's earthly existence as
God is the source of his eternal existence, man in both instances having

lost his right or claim to any benefit by his involvement in evil. The word "honor" signifies the existence man receives from the state, since honor alone lets earthly goods be good and the state restrains evil by giving or withholding honor even more than by the power of the sword. The state, however, is always tempted to make honor an eternal good and to seek an eternal sovereignty over man, over his soul and conscience. In the face of this threat the church must assert the sovereignty of God and so restrain the state. But, as anyone looking back can see, the church had already lost the battle with the state in Gogarten's theological definitions in having the sovereignty of God limited to an "eternal" realm in the life of man that could be marked off with such facility from his "earthly" life. The Lordship of Jesus Christ over the whole of life was here specifically denied and the door opened wide for the Nazi state, with only a warning to the nationalists not to go too far.

The second article, on "Creation and National Life" (*Volkstum*),[10] laid the theological foundation for nationalism from another angle. A German missionary, Siegfried Knak, in an earlier article had drawn attention to the parallel between the revival of the folk consciousness in mission lands and the development of nationalism in Germany. Both involve a recognition of organic distinctions in humanity that originate in the divine creation. Anglo-Americanism (a new name for the modern liberal individualistic mentality), however, threatens to dissolve all such distinctions in order to create a unified humanity. Gogarten wished to restate Knak's case with more carefully guarded theological definitions. Faith in God the Creator cannot be separated from faith in Jesus Christ. The Creator is not simply evident in the givenness of things. Creation is inseparable from redemption and sanctification and the three denote three sides of God's relation to us. But to belong to God is to stand under his law, and there is a threefold meaning of his law to correspond to the three sides of his relation to us. Our life in this world is the gift of the Creator, our redemption comes to us from the Redeemer and our sanctification from the Holy Spirit. But in each we come under the law which claims from us a total response in love to God and to our neighbor.

God as Creator gives us our life in this world in a particular form, and in obedience to him we dare not distort that form. Nationality belongs to this order of creation as an original bond of certain men to each other from which they draw their common life. It creates them rather than being their creation. They belong not to themselves but to their nation, and the law in which the nation makes its claim upon them is analogous to the law of God in creation. This law of the nation expresses itself in "folk customs" such as those which in an earlier Germany gave order and discipline to village life but have now been lost in industrial towns where each man is his own master in accordance with a liberal ethic. By such customs, men who belong together sustain one another. Man's true being is that he belongs not to himself but to his neighbors and draws his life from them. When he wants to be something for himself, he is evil, even though what he does is good. Gogarten concluded with a warning against making the nation an idol, but the warning is ironic coming as it does after he himself, having begun by defining the law of the nation as analogous to the law of God, has moved on to an identification of the national will with God's will (503).

In the light of these two articles it is not surprising that Gogarten for a time made common cause with the German Christians whose aim was to coordinate the Christian churches with the Nazi state. He was quite aware of the dangers inherent in an alliance of Christianity with nationalism, but his own national sentiment blinded him to the extent to which he himself was providing a theological justification for a disastrous compromise of the church's existence. He was so engrossed in the negative task of eliminating from theology and culture, which meant from church and state, every trace of the old idealistic-humanistic self-understanding and all its products that he was unaware how by his neglect of an adequate dogmatic reconstruction he had left a vacuum even in his own thinking which drew in a pagan self-understanding. It was a perfect exemplification of the house in Jesus' parable from which one demon was expelled but, being left empty, attracted seven much more evil demons.

In May, 1933, Hitler and the Nazi Party having captured control of the German government, Bultmann opened his course in the summer semester with some remarks on the situation of theology in the new Germany, to which he later gave a wider circulation by printing them in a theological journal.[11] Having observed the theological alliance between Gogarten and Bultmann during the preceding years, we are naturally anxious to know how Bultmann responded to the challenge of nationalism. Two things should be made clear at once: that Bultmann was consistently averse throughout his life to mixing in political matters,[12] and that in contrast to Gogarten, he had nothing to do with the notorious "German Christians," standing instead with the Confessional Church which so stubbornly resisted all interference of the Nazis in church affairs. Nevertheless, his remarks in "The Task of Theology in the Present Situation" show disturbing parallels to the thinking of Gogarten and would not be likely to build any significant barriers against the rising tide of totalitarian nationalism.

First, he disassociated himself both from the enthusiasts for nationalism and from the severe critics of it (such as Barth). His purpose was neither affirmation of the political events nor " to give voice to a sceptical or resentful criticism." What he attempted to do, rather, was to lay a theological foundation for Christians to cooperate in the development of the new nation while at the same time retaining a basis from which to criticize undesirable features of it. His approach was by way of the doctrine of creation and ordinances of creation. " The relation of God to the world and therefore of faith to life in the world, and thus to political life, is a peculiarly two-sided one." This prepares us for a balancing of two sovereignties such as we observed in Gogarten, one based upon the ordinances of creation which include one's nation, and the other upon Jesus Christ. Bultmann posited an " encounter with God " in the concrete situation of the moment in history. " That God is the Creator means that he encounters us as Lord in our concrete world, in the world that is determined historically in our actual life in the present. . . . That God is the Creator means that man's action (as obedience to our Lord) is not determined by timeless principles, but rather by the concrete situation of the moment." The factors that give concreteness to the situation are nationality, sex, youth or age, strength or weakness, cleverness or dumbness, etc. What Jesus Christ has to do with this encounter with God in the concrete situation is nowhere made clear. The way is left open for the historical moment of Germany's rebirth under Hitler to be interpreted as an encounter with God the Creator. " Faith in God and nationality stand in a positive relation insofar as God has placed us in our nation and state." Submission to the state is one's destiny. Here again as in Gogarten the teaching that response to the claim of the neighbor upon us is response to God comes into play. Faith in God the Creator demands of us that we let our existence be determined by others, that we be responsible for the common future, that we receive our very selves from others and thus be able to sacrifice ourselves for others in return. One is reminded here of how in the 1917 sermon Bultmann found a revelation of God in the tragic events of war.

Bultmann, however, could not stop at this point. Thus far his statement could and would be interpreted as a religious (not Christian but religious, since Jesus Christ did not enter into consideration but only God the Creator) endorsement of the nationalist development. He was quite aware that this would constitute a betrayal of Christian theology and of the church. He therefore proceeded to develop the second side of God's relation to the life of the world, based on the transcendence of God to all that is given in the world's life. God cannot be regarded as immanent in the ordinances of creation. " Nothing that encounters us as a phenomenon within the world is *directly* divine. God stands beyond the world." God is the world's judge as well as its creator so that faith must be critical in relation to the world as well as affirmative. The ordinances of creation are ambiguous in their meaning, being perverted into ordinances of sin by man's understanding of himself as lord of his own life. The nation, the family, and all the orders of life become sinful. Here one can see Bultmann preparing the way for the preservation of a critical stance in relation to the new state. " No nation is so pure and clean that one may interpret every stirring of the national will as a direct demand of God." " In a day when the nation has again been generally recognized as an ordinance of creation, the Christian faith has to prove its critical power precisely by continuing to insist that the nation is ambiguous." Obedience to it as an ordinance must be accompanied by a questioning of what it should demand. At this point comes the assertion which would have been more effective four pages earlier in the definition of man's encounter with God in the concrete moment of history: " Only he who knows the transcendent God who speaks his word of love to the world in Christ is able to extricate himself from this sinful world and to achieve a perspective from which the world's ordinances can really be known as ordinances of creation. . . . He alone has a critical perspective over against the loud demands of the day, in that he measures the good and evil in such demands by asking whether and to what extent they serve the command to love. . . . The only man who can truly serve his nation is he who has been freed to love by receiving the love of God in Christ." The criterion of conduct in relation to the state must be the love of one's neighbor. Applying that criterion, Bultmann deprecated rash changes that were being made, the insidious evil of denouncing neighbors to the government, the defamation of the character of opponents, and the injury being done to the Jews. He ended with an appeal to " keep the struggle for the German nation pure " and to guard against falsifications of the Christian faith by the confusion of it with a nationalistic religiosity.

One has to respect Bultmann's attempt to preserve a critical stance in the midst of the flood of nationalism. In 1933 he spoke out boldly denouncing the law that expelled Jews or persons married to Jews from the ministry of the church.[13] But at the same time it is only too evident that his encouragement of the concept of ordinances of creation in which God somehow reveals his will apart from Jesus Christ was a strong assist to Gogarten and others who were seeking a theological validation for their nationalism. Surely Barth was right when he branded this doctrine of ordinances of creation, in which not only Bultmann and Gogarten but also Brunner was strongly interested,[14] as a new version of natural revelation and natural theology by means of which men were seeking a divine validation for the order of life that seemed to them to have in it the highest value. It is plainly to be seen that in 1933 this doctrine neutralized for both Gogarten and Bultmann the power of the word of God in Jesus Christ (which their theology claimed to serve) to bring the whole nationalistic development in church and state under God's ruthless judgment and expose it as a peril not only to the church but to humanity. Natural revelation alongside the revelation of God in Jesus Christ means inevitably a compromise between the authority of God and the authority of man.

3. The "Dogmatics" of 1932

The most practical thing that Barth could find to do in the increasingly tense and perilous situation of 1932 was to launch afresh his project in the reconstruction of dogmatics in a much more massive form than in 1927. He was aware that it was a daring, some would say a foolhardy, thing to do at such a moment in the church's life and that he would be accused of offering dogmatic stones to people who were in urgent need of prophetic bread. But it was his way of indicating the depth and character of the dilemma in which the church found itself. This was no superficial skin disease to be lightly healed but a " sickness unto death." The crisis of the moment had merely laid bare the extent to which the very foundations of the church had over the years been gradually destroyed. The church's dilemma was the product of confusion about the nature of the faith to which it was committed, a confusion that permitted false doctrines to run riot in the church. So deep was the confusion that there was no hope of escape from it except by a return of theology to its indispensable critical task on behalf of the church, of constantly submitting all things in the life of the church, but particularly in its message, to the most thorough scrutiny under the criterion of the word of God in Jesus Christ. This should be the sole determiner of the church's faith and life. And since this was the only way of promise out of the dilemma, then the most practical action in the current situation was to go steadily forward with the construction of such a critical dogmatics. Soon, however, in 1933 Barth was to supplement this massive project with a succession of pamphlets [15] which were distributed in the thousands and in which he and others spoke directly to the situation of the moment, but always making clear that every problem confronting the church was a problem of faith versus unbelief and therefore at root a theological problem.

In the foreword to the volume Barth stated the reasons that prompted him to begin again at the beginning and rewrite the first volume of his

dogmatics, even as he had rewritten his " Romans " ten years earlier. Colleagues as close to him as Gogarten, Bultmann, and Brunner had not
rightly understood him in 1927, so that he was determined to say everything more sharply and to define his differences from them more plainly
in order to remove as far as he could the possibility of misunderstanding.
The shifts that had taken place not only in theology and the church but
also in the general situation called for a fresh approach. Moreover, he
had lived and thought for seven more years and could no longer say the
same things in the same way. The bird in flight had moved on and a new
description could not merely repeat the old. More room was needed for
the elaboration of the Biblical and theological presuppositions, to trace
out the historical connections and to indicate the polemical relations, making the new volume grow to more than three times the size of the old.
The new volume had also a new name, " Church Dogmatics " instead
of " Christian Dogmatics," expressing the conviction that dogmatics is
a science that is possible only within the church. Barth's desire to dis-
associate himself from his former colleagues came to expression most
forcefully in his warning against his book's being regarded as the dogmatics of a school of dialectical theology. The only colleague to whom he
still felt himself close was Thurneysen.

The change that holds most interest for us is the clearing away of all
that had the appearance of a basing of the dogmatics on existential philosophy. Existentialism had never entered far into the substance of Barth's
thinking but had been used by him chiefly as indicating philosophical
parallels to the theological phenomena. The existential terminology could
be stripped away without any effect whatsoever upon the basic theological structure. One has to remember how close Barth's association was
in the earlier twenties, not only with Bultmann and Gogarten who were
captured by existentialist philosophy, but also with his own brother, Heinrich, who was an existentialist philosopher. Also, in the twenties the air
was thick with the terminology of existentialism. Indeed, there was a valid
Christian concern to be recognized in existentialism, the involvement of
one's own existence in one's thinking about God and man and the impossibility of maintaining a spectator attitude. But it was not necessary
to become an existentialist to recognize the validity of this insight.

What caused most misunderstanding in 1927 was Barth's introduction
of the terms " phenomenological " and " existential." It had seemed to him
that, in beginning with the church's human speech concerning God, his
approach was phenomenological (by which he meant, rather inexactly,
that it was from an objective spectator standpoint) but that at a certain
point he was making a transition to an existential way of thinking (by

which he meant only that he was recognizing his self-involvement in the statements). Th. Siegfried [16] had attacked him for basing his theology on existentialist philosophy while Gogarten had criticized him [17] severely for adopting an existentialist approach and failing to carry it through effectively. Both had misunderstood his intention. So now he swept away every trace of existentialist terminology, declaring that the concepts "phenomenological" and "existential" have no place in a theological development and that they were quite unnecessary in 1927 for what he wanted to say. He now asserted that the first section of the book was not at all from a spectator standpoint. "It would have been fatal if in the earlier part we had not thought and spoken as those whose existence was involved in the things." Nor would it have been possible really to make a transition from a spectator attitude to one of involvement. We have no control over our own involvement. We always see things from *both* outside and inside.

A second concession to existentialism, which showed a larger degree of confusion in 1927, occurred in sections five, six, and seven of the 1927 "Dogmatics," where Barth attempted to deduce the essential nature of the word of God from an analysis of the concrete situation of man as preacher and hearer of the word, who in preaching and hearing possesses a knowledge of the word. The analysis in each section was followed by statements about the word which had the appearance of being conclusions drawn from the analysis. But now Barth recognized that these statements had their basis elsewhere than in the analyses, and indeed could not validly be reached in the attempted fashion. The offending sections were therefore eliminated in 1932 and the essential content included in two earlier sections. In discussing these changes, Barth makes the statement that he was "on the way to a real anthropology in 1927," which gives the impression that he was then moving in the direction of an alignment with Bultmann and Gogarten in their anthropological project. But our examination of the literature of the period has shown that for some time before 1927 he had been determinedly asserting in contrast to Bultmann and Gogarten that theology must be focused on the word to which faith responds rather than on the faith of man which responds to the word. No concessions that he made to existentialism in language or approach ever touched or endangered this basic decision.

Barth at several points made clear at least a few of the reasons for the repudiation of his former colleagues. Gogarten, in his development of an anthropology and in making it central to theology, was allowing an apologetic concern to take precedence over the urgent need of the church for dogmatic clarification.[18] Because the humanism of modern man involved him in a false self-understanding, Gogarten was demanding that the construction of a Christian anthropology should be made primary. But, answered Barth, theology dare not let its questions be set for it by the world; it must begin, rather, with what it hears when it is questioned by the word of God in the concrete situation of the present in the church. Gogarten professed to be starting from the incarnation, but it was the *man* whose life has been determined by the word of God with whom he began rather than with Christ as *God* become man. Gogarten held that man's understanding of himself was dependent upon revelation, but he began with a revelation in the created order and not with revelation in the gospel, and on this basis made man's self-understanding precede the understanding of God. How, then, could Gogarten's claim to reject natural theology be valid if he recognized a revelation of God in the created order? In a Reformation theology, the revelation of God in his creation is concealed by man's sin and an anthropology can only be a demonstration of man's true nature as revealed in Jesus Christ and of his corrupt nature in antithesis to the true. Gogarten had called for a philosophical clarification of concepts, by which he meant the purging from man's self-understanding of all false elements, as a preliminary to theological thinking. Barth regarded this as a project which, even if it were desirable, would not be feasible. Man comes to a right understanding of himself only as he comes to a right understanding of God. Revelation at one and the same time reveals both God and man. Therefore the clarification of concepts can take place only in the fulfillment of the dogmatic investigation. Barth also rejected Gogarten's existentialist elimination of the subject-object relation. Gogarten spoke of the event of revelation as though in it God's relation to man and man's relation to God become so merged that neither can any longer be conceived apart from the other. He had criticized Barth for transgressing this principle. Barth agreed that man must never be spoken of in isolation from God, but he insisted that God *must* at times be spoken of in isolation from man. God's existence must not be conceived as consisting only of his relation with us and as being comprehended entirely in his revelatory speech with us. The word of God must first have its own truth and glory. God must be free to speak it or not to speak it. To eliminate subject and object in the concept of the word of God as Gogarten did was to compromise and limit the freedom of God.

Bultmann was included in several of the criticisms of Gogarten but received special attention for his provision of a philosophical foundation for Christian theology.[19] Methodologically, because of his philosophical pre-understanding, Barth placed him in line with Schleiermacher. Philosophy for Bultmann was able to demonstrate objectively the possibility of faith and to provide criteria for the correction of a science of faith. The assumption was that an existential-ontological or formal knowledge of all human reality, including the realities involved in faith, is open to philosophical, that is, rational comprehension, while the *ontic-existentiell,* or inner content of these realities, alone remains hidden and known only to faith. The philosopher can define with exactness all the possibilities of human existence even though the inner reality remains beyond his comprehension. But in defining possibilities he defines limits. Faith he describes as " a way in which human existence is historical." The nature of dogmatic knowledge thus is defined not by dogmatics but by philosophy. The church becomes a human possibility rather than possible only through a divine act. The introduction of an alien philosophic criterion not only limits but contradicts the authority of the word of God for theology.

Apart from the small changes that have been mentioned, the general structure of the " Dogmatics " of 1932 corresponds closely with the structure of that of 1927. In fact a reader who is familiar with the 1932 edition may be perplexed when he later reads the 1927 volume to say precisely what is different, beyond the added historical and controversial sections. The basic thinking seems to be the same, and in the more concise form of 1927 is easier to see in its unity. Von Balthazar is justified in his comment on the 1927 volume that " by its brevity and concentration, by the beauty and forcefulness of its language and by the positive and unpolemical character of its presentation, it remains one of the best introductions to the thinking of Karl Barth." [20] Von Balthazar, however, has given currency to the idea that there was an important transition in Barth's theology between 1927 and 1932, from dialectic to analogy, and this has been repeated and interpreted by others as though Barth abandoned the use of dialectic and in its place developed an analogical mode of thinking. The fact of the matter is that analogy plays a part in his thinking very early, long before 1927, and that dialectic is so intrinsic to his concept of how man thinks about God that its abandonment would have meant the scrapping of the whole of the earlier structure and the development of an entirely new methodology. What is true is that dialectic and paradox become less obvious and analogy becomes more prominent.

It lies beyond the bounds of this study to follow Barth and Bultmann through the years of the German Church conflict and of the Nazi state. Our limited concern has been to trace the course followed by each of them during the first quarter century of their theological development, since only against this background can we rightly understand the later developments in their theologies which have created such an enormous division in the theological world.

Chapter XI

THE FINAL ISSUE

OUR INTEREST has been in seeing what brought Barth and Bultmann together and what it was that sent them apart so decisively and deeply that the cleft between them has become a paralyzing division in the structure of modern theology. The survey of their writings has not been all-inclusive. The focus has been upon the theological issues, and because Barth's concern from the beginning has been primarily that of a systematic theologian, whereas Bultmann's has been primarily that of a critical literary and historical scholar, more of Barth's publications than of Bultmann's have received attention. Bultmann's major work, *The History of the Synoptic Tradition,* and the essays that he began to publish in the twenties in preparation for his commentary on the Gospel according to St. John had little contribution to make to the discussion of theological issues which has been our concern.

Full account must be taken of this distinction between the two men. There is an unbroken continuity in Bultmann's participation in the work of the " history of religion " school in New Testament scholarship. Theologically, he revolted against the mysticism of a Bousset and the immanentalism of a Johannes Weiss but in his critical judgments and in his reconstruction of the development of early Christianity he could perhaps be called a typical representative of the school. He shares its ruthless determination to let the facts be what objective research shows them to be and to make no judgments about the theological content of a document until full cognizance has been taken of the influence of contemporary religious forces upon its concepts. He also shares with his colleagues in the same school the conviction that in the work of New Testament authors he can and must distinguish between that which witnesses to the eternal kerygma and that which belongs only to the transitory conceptuality of the age. Whether or not one agrees with this latter point, one has to recognize the magnitude and importance of Bultmann's contribution to historical and literary scholarship. He saw that tradition endangered by Barth's subordination of the historical to the theological concern, which in some quarters led men to disparage the importance of historical and critical research and to act as though they could extract the theological content directly from the Biblical text.

A valid criticism of Barth through the years is that he never seems to have recognized the *theological* necessity of a thoroughly historical and critical understanding of Scripture in the church if men are to be free to hear what the text really says. It is significant that in the Roman Catholic Church the encyclical which twenty-five years ago liberated critical scholarship has set bishops and laymen alike free to give their obedience to the word of the gospel in a way that is already transforming many aspects of the church's life. It is completely unfair to accuse Barth of negating the work of historical criticism. He has always recognized its validity as a preparatory discipline. But in separating the historical from the theological so sharply and setting all emphasis upon the theological, he has contributed, perhaps unintentionally, to the divided mind of modern theology. The theological and the historical elements are so intertwined in the text of the Scriptures that in their interpretation the historical and the theological questions must be considered constantly in the closest interrelation.

While Bultmann has been mainly occupied with the work of historical criticism, and with theological issues only as the outcome of his recognition that the ultimate content of Scripture is a unique revelation of God, Barth has from the beginning been a systematic theologian who published his commentaries on New Testament books because as a theologian he discovered a revelational content in those books which was being overlooked by critical commentators. There is a breadth and depth in his theological writings that one cannot expect in those of Bultmann. By 1917 he had moved out of continuity with the Schleiermacher-Ritschl tradition of the nineteenth and early twentieth centuries, with a full consciousness of what he was rejecting, while Bultmann even by 1920 had only a vague consciousness of a new theological era beginning. It took the stimulus of Barth's 1922 "Romans" and the influence of two philosophers, Kierkegaard and Heidegger, to set Bultmann on his way as a theologian and to break in some degree his continuity with the liberal theology of the past. But there are no writings in which Bultmann consciously clarifies the issues involved in that break, to correspond with Barth's detailed evaluation of his relation with earlier theologies. In line with this is the fact that Bultmann has not let himself be drawn into discussion of his theological differences with Barth, while Barth for forty years has debated the theological consequences of positions taken by Bultmann.

There has not been much movement in Bultmann's theology since he adopted his basic standpoint in the twenties, only elaborations of the standpoint. Jaspers, after meeting him in the twenties, complained of a rocklike immovability. He tends to absolutize a principle. Nowhere is this more evident than in the significance for him of Kierkegaard's infinite qualitative difference between eternity and time which issues in his thought in a rigid separation between history and eschatology, between this world and the Beyond, and makes him deny the possibility both of the word of God becoming flesh and of history having an eschatological goal. He has much to say of openness to the future as the very essence of faith, but one may ask whether his theology is not robbed of its mobility by this abandonment of the futurist element in eschatology and by this tendency to regard certain principles as fixed and final, not even to be discussed. This rigidity is perhaps Bultmann's primary contribution to the divided mind of modern theology. At this point the contrast with Barth is striking. Barth's eschatological perspective has relativized all theologies including his own. Because God is a living God he is constantly moving on beyond us in his dealings with our world, hastening toward his goal. We have to be ready and willing to move with him. The goal of the entire movement has already been revealed in Jesus Christ, but that gives us no final answers to our theological questions. Rather, it sets us in motion toward the goal in response to the promise of God that we have heard in Christ. We can never take possession of the word of God in our theologizing because to possess it would be to have mastered God himself in our human categories, which would be the ultimate blasphemy. The outcome of this is that Barth's theology has been constantly in motion, not like a ship sailing before the wind but more like a ship tacking against the wind. There is no arbitrariness in his movement. We have seen him at twenty-eight begin his first revolt against the theology of his teachers and then at thirty-four revolt with equal severity against the theology of his own first publication. While others were still trying to decipher the language of his 1922 " Romans," he was beginning to free himself from certain elements in Kierkegaard's existentialism which had captured Bultmann and Gogarten. At the end of the twenties he was using Anselm to clarify the basic problem of how theology is possible, in order to prepare the way for a second start on his " Dogmatics." Theology for him requires an unconditional openness to what God is saying *now* in the human situation. Because God and the human situation are both in

constant movement, a theology that absolutizes anything in its own structure is unfaithful to its task.

Where Barth and Bultmann went apart theologically stands out plainly
in their writings. Were we to move beyond 1933 we would trace the full
consequences of their separation and see how it has split modern theology
into two streams. Our concern has been to get at the source of the division.
And there the judgment of theologians as to which of the two took the
wrong turning will vary. But there can be no question about the character of the issue. Shall theology be based on the word to which faith responds or shall it be based on the faith which responds to the word? Here
two roads divide. On the first, theology is possible as a knowledge of God
that has within it the only true knowledge of man. On the second, theology is possible only in the form of statements about the self-understanding of man which has been determined by God and it becomes difficult
to prevent theology becoming no more than anthropology and soteriology.
It is perhaps significant that as yet no dogmatics has been produced on
the basis of Bultmann's theology, and he himself may regard that as no
misfortune for the church. But the question of truth posed for us by these
two theologies cannot be evaded without deepening the division, the schiz-
ophrenia, in the mind of modern theology. Theology for the sake of its
own and the church's future must let the two isolated streams become
two poles in a theological discussion.

NOTES

In the text the numbers in parentheses after quotations denote the pages in the book or other work referred to in the footnote immediately preceding.

Abbreviations

ChrW	*Die christliche Welt*
EvTh	*Evangelische Theologie*
RGG	*Die Religion in Geschichte und Gegenwart*
ThBl	*Theologische Blätter*
TR	*Theologische Rundschau*
ZdZ	*Zwischen den Zeiten*
ZNW	*Zeitschrift für die neutestamentliche Wissenschaft*
ZThK	*Zeitschrift für Theologie und Kirche*

CHAPTER I   BARTH AND BULTMANN IN THE ENGLISH–SPEAKING WORLD

1. Hermann Diem, *Dogmatics* (London: Oliver & Boyd Ltd., 1959; The Westminster Press, 1960). Translation of *Dogmatik: Ihr Weg zwischen Historismus und Existenzialismus* (Munich: Chr. Kaiser Verlag, 1955).

2. Heinrich Ott, *Geschichte und Heilsgeschichte in der Theologie Rudolf Bultmanns* (Tübingen: J. C. B. Mohr, 1955).

—— *Denken und Sein: Der Weg Martin Heideggers und der Weg der Theologie* (Zollikon: Evangelischer Verlag, 1959).

—— *Dogmatik und Verkündigung* (Zurich: Evangelischer Verlag, 1961).

3. Helmut Gollwitzer, *The Existence of God as Confessed by Faith* (The Westminster Press, 1965). Translation of *Die Existenz Gottes im Bekenntnis des Glaubens* (Munich: Chr. Kaiser Verlag, 1964).

4. *Post Bultmann locutum*, Vols. I and II (Hamburg-Bergstedt: Herbert Reich Verlag, 1965).

5. Karl Barth, *Rudolf Bultmann: Ein Versuch, ihn zu verstehen*, Theolo-

gische Studien, Vol. 34 (Zurich: Evangelischer Verlag, 1952).

6. Arnold B. Come, *An Introduction to Barth's* Dogmatics *for Preachers* (The Westminster Press, 1963).

7. Schubert M. Ogden, *Christ Without Myth: A Study Based on the Theology of Rudolf Bultmann* (Harper & Brothers, 1961).

8. Rudolf Bultmann, *The History of the Synoptic Tradition* (Harper & Row, Publishers, Inc., 1963. First German edition, 1921).

9. Karl Barth, *The Epistle to the Romans* (London: Oxford University Press, 1933). Translation of *Der Römerbrief* (Munich: Chr. Kaiser Verlag, 1922), by Edwyn C. Hoskyns.

10. *Revolutionary Theology in the Making,* Barth-Thurneysen correspondence, 1914–1925, translation by James D. Smart (John Knox Press, 1964), p. 164.

11. Karl Barth, "Brunners Schleiermacherbuch," *ZdZ,* 1924, p. 49.

12. Karl Barth, *Nein! Antwort an Emil Brunner* (Munich: Chr. Kaiser Verlag, 1934).

13. Karl Barth and Eduard Thurneysen, *Suchet Gott, so werdet ihr leben!* (Bern: G. A. Bäschlin, 1917; Munich: Chr. Kaiser Verlag, 1928).

14. Eduard Thurneysen, *A Theology of Pastoral Care* (John Knox Press, 1962). Translated from German edition, 1946.

15. Eduard Thurneysen, *Das Wort Gottes und die Kirche* (Munich: Chr. Kaiser Verlag, 1927). Translation made but never published.

16. Hans Werner Bartsch, ed., *Kerygma und Mythos: Ein theologisches Gespräch,* Vol. I (Hamburg-Volksdorf: Herbert Reich, Evangelischer Verlag, 1948).

17. Translation of above (London: S.P.C.K., 1953).

18. James M. Robinson and John B. Cobb, Jr., *The New Hermeneutic* (Harper & Row, Publishers, Inc., 1964).

19. H. H. Halley, *Bible Handbook* (Zondervan Publishing House, 23d edition, 1962). Widely recommended by evangelist Billy Graham. Represents an eighteenth-century level of Biblical scholarship.

20. Barth recognizes the problem too in the third stage of his hermeneutical process, *selberdenken,* in which the modern interpreter has to take responsibility for reformulating the message of the Biblical author. See p. 173.

21. Charles N. Cochrane, *Christianity and Classical Culture: A Study of Thought and Action from Augustus to Augustine* (London: Oxford University Press, 1940). An impressive exposition of how the uniqueness of the Christian faith in God as it invaded the Greco-Roman world came to expression in the doctrine of the Trinity.

CHAPTER II BEFORE THE EARTHQUAKE

1. *Revolutionary Theology,* pp. 37, 42. In *Die Protestantische Theologie im 19. Jahrhundert,* p. 56, he notes Beck's influence on his father, Fritz Barth. Published in German (Zollikon-Zurich: Evangelischer Verlag) in 1952, *Prot-*

estant Thought: From Rousseau to Ritschl (Harper & Brothers, 1959) being the English translation of eleven chapters by Brian Cozens.

2. *Existence and Faith: Shorter Writings of Rudolf Bultmann,* selected, translated, and introduced by Schubert M. Ogden (Meridian Books, Inc., 1960), pp. 31, 32.

3. Albert Schweitzer, *The Quest of the Historical Jesus* (The Macmillan Company, 1948). Translation of German edition of 1906.

4. Adolf von Harnack, *What Is Christianity?* with an introduction by Rudolf Bultmann (Harper & Brothers, 1957).

5. Karl Barth, *Die Theologie und die Kirche* (Munich: Chr. Kaiser Verlag, 1928), p. 240. English translation by Louise Pettibone Smith, *Theology and Church: Shorter Writings, 1920–1928* (London: SCM Press, Ltd., 1962).

6. Wilhelm Herrmann, *Gesammelte Aufsätze* (Tübingen: J. C. B. Mohr, 1923), p. 12.

7. *Ibid.,* p. 24.

8. *Ibid.,* p. 159.

9. *Ibid.,* p. 131.

10. Johannes Weiss, " Die Bedeutung des Paulus für den modernen Christen," *ZThK,* 28, 1919/20, pp. 129 f.

11. Wilhelm Wrede, *Paulus* (Tübingen: J. C. B. Mohr, 1906). English translation by American Theological Library Association, 1962.

12. Adolf Jülicher, *Paulus und Jesus* (Tübingen: J. C. B. Mohr, 1907).

13. Paul Wernle, *The Beginnings of Christianity,* Vol. I, *The Rise of the Religion* (Williams and Norgate, 1903). Translated from the German edition of 1901.

14. O. Eissfeldt, " Religionsgeschichtliche Schule " in *RGG²,* Vol. IV, col. 1898.

CHAPTER III   TWO DEVOTED LIBERALS

1. Johannes Rathje, *Die Welt des freien Christentums,* on the life and work of Martin Rade (Stuttgart: E. Klotz, 1952).

2. *Revolutionary Theology,* p. 109.

3. Karl Barth, " On Systematic Theology," *Scottish Journal of Theology,* September, 1961, p. 225.

4. Jürgen Fangmeier, *Erziehung in Zeugenschaft. Karl Barth und die Pädagogik* (Zurich: Evangelischer Verlag, 1964), pp. 21 ff.

5. Karl Barth, " Moderne Theologie und Reichsgottesarbeit," *ZThK,* 19, 1909, pp. 317, 475.

6. Karl Barth, " Der christliche Glaube und die Geschichte " (Referat October 5, 1910), *Schweizerische Theologische Zeitschrift,* 1912, pp. 1–18, 49–72.

7. Karl Barth, " Der Glaube an den persönlichen Gott," *ZThK,* 24, 1914, pp. 21 ff., 65 ff.

8. Rudolf Bultmann, *Der Stil der Paulinischen Predigt und die kynisch-stoische Diatribe* (Göttingen: Vandenhoeck und Ruprecht, 1910).

———— "Das religiöse Moment in der ethischen Unterweisung der Epiktet und das Neue Testament," *ZNW*, 13, 1912, pp. 97–110.

9. R. Bultmann, *Existence and Faith*, p. 24.

CHAPTER IV   THE BEGINNINGS OF REVOLT, 1913–1917

1. Stephen Neill, *The Interpretation of the New Testament, 1861–1961* (London: Oxford University Press, 1964).

2. Karl Barth, "A Thank You and a Bow: Kierkegaard's Reveille," *Canadian Journal of Theology*, January, 1965, pp. 3 f. Translation of "Dank und Reverenz," an address in Copenhagen, April 19, 1963. Published first in *EvTh*, 23, 1963.

3. Walther Schmithals, *Die Theologie Rudolf Bultmanns* (Tübingen: J. C. B. Mohr, 1966), p. 9, quotes a letter to Erich Förster in 1926 in which Bultmann denied that the war caused any revision in his concept of life or the character of his theology, asserting that debate with his teachers was the primary force in effecting changes. But his 1917 sermon printed in *Existence and Faith* suggests a greater significance than he remembered in 1926.

4. *Revolutionary Theology*, p. 72; also, in a preface to the unpublished translation of Thurneysen's essays.

5. Eduard Thurneysen, *Christoph Blumhardt* (Munich: Chr. Kaiser Verlag, 1926).

Fr. Zündel, *Johann Christoph Blumhardt, ein Lebensbild* (Basel: Brunnen-Verlag, 15th edition, 1948).

6. *Revolutionary Theology*, p. 217.

7. Hermann Kutter, *They Must, or God and the Social Democracy* (Cooperative Printing Company, 1908).

8. Leonhard Ragaz, *Mein Weg*, Vol. I (Zurich: Diana Verlag, 1952), p. 114.

9. Eduard Thurneysen, "Zum religiös-sozialen Problem," *ZdZ*, 1927, pp. 513 ff.

10. Eduard Thurneysen, *Dostoiewski* (Munich: Chr. Kaiser Verlag, 1921). Translation 1966 by John Knox Press.

11. Emil Brunner, *Christianity and Civilization*, Vol. I (Charles Scribner's Sons, 1948).

12. *Revolutionary Theology*, pp. 12, 13.

13. Karl Barth, *The Word of God and the Word of Man*, translated by Douglas Horton (The Pilgrim Press, 1928).

14. *Revolutionary Theology*, p. 26.

Karl Barth, *God, Grace and Gospel*, translated by James Strathearn McNab (Edinburgh: Oliver & Boyd, Ltd., 1959), p. 57.

15. R. Bultmann, *Existence and Faith*, p. 288.

16. *Ibid.*, pp. 23 ff.

17. Rudolf Bultmann, *Glauben und Verstehen*, Vol. I (Tübingen: J. C. B. Mohr, 1933; 2d ed., 1954), p. 2.

18. *Existence and Faith*, p. 30.

19. *Ibid.*, p. 31.
20. Rudolf Bultmann, "Der Gottesgedanke und der moderne Mensch," *ZThK*, 60, 1963, pp. 335 ff.
21. Rudolf Bultmann, "Die Bedeutung der Eschatologie für die Religion des Neuen Testaments," *ZThK*, 27, 1917, pp. 76 ff.

CHAPTER V   OPEN REBELLION, 1917–1920

1. Friedrich Gogarten, "Between the Times," *ChrW*, 24, 1920, pp. 374 ff.
2. *Revolutionary Theology.*
3. K. Barth, *The Word of God and the Word of Man.*
4. Karl Barth, "The Pastor Who Pleases the People," *ChrW*, 14, 1916, pp. 262 ff.
5. Now in *The Word of God and the Word of Man.*
6. Karl Barth and Eduard Thurneysen, *Suchet Gott, so werdet ihr leben!* (1917).
7. *Ibid.*, p. 93.
8. Karl Barth, *Der Römerbrief* (Bern: G. A. Bäschlin, 1919. Reprinted 1963 by Evangelischer Verlag, Zurich).
9. P. Wernle, *The Beginnings of Christianity*, Vol. I.
10. In *The Word of God and the Word of Man.* George Merz in *Wege und Wandlungen* (Munich: Chr. Kaiser Verlag, 1961) describes the enthusiastic response of the conference to Barth's address.
11. In *The Word of God and the Word of Man.*
12. Rudolf Bultmann, *The History of the Synoptic Tradition*, 1921. English translation, 1963.
13. Rudolf Bultmann, "Die Frage nach dem messianischen Bewusstsein Jesu und das Petrus-Bekenntnis," *ZNW*, 19, 1919/20, p. 165. Schmithals, *op. cit.*, comments on the slow development of independent theological thought in Bultmann before the middle twenties. But when allowance is made for his concentration on critical problems, the evidence seems to show considerable significant development.
14. Wilhelm Wrede, *Das Messiasgeheimnis in den Evangelien* (Göttingen: Vandenhoeck und Ruprecht, 1901).
15. Rudolf Bultmann, "Ethische und mystische Religion im Urchristentum," *ChrW*, 34, 1920, pp. 725 ff., 738 ff.
16. Wilhelm Bousset, *Kyrios Christos* (3d edition, Göttingen: Vandenhoeck und Ruprecht, 1926. First edition, 1913).
17. Karl Barth, "Persönliche Nachklänge zu Professor Bultmanns Vortrag über ethische und mystische Frömmigkeit im Urchristentum," *ChrW*, 50, 1920, p. 791.
18. Rudolf Bultmann, "Religion und Kultur," *ChrW*, 29, 1920, pp. 450 ff.
19. Rudolf Bultmann, *Glauben und Verstehen*, Vol. III (Tübingen: J. C. B. Mohr, 1960). Also in *The Christian Century*, Aug. 27, 1958, pp. 97–99.

CHAPTER VI   A CHANGE OF COURSE, 1920-1922

1. Ch. 1 entitled "Unerledigte Anfragen an die heutige Theologie" in *Die Theologie und die Kirche.*
2. *Revolutionary Theology,* p. 48.
3. *Ibid.,* p. 51.
4. *Ibid.*
5. *Die Theologie und die Kirche,* p. 2.
6. *Ibid.,* p. 23. Direct quote of Overbeck.
7. *Ibid.,* p. 7.
8. See Note 2 in Chapter IV.
9. Bultmann in "Ethische und mystische Religion" praised Gogarten's *Religion weither* (1917).
10. *Revolutionary Theology,* p. 89.
11. *Ibid.,* p. 117.
12. H. C. Wolf, *Kierkegaard and Bultmann: The Quest of the Historical Jesus* (Augsburg Publishing House, 1965).
13. In *Revolutionary Theology,* p. 122, Barth uses the term "the known Unknown."
14. Rudolf Bultmann, "Karl Barths *Römerbrief* in zweiter Auflage," *ChrW,* 18, 1922, pp. 320 ff., 329 ff., 358 ff., 369 ff.
15. *Revolutionary Theology,* p. 94.
16. H. W. Bartsch, ed., *Kerygma and Myth,* pp. 6, 7, 22.
17. K. Barth, *Der Römerbrief,* p. XX. Foreword to the third edition in which he answered Bultmann.
18. Ch. IV in *The Word of God and the Word of Man.*
19. *Ibid.,* p. 120.
20. Ch. V in *The Word of God and the Word of Man.*

CHAPTER VII   AGREEMENT AND DISAGREEMENT, 1923-1926

1. Hermann Friedrich Kohlbrügge, 1803-1875, a Dutch Reformed pastor who had a remarkable ministry in Elberfeld, Wuppertal. Barth was impressed with his emphasis that the converted man is to his dying day wholly flesh and sinner, so that he is thrown completely upon Christ and cultivation of a sanctified self is ruled out.
2. *Revolutionary Theology,* pp. 49, 50.
3. The contributions of both Harnack and Barth to the discussion appeared in *Die christliche Welt* in 1923 but have been reprinted in Barth's volume, *Theologische Fragen und Antworten* (Zollikon: Evangelischer Verlag, 1957).
4. *ChrW,* 16/17, 1923, p. 245. Also, in *Theologische Fragen und Antworten.*
5. Paul Tillich, "Kritisches und positives Paradox. Eine Auseinandersetzung mit Karl Barth und Friedrich Gogarten," *ThBl,* II, 1923, pp. 263 ff.
6. Karl Barth, "Von der Paradoxie des positiven Paradoxes. Antworten und

Fragen an Paul Tillich," *ThBl*, II, 1923, pp. 287 ff.

7. First printed in *ZdZ*, 1923, and then as Ch. II in *Die Theologie und die Kirche*.

8. Ch. VII in *The Word of God and the Word of Man*.

9. Karl Barth and Eduard Thurneysen, *Come Holy Spirit* (Munich: Chr. Kaiser Verlag, 1923).

10. Published in *ThBl*, III, 1924, pp. 73 ff., and in *Glauben und Verstehen*, Vol. I (1933), pp. 1 ff.

11. *Existence and Faith*, p. 288.

12. *ThBl*, IV, 1925, pp. 129 ff., and *Glauben und Verstehen*, Vol. I, pp. 26 ff.

13. *ZdZ*, 1925, pp. 334 ff. Reprinted in Moltmann-Anfänge. The fact that it was not included in the collected essays may indicate how quickly Bultmann abandoned some of the positions which were taken in it.

14. Karl Barth, *Die Auferstehung der Toten* (Munich: Chr. Kaiser Verlag, 1924. English translation published by Hodder & Stoughton, Ltd., London, 1933).

15. *ThBl*, V, 1926, pp. 1 ff. *Glauben und Verstehen*, Vol. I, pp. 38 ff.

16. Karl Barth, *The Resurrection of the Dead*, p. 86. Quotations are from the English edition.

17. R. Bultmann, *ThBl*, V, p. 14.

18. In *ZdZ*, 1926, pp. 40 ff. An essay provoked by one of Erik Peterson's which attacked the use of dialectic by Barth, Gogarten, and Bultmann. Barth, too, answered Peterson in his article " Church and Theology."

19. Chs. IV and V in *Die Theologie und die Kirche*.

20. *Die Protestantische Theologie im 19. Jahrhundert*, p. 380.

21. " Die dogmatische Prinzipienlehre bei Wilhelm Herrmann," *ZdZ*, 1925, pp. 246 ff. Ch. VIII in *Die Theologie und die Kirche*.

22. Reinhold Niebuhr and Paul Tillich, both of them religious socialists like Barth, focused their theological work on the problems of society and culture rather than upon the problems of the church in its relation to society and culture.

23. Karl Barth, "Kirche und Theologie," *ZdZ*, 1926. Reprinted in *Die Theologie und die Kirche*, p. 302.

24. In *ZdZ*, 1926, pp. 363 ff. Ch. XII in *Die Theologie und die Kirche*.

25. *Ibid*.

26. This is Barth's version of the divine immanence in nature, history, and man.

CHAPTER VIII THE WIDENING GULF, 1926–1927

1. In *ZdZ*, 1927, pp. 11 f. Ch. VII in *Die Theologie und die Kirche*.

2. *Ibid.*, pp. 33 f.

3. Friedrich Gogarten, " Offenbarung und Zeit," *ZThK*, 30, 1922, pp. 347 ff.

4. *Revolutionary Theology*, p. 88.

5. In *ZdZ*, 1926, pp. 451 ff.

6. Rudolf Bultmann, *Jesus* (Berlin: Deutsche Bibliothek, 1926). Translated as *Jesus and the Word* (Charles Scribner's Sons, 1934).

7. Karl Barth, *Die Lehre vom Worte Gottes: Prolegomena zur christlichen Dogmatik* (Munich: Chr. Kaiser Verlag, 1927). Vol. I of *Die christliche Dogmatik im Entwurf.*

8. In *Glauben und Verstehen,* Vol. I, pp. 245 ff.

9. *Revolutionary Theology,* p. 149. The first suggestion was on September 13, 1923.

10. " The Word of God and the Task of the Ministry " in *The Word of God and the Word of Man.* An address delivered in 1922.

11. At the end of his review of Barth's *Resurrection of the Dead,* in *ThBl,* V, pp. 1 ff.

12. Heinrich Ott in his *Geschichte und Heilsgeschichte in der Theologie Rudolf Bultmanns* has pointed to a confusion both in Bultmann's conception of history and in his ontology. There is an outer realm of history in which the phenomena are objectively available to the scientific historian, but where man's existence is concerned in history no such objectivity is possible. Here the past discloses itself only as the interpreter, aware of his preconceptions, enters into an unending dialogue with it, willing to have his very existence modified by what he hears from it. But the word that alone brings man to his fulfillment comes from the Beyond, beyond history, yet is heard by man only in existential confrontation with a message in specific human words which the historian is able to isolate for him in the record of the past. The realm of the Beyond is sharply distinguished from the entire historical realm by being eschatological, but at times the inner realm of history disclosed by existential understanding seems to participate more in the eschatological than in the historical. Barth in his insistence upon the inseparableness of history and *Urgeschichte* sees eschatology as the revelation of the hidden depths of history and of all historical events. He permits no such hard lines of separation between outer and inner events in history and between this world and the Beyond. There are only two basic realities: God and all that exists in the visible and invisible realms as God's creation.

13. Friedrich Gogarten, " Karl Barths Dogmatik," *TR,* N.F.1, 1929, pp. 60 f.

14. Karl Barth, *Erklärung des Philipperbriefes* (Munich: Chr. Kaiser Verlag, 1927. English translation published by John Knox Press, 1962).

15. Ch. IX in *Die Theologie und die Kirche.*

16. Hans Urs von Balthazar, *Karl Barth, Darstellung und Deutung seiner Theologie* (Köln: Hegner-Bücherei, 1951).

17. Most significant, the three-volume work by the French scholar, Henry Bouillard, and Hans Küng's *Justification by Faith,* but these are by no means the only Roman Catholic works that are deserving of attention.

Chapter IX THEOLOGY VERSUS ANTHROPOLOGY

1. K. Barth, *Nein! Antwort an Emil Brunner*.

2. H. M. Müller, *ThBl*, VII, 1928.

3. "Die Theologie und der heutige Mensch," *ZdZ*, 1930, p. 374.

4. One has only to contemplate the 780 pages of Christological anthropology in *Dogmatik* III, 2, to see that Barth had no intention of bypassing the subject.

5. See Rudolf Bultmann, "The Historicity of Man and Faith." Published in 1930 in *ZThK*, N.F. XI, pp. 339 ff., and later translated in *Existence and Faith*, p. 102.

6. Rudolf Bultmann, "Die Bedeutung der 'dialektischen Theologie' für die neutestamentliche Wissenschaft," *ThBl*, VII, 1928, pp. 57 ff., and *Glauben und Verstehen*, Vol. I, pp. 114 ff.

7. Published in Germany by J. C. B. Mohr in 1929 and translated in *Existence and Faith*, pp. 58 ff.

8. Rudolf Bultmann, "Das Problem der 'natürlichen Theologie.'" First published in *Glauben und Verstehen*, Vol. I, pp. 294 ff.

9. Friedrich Gogarten, "Das Problem einer theologischen Anthropologie," *ZdZ*, 1929, pp. 493 ff.

10. This doctrine of the hiddenness of God even in the moment of his revealing of himself to us in his Word and Spirit remains primary for Barth in all his writings. We know the revelation only in memory and in anticipation, never directly in the event itself. Our faith lives in the memory and in the anticipation of the event. Hence, the engrossment of Scripture with history and eschatology.

11. *RGG*², Vol. II, col. 1687. Article on Heidegger.

12. T. F. Torrance, *Karl Barth: An Introduction to His Early Theology, 1910–1931* (London: SCM Press, Ltd., 1962).

13. *Revolutionary Theology*, p. 55.

14. Karl Barth, "Parergon. Karl Barth über sich selbst," *EvTh*, 1948, p. 268. Reprinted from *The Christian Century*.

15. Karl Barth, *Anselm: fides quaerens intellectum; Anselm's Proof of the Existence of God in the Context of His Theological Scheme*, translated from the 2d German edition by Ian W. Robertson (London: SCM Press, Ltd., 1960), p. 11.

16. "A Thank You and a Bow," *loc. cit.*

17. Barth, *Anselm*, p. 38.

18. *Revolutionary Theology*, p. 37.

19. *Die Protestantische Theologie im 19. Jahrhundert*. In English *From Rousseau to Ritschl*.

20. "Schicksal und Idee in der Theologie," *ZdZ*, 1929, pp. 309 ff. Reprinted in *Theologische Fragen und Antworten*.

21. Comment to a group of English and American students at his home in 1955.

Chapter X　A MATTER OF LIFE OR DEATH

1. Emil Brunner, *Die Mystik und das Wort* (Tübingen: J. C. B. Mohr, 1924).

2. *Revolutionary Theology,* p. 175.

3. *ZdZ,* 1930, pp. 1 ff.

4. " Die Bedeutung des Bekenntnisses," *ZdZ,* 1930, pp. 353 ff.

5. " Die Not der evangelischen Kirche," *ZdZ,* 1931, pp. 89 ff.

6. Otto Dibelius, " The Responsibility of the Church. An Answer to Karl Barth." Published February 12, 1931.

7. Note its expression in Brunner's " Misunderstanding of the Church " in which the church in becoming an institution ceases to be the church of the Spirit.

8. Friedrich Gogarten, " Wahrheit und Gewissheit," *ZdZ,* 1930, pp. 96 ff. Rudolf Bultmann, " Das christliche Gebot der Nächstenliebe," *Revue d'Histoire et de Philosophie religieuses, 1930,* pp. 223 ff. Also, in *Glauben und Verstehen,* Vol. I, pp. 229 ff.

9. " Staat und Kirche," *ZdZ,* 1932, pp. 390 ff.

10. " Schöpfung und Volkstum," *ZdZ,* 1932, pp. 481 ff. Gogarten quotes Knak's article published in *ZdZ,* 1932.

11. " The Task of Theology in the Present Situation," *ThBl,* XII, 1933, pp. 161 ff. Translated in *Existence and Faith,* pp. 158 ff.

12. " Autobiographical Reflections " in *Existence and Faith,* p. 286.

13. Rudolf Bultmann, " Der Arier-Paragraph im Raume der Kirche," *ThBl,* XII, 1932, pp. 359 ff.

14. Emil Brunner, *Das Gebot und die Ordnungen.* The reference to the " orders " is not evident in the title of the translation, *The Divine Imperative.*

15. *Theologische Existenz heute.* A series of pamphlets by Barth and others which attempted to clarify the different aspects of the situation confronting the church.

16. Th. Siegfried, *Das Wort und die Existenz* I (Gotha: L. Klotz, 1930).

17. Review of " Christian Dogmatics " in TR, N.F.1, 1929.

18. *Dogmatik,* I, 1, pp. 131 ff.

19. *Ibid.,* pp. 36, 37, 421.

20. Hans Urs von Balthazar, *Karl Barth, Darstellung und Deutung seiner Theologie* (Hegner-Bücherei im Summa-Verlag zu Olten, 1951), p. 94.

INDEX